THE
SPECTATOR
ANNUAL
1994

THE SPECTATOR ANNUAL 1994

Edited by Dominic Lawson

Foreword by John Osborne

JOHN MURRAY

Albemarle Street, London

A catalogue record for this book is available from the
British Library

ISBN 0-7195-5704-6

Typeset in 11/13pt Trump Medieval
by Servis Filmsetting Ltd, Manchester
Printed and bound in Great Britain by
The University Press, Cambridge

CONTENTS

FOREWORD

My ex-agent, in his happy venal way, was mystified and disapproving whenever I told him I was writing something for *The Spectator*. He considered that to write for a small fee for a publication with a modest circulation was a waste of my time and that his own cut would not cover a bottle of supermarket claret. Useless to point out that it would be most likely read by the great, the good and the literate and that if one did not exactly know one's audience intimately, at least one had a fair idea of how to provoke, amuse and, very occasionally inform.

None of those represented in this annual cull of cream contributions will have done it for the money. Perhaps that is why so many bear scrutiny and re-reading under the glare of hard covers. As always, it is a fascinating mixture of informed yearbook and intelligent comment, a reminder of the transience of supposedly 'pressing' issues and of the abiding life of good-natured relish or eccentricity. More surprising, in the light of sneering envy from scribblers of a *Guardian* persuasion, a random dip reveals a range and a tolerance, albeit sometimes masked by stringency, despair, even gallant flippancy, almost unique in these wearily proscribed times.

The Spectator is the only publication I know which rarely produces a dud issue. Week by week, I find myself reading at length about something or somewhere or somebody I am not remotely interested in simply because it is, unfashionably, 'well written'. By comparison, standards elsewhere – in the dailies, the Sundays and the weeklies – seem slipshod, conformist and, most damning of all, *worthy*. No, no comparisons, they just *are*. Reporting is flaccid, criticism moribund and dreaded 'opinion' pretentious at best and vicious at worst. The old 'Posh Papers' (a phrase I invented and which nightly raised a rare laugh) are no more.

There seems to me to have been a spectacular decline in journalism over the past thirty years. Star writers and columnists have all but vanished. Perhaps the trade is no longer considered respectable for Real Writers, although Arnold Bennett, Conrad, Dickens, Wells, Shaw, even Henry James never believed it beneath them. In the late fifties and early sixties the *Sunday Times* and *The Observer* fielded teams of reporters and reviewers – Tynan and Hobson, Connolly and Toynbee –

which were seized on avidly each Sunday in the hopes of delight, enlightenment or hearty derision.

No more. Fillet the Business Section, Sport, Classified, Cartoons. What is left is bloated, indigestible and dispiriting. Only when *The Spectator* flips through the letter box on a Friday morning is there the promise of a small but tasty treat of selective, civilised reading: Bernard and Waugh, Johnson and Kavanagh, Taki or Patterson; a good grumble at the inanities of the theatre column; reviews of lady novelists I shall never buy, restaurants I shall never eat in; a sparkling diary from the Duchess of Devonshire and, always, the expectation of some cherishable larkiness as well as a salutary surprise or two.

Not then, just a pat on the back for this collection, but a whoop of joy and welcome for a weekly dose of sanity, grace and rare lucidity in a very batty, over-serious world.

John Osborne

GUESTS OF MR RAMBLER

P.J. Kavanagh

Having walked the Severn from estuary to source – in snatches, it took us about ten years – a couple of years ago we decided to walk the Wye the other way round, from source to estuary. This was partly because the Wye rises only a mile or two from the source of the Severn, on Plynlimmon, and we wanted an excuse to visit again that haunting place, but there was another, odder, reason.

On our first climb to Plynlimmon, which is in effect a high sand-coloured moor, we were triumphant that we were at last to reach our destination, had grown so fond of companionable Sabrina by this time that we felt we had earned the right to be in at her beginning. We stood at the top, stared at the map, and slowly admitted to ourselves that we were lost. The place was more or less featureless; we had meant to bring a compass, but we had not. Small birds, their feathers blown forward by the wind, perched on low rocks to examine our dismay. Just at the moment when we decided where the source must lie (wrongly, as we immediately learned) a figure strode round the corner, feathers of white hair blown forward from its face, and with some impatience put us right. The point was that there seemed no corner that he could have come round – the place was nearly flat and you could see for 50 miles. When told what we were doing the figure crossly said, '*I* would have *begun* at the source!' Then, as we stared in the direction he indicated, checking our map, he disappeared. The point, again, was that there was nowhere he could disappear to. Laurie Whitfield, sculptor, sceptic, Mancunian-practical, voiced my own woozy suspicion. '*Was* that an angel?' he said, round-eyed, pixillated. We had seen no one else that day, and were to see none for the rest of it.

At all events, the implied rebuke stayed with us, and is part of the reason why the year before last we climbed Plynlimmon again, found the source of the Wye and, cursing, dragged ourselves through the high quagmires that attend its birth. We were innocents then; the Severn had not taught us about acid bogs. We thought that if we climbed away and up from the nursling river we would reach drained ground. But where there is excess of acid there are insufficient bacteria, so dead vegetation accumulates, layer upon layer in water; on the way, presumably, to becoming peat.

Last year we reached Newbridge, or nearly reached Newbridge. One of the things we learned quickly about the Wye is that it does not demand, or facilitate, constant attendance on its banks, as does the Severn. You can follow the Severn for almost its whole course, the interruptions being rare and brief. The Wye seems trickier; often there are no paths, or the road runs so immediately alongside there is no point in stumbling over rocks and through reed-beds in the slipstream of lorries.

So, Newbridge was good enough, and we drove to Builth Wells, had time to observe that it was awash with holiday-makers, booked ourselves a couple of beds, parked the car, hired a taxi to Newbridge, consulted the village elders in their sadly refurbished pub – they seemed both dazed and defiant amid the new formica – and took to the riverside with relief.

It was mostly old oaks along the banks, striking into it with huge curved roots, like claws. The river itself was curiously varied; sometimes chocolate coloured, when feathers floated on it they seemed barely to move; at other times it bubbled noisily over stones. Certainly hereabouts it lacks the settled and powerful personality of the Severn, but we are still besotted with memories of that river.

There were well-built stiles at field intersections, with helpful arrows pointing our way and fingerposts with a striding logo-figure we christened Mr Rambler, who diminished the *numen*, the sense of discovery, but we were grateful not to have to consult the map. We wondered what the Builth holiday-makers did with themselves, because we were quite alone. Perhaps they were nervous of the instructive Mr Rambler, with reason. Next day, when we lost him for a while and pondered a possible turning we were confronted by a notice, YOU HAVE BEEN WARNED!

That first afternoon we sat in the roots of an oak and Laurie found the dry skeleton of a lamb curled in the surface roots in the position it must have died in, and while he held its skull, Hamlet-like, trying to fit back the lower jaw, there flashed the dragonfly iridescence of a kingfisher, which obligingly perched and posed for us. That indescribable stab of colour – 'the blueness of blueness' an Irish bard might untranslatably have called it – is always thrilling.

We rolled into Builth Wells around opening-time – extraordinary how often that happens to us – past a mown riverside sward with swimming pools, tennis-courts, playground, all empty. On a late July evening, when England were losing to Australia by a bagful of runs, not a couple of boys with a bat and a ball. 'Lack of facilities for sport at the grass-roots'? Plenty here, unused. The pubs were mostly for the young, flashing lights and rock videos, so we drove down the road to a poshery where the wine tasted like the smell of old laundry.'We never had a complaint before,' we were told – so we left there too.

Next day Mr Rambler forced us from the river and onto the 'Wye Valley Walk' – the river, along this stretch, is rather landownery and salmony – but this did not matter much, because it led up, along a hazel-enclosed track, a lime-green tunnel, until we came out on the hip of the hills looking down at the Wye and along it, and across to Aberedw where the last Welsh Prince of Wales spent the night in a cave before being killed next day, his head sent to London to be put on a spike. There were wild raspberries, and foxgloves with their last two or three bells remaining, bowed down by rain so that they stuck horizontal from the hedge like purple fists punching out – maybe at this stage they should be called boxing-gloves. Eventually, past herons and buzzards and glossy ponies grazing among bracken, this track led down to the main road near Erwood, where it runs only a few feet from the river.

Down there I asked about the invasion of weed that we spotted everywhere in the river, greeny-white, waving just under the water. Did it affect the fishing? Everyone declared at once that they knew nothing of the weed or the fish or the river, although they lived there. At last I cornered a man before he could dash and hide his waders in the Gents, and he conceded that it might have some effect . . . A mystery. There is money in the Wye and this sounded like money-caginess. Next year, beginning at Erwood, the two tramps will carry on asking until they get the answer. Bland Mr Rambler, helpful as he is, cannot be allowed to have it all his own way.

7 August 1993

ARTS

UNRAVELLING A TASTE FOR MONARCHS

Tanya Harrod

Saturday 7 August 1993
5. 00 a.m. I arrive at Buckingham Palace to find a small queue.

5.30 a.m. The queue is tidied up by the police. We are asked to get in line on the gravel and move sleeping bags out of the park. Benders are dismantled. As we regroup an aggressive American accuses a small, fellow-countryman of queue jumping. 'I've not come 6,000 miles for this,' replies the small man stoutly. Although there are some oddities – Screaming Lord Sutch, for instance, a lady dressed in a Union Jack and a handful of dreamers in Royal-Garden-Party outfits – my immediate neighbours are pleasant. None of us – Carol and Sheena from Essex, Paul, a trainee cab driver, Debbie and Francis, dressed in hi-tech cycling gear but with startlingly grand voices – are quite sure why we are here. There is a general feeling that it would be an achievement to be among the first visitors.

6.00 a.m. Police arrive with golden retrievers, which our group knowledgeably identify as 'sniffer dogs'. Camera crews from round the world walk up and down. The aggressive American manages to look the appropriate voice of the Mid-West and is interviewed four times. Vendors of newspapers, sweets and juggling balls pass to and fro but are soon asked to leave by the police. For those of us who lead quiet lives, we briefly seem to be at the epicentre.

7.30 a.m. Francis, the posh cyclist, says gravely, 'This is really an historic day.' The Queen is a presence in our group and her money problems re Windsor Castle are discussed fairly sympathetically.

8.30 a.m. We are certainly being looked after, what with the police, the dogs and the stream of Palace staff in blue trousers with red piping. 'We're mostly fresh off the dole,' says one cheerily. There is even a glimpse of the Lord Chamberlain himself, exquisitely suited, every grey hair in place. He chats pleasantly to the crowd and looks so elegant that his sexuality is called into question. 'He's obviously gay,' says John from Fulham Palace Road. 'No, he's upper class,' says John's girl friend wisely.

9.30 a.m. There is something publicly humiliating about queueing in The Mall, parting with £8 and being escorted by functionaries round the top of St James's Park, across Birdcage Walk and Buckingham Gate and into the so-called Ambassadors' Entrance. This is the sole opportunity to buy a 50p leaflet which lists all the works of art in the state rooms (much better value than the lavishly illustrated *Buckingham Palace*, Pitkin £2.50).

10.00 a.m. Through an airport-style security check and heading for the Central Courtyard and Grand Entrance. It is hard to resist the wistful reflection that it would have been nicer to have been invited by the Queen herself to one of those hospitable occasions, 'both formal and welcoming' described by the emollient Colin Amory in his courtly introduction to *Buckingham Palace: A Complete Guide* (Apollo £8). For many the feeling of loss and rejection at not seeing the Queen – nor any photograph or painting of her, nor associative object – will be intense and might well spark off psychopathic behaviour.

10.15 a.m. The taste of monarchs is on display but needs unravelling. The constant crackle of the intercoms carried by the attendants is distracting.

Despite Charles I's superb Van Dycks and George III's high-minded commissions from Benjamin West depicting scenes of civic virtue, it is the opulent aesthetics of George IV which dominates most of the 18 staterooms open to the public. George IV collected great paintings, too, but these were more easily examined when recently on show at the National Gallery. The chief reason to visit Buckingham Palace is surely an architectural one, to study the boundless creativity of John Nash's work for George IV, his Grand Staircase, his exquisite little Guard Room and his lavish, mannered ceilings. Nash did not work alone and he incorporated brilliant etched glass, marble work by Joseph Browne and numerous sculptured plaster reliefs designed by Thomas Stothard and William Pitts which in different ways reflect on English themes, both pastoral and historical.

As a tour of Buckingham Palace makes clear, George IV's death meant the end of a high point in monarchical patronage. Nash was sacked and Edward Blore, 'Blore the bore', was brought in to complete rooms and enlarge, adding a dismal east frontage closing Nash's courtyard and removing the Marble Arch to its present site.

Prince Albert was the second, and last, royal to have a creative impact on the Palace but sadly we have to imagine his contribution. His artistic adviser was Ludwig Gruner, a scholarly German artist and connoisseur who created Raphaelesque polychrome schemes for the Grand Staircase and the Ballroom. (The Ballroom scene of investitures, is at present closed to the public as it is undergoing restoration.) Gruner also designed a charming garden pavilion for Prince Albert as part of an experimental revival of fresco painting which, shamefully, was demolished in 1928. The Gruner-Albert collaboration – though very different from Nash's plaster/gilt/scagiola effects for George IV – looks ravishing from the evidence of contemporary watercolours.

Gruner, who deserves a full-length biography, always felt that he and Albert were fighting a rearguard action against the philistine English. How right he was! Only his work at Osborne on the Isle of Wight remains. On the death of Queen Victoria, Edward VII brought 'the decorators' into the Palace and painted Gruner out with white and gold schemes enlivened by the odd otiose pilaster. It is this dreary white and gold combined with red carpeting which dominates the Grand Entrance, the former Sculpture Gallery and Grand Staircase today. The Picture Gallery was also made dull this century by redecoration, with Nash's eccentric lively ceiling replaced by a bland, curved, glass roof.

12.00 p.m. Of course, some part of this building should be open to the public on a regular basis, not just as a stop-gap fundraiser. The queues would die down, the royalists would have their fill and the experience could become as pleasant as a visit to the peaceful Queen's Gallery round the corner. On 7 August this was virtually empty even though the exhibition *A King's Purchase: King George III and the Collection of Consul Smith* is a fascinating one. It draws on pictures, drawings and books bought by George III *en bloc* from Smith in 1762, including Vermeer's 'A Lady at the Virginals', Canalettos, and a Raphael study for the 'Massacre of the Innocents'. In the Queen's Gallery there is also a decent shop, preferable to the stark little tent where visitors to the Palace may buy a selection of depressingly expensive gifts. These are marketed by Royal Collection Enterprises Ltd – a title which seems to sum up the less pleasant aspects of the Buckingham Palace experience.

1.00 p.m. Homeward bound. The queue stretches a third of the way down The Mall. It is apparently shorter than expected and moving at speed.

14 August 1993

THEATRE

GOD-AWFUL

Sheridan Morley

Grease (Dominion)
Godspell (Barbican)

Joseph and that bloody *Technicolor Dreamcoat*, followed hotly as it was by *Jesus Christ Superstar*, has a lot to answer for: indeed it could have been argued, had Rice and Lloyd Webber not progressed to the vastly better *Evita*, that what they had done was not so much revive the stage musical as kill it stone dead. True, this was not exactly their fault: it just so happened that their first two shows came at the most appalling time for the West End and Broadway musical theatre. Late in the Sixties or early in the Seventies that theatre lost, either by death or retirement, Noel Coward, Lerner/Loewe and Rodgers/Hammerstein, and a kind of producer-panic set in. The success of *Joseph* and *Jesus* seemed to offer an alternative: a kind of God-rock-pop mishmash, somewhere between a church service and a teenybopping open-air concert, at which nobody would be old enough to care that these shows stood in the same relation to real stage musicals as Sandra Dee did to Peggy Ashcroft among actresses.

And producers are a copycat lot: in the wake of *Joseph* and *Jesus* came a whole raft of stadium shows like *Hair* and *Grease* and *Godspell*, and the God-awful truth is that 20 years later, just when we thought it was safe to go to a musical again, they're all back or (as in the case of *Hair*) threatening imminent reappearance.

Moreover, they have now found a new source of supply: whereas the original casts were at least vaguely theatrical (*Godspell* indeed boasted Jeremy Irons among its first players) the new lot have been almost exclusively recruited from Australian daytime soap operas or breakfast television children's shows, and wander around West End stages looking uneasily as if they might be about to fall through them.

If only they would: what is so horrendous about *Grease* is that it is currently taking more money than any other show in town, despite a score which seems to have been reconditioned from old Pat Boone rejects by a team of manic cheerleaders. A dozen blokes in silver leather jackets leaping cautiously off a parked car does not constitute choreography in the *Crazy for You* sense, nor does an orchestra moving slowly up and down on a stage lift exactly correspond to the Heavyside Layer in *Cats*.

This is, in short, a production which should be happening in a tent at the Birmingham Exhibition Centre for about a week, and before you write to ask me what is wrong with a show which clearly introduces thousands of contented theatre-goers to the West End, I will tell you exactly: the fact that they are not theatre-goers at all. They are pop concert-goers who have drifted into the Dominion because they saw the film on TV and wish, for some unfathomable reason, to repeat the experience live. The idea that they or *Grease* itself will be of any future use to the British or American musical theatre is very nearly as daft as the show's book, which would seem to have been cobbled together in capital letters on the back of a drive-in movie ticket stub sometime in 1956.

And if you thought that *Grease* was awful, try *Godspell*: this one comes back to us at the Barbican Concert Hall with the requisite kiddie-telly presenters, plus Gemma Craven who, as the only legit talent among them, at least has the grace to look deeply embarrassed throughout. Loosely based on the Old Testament, and now given a mindless and pointless rock-concert setting in place of the original pierrot show, *Godspell* is a shapeless, aimless, hopeless show which again nobody ever bothered to write, and the score of which has been composed for the brain-dead by the lyrically challenged.

Neither *Grease* nor *Godspell* is a 'musical' in the sense that *Carousel* or *City of Angels* are musicals: they are events, cynically packaged by American producers in the Seventies to try and catch an altogether other audience, one with no knowledge of or respect for the Broadway big-band tradition which was once the proudest boast of the American theatre. They did not belong on stage in the Seventies, and they do not belong there 20 years later. Now ask me if I enjoyed them.

21 August 1993

INHERITANCE

Peter Meinke

I seem to have inherited the wrong
things from my father: a fondness
for simple rhyme, a thirst for strong
drink, a tendency to get fat.

Above all, a certain meanness
of spirit, an inability to forgive
and forget even minor transgres-
sions. I'll get him for that.

21 August 1993

THE RISE OF THE BIG BUCKS NANNY

Nicholas Coleridge

I returned home unexpectedly early from the office one afternoon to
find the following scene in our kitchen: 11 nannies of all shapes and
sizes sitting around on chairs, supervising 12 children under the age of
two. This was 'nannies playgroup', which, for those unfamiliar with
this particular social powwow, is a forum for superior nursery nurses
to swap gossip about 'their' families, to compare notes on holidays and
cars, and periodically to scoop their charges off the floor to dab at them
with muslin cloths. Viewed *en masse,* the nannies in our kitchen
didn't look at all like the comfortably wrinkled old-school nannies,
smelling of barley sugar and Vick's vapour rub, that I recall from my
own childhood, with their Scottish or West Country accents and navy
orthopaedic shoes. These new-school nannies, extrovert and buxom in
stretch pants and T-shirts, looked more like aerobics teachers.

The manner, however, reminded me of thrusting young business executives: confident and purposeful, and talking about the job of nannies as a career rather than a vocation. And then it struck me that, in terms of the package most of them are receiving from their employers, these new-school nannies are actually far *better off* than the majority of young business executives. It wasn't simply 11 boisterous child-minders that were eating my biscuits in my kitchen, it was a quarter-of-a-million-pounds' worth of aggregate salary and perks.

What the average modern nanny earns is, of course, one of those questions, like the median salary of barristers or journalists, that's impossible to gauge definitively. Market forces prevail. You can find a Portuguese au pair for £30 a week or a captain-of-industry-style nanny who commands £350 (and I have been told of a nanny who was offered performance-related bonuses, too, if the baby learned to talk and read by a particular date).

In our part of West London most nannies seem to get £160–200 a week (let's say £10,000 a year) *after tax*. If there is another profession where your salary is reviewed in net figures, as if there were no tax to pay, then I've not heard of it. Ask anyone else what they earn and, if they tell you, they give you their gross salary, but not nannies. So the employer (and this is another perk exclusive to the nannying profession) is liable for her tax, as well as national insurance (both parts: the employer's bit *and* the employee's bit), which totals about another £2,500 a year. Your nanny in addition lives free in your house (value, say, £80 a week) with free food and drink (£40 a week) and lighting, heating, telephone, community charge, use of car, laundry (£50 a week), making a grand total of £21,340. The employers must themselves earn about £30,000 a year before tax merely to cover all this.

The amorphous role and status of the big bucks is one of the most vexed conundrums of the modern household. After mortgage and school fees, the nanny is the single greatest expense (ten years' nannying beginning now will cost you, allowing 6 per cent compound inflation, about £283,000; astonishing, really, that one isn't pestered all day long by Towry Law salesmen pitching nanny-fee schemes). Nannying is one of the only careers that appears to have been entirely recession-proof (have you heard of one who's dropped her salary lately?) and the only luxury service which actually became more, not less, essential as the economy deteriorated. As more families saw both parents having to go out to work, the more indispensable a really good nanny (notwith-standing the fact that, unless the mother is earning a pretty large net salary, it would often actually be more economical for her to remain at home looking after her own children herself). There are now an estimated 400,000 full-time or part-time nannies in Britain, only half of them British, the rest predominantly Australians, New Zealanders, Filipinos and Irish. The total nanny economy, much of it black, is, I estimate, worth about £40 billion a year, comparable with the North Sea oil industry.

At the same time, the very concept of nannying has altered (anyway in the minds of nannies themselves) and it is this remorseless upgrading of the job that causes confusion. In the past it was simple. An unmarried woman who loved children became a nanny and devoted her life to looking after other people's. That at least was the theory. With luck she worked for two or three families at most, and one of them eventually adopted her, giving her when she retired a cottage on the estate for life or a flat in a neighbouring village. English literature is full of these loyal old retainers who seldom took any time off because they had nowhere better to go.

For the modern nanny, nannying is usually a short-term career. This is not to suggest that they love the children less, or look after them less well. It is simply that nannying is a means to another end. Eventually, at some unspecified future date, they want to do something else, be their own boss – start a nursery school, open a shop, an aerobics studio – and it is to fund this project that you are handing over the £175 a week. Since nannies live free, all of this money is salted away. A friend of ours chanced upon their nanny's deposit account statement tucked between cereal packets, and almost died of envy, since her five-figure credit exactly matched his mighty overdraft.

With nannying as a career have come not just certificates and training but rules, some as fierce and rigid as old union practices: maximum number of nights baby-sitting, statutory rights on Bank Holiday time off, weekends, double time. For a while we had a very prim Norland nanny (until she left us for a pornographer, lured by £300 a week and the black BMW convertible placed at her disposal) who began most sentences, 'At Norland's they suggest . . . ', which generally opened the way to some unforeseen perk. Almost no modern nannies work weekends, which means they disappear off-duty precisely when you most need them, leaving their stressed-out employers to extend a five-day working week into a seven-day one.

For the employers, this latter-day unionism can be rather irritating. If your nanny regards herself as a career executive rather than an intrinsic part of the family, then it follows that the family holiday isn't really her holiday. My old childhood nanny looked forward to the family's summer holiday. 'We're going to France this year on our holidays,' she would tell everyone. The modern nanny says, 'They're going to Italy for two weeks in August. They want me to come along, and then I'm going away on my own holiday to Corfu in September.' So the family holiday is no longer seen as a holiday at all, it's a business trip with 14 consecutive days of work. These on-duty days are meticulously counted and caught up later. The modern nanny sees nothing odd in stating, after three weeks of being paid for watching the children from the side of the swimming pool in Umbria, and piling her plate high with prosciutto and melon, 'I'm owed five extra days off because I worked right through in Italy.'

One can, of course, see their point. If you examine the hundreds of classified advertisements for nannies in the *Lady* magazine, with their sometimes unintentionally revealing job descriptions, you realise many advertisers aren't really looking for a nanny at all, they're seeking a slave. Last week's issue dangled a job in 'a busy happy home. Duties include children's care, cooking, chauffeuring, laundry, dog walking, shopping.' And why stop there? Why not turning down beds, emptying and refilling dishwashers (sole charge), lawn mowing, pool sweeping, word processing? In a society that operates, except in the very grandest houses, without other staff aside from cleaning ladies, where do the duties of the modern nanny begin and end? Until the middle of this century the nanny occupied a precise position in the hierarchy of the household, superior to the other servants (evidenced by her eating Sunday lunch with the family) and required to do very little apart from care for the children. As the other staff evaporated, the nanny was left vulnerable, as the sole hired pair of hands, to every domestic chore. This further is exacerbated by the expense. The employer who has just handed over a couple of hundred quid, most of it in cash, can be forgiven for feeling that the ferrying of some empty wine cases out to the dustbin could hardly be his affair. And yet for the nanny, the expensively trained (£24,000 of her own money for three years at Norland's) *summa cum laude* nanny, the removal of old wine boxes exceeds her brief. Part of the problem is that, for most middle-class families, the nanny is the only full-time employee they pay themselves. Even if you happened to run a company employing hundreds of people, it is improbable that you would be dishing out your own cash, and there would, in any case, be a personnel department to adjudicate on job demarcations.

One of the great mysteries is why it is, when so many girls seek nannying posts, that there are so few good ones. Friends who have experimented with budget nannies (i.e., £90 a week) have invariably had cause to regret it. There is a species of British girl, generally originating in the Midlands, that gravitates to a nannying job in London specifically for the nightlife. One rather gave the game away at her interview by producing a long list of nightclubs – the Hippodrome, Stringfellows etc. – and asking her future employer exactly how long the travelling time would be from their house in Wandsworth. Another nanny moonlighted, on her many evenings off, at a topless club in Beak Street (a fact which only emerged when she began giving out her 'nanny line' telephone number to favoured punters). Others are bolters. A couple we know took a new teenage nanny with them to Scotland, to a rented lodge 30 miles north of Ullapool. She rapidly found the set-up too remote for her taste, so summoned a taxi to Inverness station in the middle of the night, and escaped on her return ticket. She left a 'Dear John' letter pinned to the baby's cot. When we ourselves advertised in the *Lady* and the Australian freesheet *TNT*, we drew 90 responses in two days, but nine-tenths sounded educationally subnormal or depressive. To coax a top-flight nanny, your advertisement must be as alluringly worded as a restaurant menu, full of evocative details like 'large, sunny house'. Many people offer bribes – 'Annual European skiing holiday' is on offer in the *Lady* this week – which will, I suppose, deter those nannies who prefer to ski in Aspen. A popular device is to word the advertisement as though it has been written by the baby; for example, 'I am looking for a caring nanny to be kind to me. I am ten months old and a girl. Own room with colour TV, own bathroom, use of car.' It is the notion of the baby offering the colour TV to her nanny that strikes me as particularly sickmaking.

Our own high-powered nanny, a bright Australian, is so widely admired that we live in constant fear she will be headhunted, like Aunt Dahlia's chef Anatole in the Wodehouse stories. We consequently feel rather protective towards her and try, not infallibly, to be considerate. This is most difficult to achieve when she accompanies us to stay with friends for the weekend. It is a peculiarly English failing to treat visiting nannies like Indian drivers, allocating them tiny linoleum-covered bedrooms and then leaving them to sink or swim with the other staff. Or else she is given inferior food to the guests, or marooned at meals in the dining-room, the only adult at a subsidiary 'children's table', expected to supervise all the offspring of the party on her own. This is indicative of the curiously ambivalent social attitude we now have to nannies: one moment you hear them described as 'my best friend', the next they're expected to melt deferentially into the background.

Almost in the same breath you hear people state that they 'couldn't survive' without their nanny, and that she is grossly overpaid 'for what she does'. This last, widespread criticism is fuelled by the fact that nannying is the least technological of skills. When a plumber demands

£150 for two-and-a-half hours' work fixing the boiler you pay gratefully, because you couldn't fix it yourself. But the stock-in-trade of a nanny is largely common sense and patience, and so easier to resent financially.

Anybody can do a nanny's job. That is what I tell myself before those weekends when we look after the children ourselves. By Sunday evening the house is a shambles of toys, clothes and goblets of rusk strewn up and down the stairs, fractious children and a terrible pall of exhaustion hanging over us. But when I return home on weekday evenings after work, I can see exactly what I'm bankrupting myself for: two children sitting in their nanny's comfortable lap, in ironed pyjamas and hair sweetly smelling of Johnson's baby shampoo, happily engrossed in *Orlando the Marmalade Cat*.

28 August 1993

FEAR AND LOATHING IN THE SAVOY

Dominic Lawson

I find it hard to pinpoint the exact moment when Nigel Short first began to loathe Garri Kasparov. Probably it was during their game in a tournament in Andalucia in the spring of 1991. Short played a new move against one of the world champion's favourite openings. It was an idea of startling originality: Nigel advanced the pawn which defended his own king's position, in deliberate contravention of the most basic of chess principles. Kasparov, who at that time was experimenting with spectacles, stared wide-eyed at the miscreant pawn, whipped out his glasses, and ostentatiously peered through them at the board. Then he opened his mouth. And laughed. Other grandmasters immediately gathered round, as perhaps the world champion had intended, to see the move which had provoked such mirth.

It is the sort of behaviour which one might – in a bad neighbourhood – expect from an arrogant local champion condescendingly playing a game against the club duffer. But Kasparov is the world champion, a figure who, Short protested to me after the game, 'should behave with dignity and decorum at the board no matter who he is playing'. And the

28-year-old Short is not a duffer, even by Kasparov's stellar standards. He is the strongest British player in the long history of chess. He is the only Briton ever to qualify as the official challenger for the world chess championship, and, with the ephemeral exception of Bobby Fischer, the only non-Russian to contest such a match for almost 60 years. When a man like Short plays a new move in a familiar opening and against the world champion, he will have invested enormous intellectual effort and pride in the discovery; to have it instantly dismissed by mocking laughter is an unimaginable insult, a slight which cannot be forgotten, and has not been forgiven.

In other, more recent games, the world champion has persistently fixed Short with long, cold stares from his khaki-grey eyes, and, during his opponent's thinking time, has paced up and down in the Englishman's line of vision – 'deliberately . . . like a baboon', Nigel would complain to me. But perhaps it is precisely because Kasparov has long been aware that Short was a potential threat to his supremacy, rather than a figure of fun, that he has regularly sought to humiliate him. At the very highest level, chess is as much psychology as skill, and this world champion, more than any of his predecessors, sets great store by the undermining of the opponent's ego through psychic intimidation.

Kasparov, now 30, has for many years brooded over the idea that he would, one day, face a challenge from the apparently diffident and taciturn Lancastrian, long before other commentators took Short's chances seriously. In his autobiography, written immediately after he became world champion in 1985, Kasparov wrote:

> Nigel Short is destined, in my opinion, to become the leading grandmaster in the West . . . In fact his career has closely paralleled my own, beating a grandmaster at the age of 12, becoming national champion at 13, and, at 18, becoming one of the few foreigners ever to win a tournament on Soviet soil. All that now seems to stand between Nigel and the prospect of the world crown is the unfortunate fact that fate brought him into this world only two years after Kasparov.

Short himself was quick to see the back-handedness and egotism of this apparent compliment, when I asked him to write a review of Kasparov's autobiography for *The Spectator*. Quoting Kasparov's self-portrait – 'many a player who becomes world champion realises that he can go no higher and begins to descend . . . I see no danger of this for myself. I see only new peaks before me and no descent' – Nigel wrote:

Unashamed conceit runs like a connecting thread throughout the book. We have repeated references to Kasparov's brilliant memory, which he imagines knows no limits. My own experience is different. I witnessed a game between Kasparov and ex-world champion Boris Spassky, where the younger man tried and failed miserably to recall his own previous analysis . . . Another facet of Kasparov's personality is his ability to manipulate a set of circumstances into a simplistic theory to suit his own emotional needs. Of course, this defence mechanism is present in us all, but in Kasparov it seems to be in permanent over-drive.

Kasparov, concluded *The Spectator*'s occasional book reviewer, was 'a grandmaster of self-delusion'.

Cynics – and the chess world consists of little else – have seen in Short's verbal attacks on the world champion a vicarious attempt to score the points he has miserably failed to achieve over the chess board. Nigel has only beaten Kasparov once in fully-fledged tournament play, and that was in 1986. Kasparov described that result as 'a fluke', and since then has beaten the Englishman eight times, usually in crushing style. This record is the main reason why there are few grandmasters who give Short much of a chance in his forthcoming match against Kasparov for The Times World Chess Championship and a prize of £1.7 million.

The second reason is that Kasparov is the strongest chess player of all time. His rating, on a universally recognised scale of measurement, is higher than Bobby Fischer's at the American's peak. He regularly takes on entire national sides in simultaneous multi-board displays. In recent years the Argentine, American and German chess teams have experienced such national humiliations at the hands of this one man. There are times when Kasparov seems to believe that he is unchallengeable by mere human opponents (one of whom, defeated, described him as a 'monster with a hundred eyes') and has taken to playing matches against Deep Thought, the world's most powerful chess-playing computer, which is capable of analysing over 2 million positions a second (Kasparov won). During his most recent defence of his title, against the former world champion Anatoly Karpov in 1990, Kasparov pronounced, 'I want the best, best, best. I'm not playing against Karpov. I'm playing against God.'

There is a third facet to Kasparov's success and it is the one which most terrifies other players. He has an extraordinary, almost animal energy. To meet the man, let alone play chess against him, is an intimidating experience. He seems to be in a state of perpetual motion. Even when he is sitting down he gives the impression of hovering a few inches above the chair, like a human humming-bird. His nails are bitten almost to the quick, and his face tends to break out into bright red pustules, as if the sudden surges of energy have no other means of release. Kasparov's opponents, seated toe to toe against the world champion, find these waves of energy and aggression every bit as difficult to cope with as the play of the champion on the board. Indeed, his opponents' terror makes the champion's moves even more destructive than they need be, and it is this, rather than any unbridgeable gulf in chess talent, which has in the past prevented Nigel Short from showing his true mettle against Kasparov.

When I spoke to Nigel just after he had qualified for the match against Kasparov, which itself involved three years of tournament and match victories over all other contenders, he wearily conceded, 'At the moment I would be utterly crushed if I played Kasparov. Not a chance. I have to build up my inner strength. It's like a muscle. You have to exercise it the whole time.' This is what Nigel has been doing for the past few months, through a mixture of intense study of the champion's games, meditation, and – for almost the first time in his 28-year-long life – regular physical exercise.

Last week I visited Short at his pre-match safe-house, the Fenja Hotel in Chelsea. Although I had seen him several times in the interim, I was still amazed by the transformation from the pale and exhausted survivor of the three-year world championship eliminating cycle. He was serenely confident. We sat up until late talking and drinking, until, looking at my watch, I asked him whether or not he ought to be doing some work, since it was only a week before the match was to start. 'No. I've done all the work I need to. If I'm not ready now I never will be. I feel good.'

Physical well-being, ultimately, could decide the contest between two mighty intellects. The match is scheduled for 24 games over eight weeks. Ferocious concentration over such a long period places as much a strain on the body as it does on the mind. As Kawabata wrote of the similarly interminable struggle for the supreme title in the Japanese chess equivalent, Go: 'The required concentration cannot be maintained or the tension endured for whole months. It means something akin to a whittling away of the player's physical being.'

Generally, the contestants in world chess championship matches lose about ten per cent of their body weight, through a mixture of extreme stress and calorie burn-up. It is, quite literally, the survival of the fittest, and explains why, to the mystification of some members of the public, the peak age for a chess player is not much older than the peak age of an athlete.

Pictures published in the *Sunday Express* last week showed Kasparov lifting 100-kilogram weights at his training camp in Croatia, under the careful attention of his full-time 'fitness instructors', Alexander Kosik and Yevgeny Borisov. When, a few weeks ago, I went to a gymnasium with Nigel, the British challenger was instead concentrating on exercises which demanded endurance rather than explosive physical strength. These choices reflect the players' differing approach to the game itself. We can expect Kasparov to mount massive attacks right from the opening and to go for quick, concussive knockouts. Short, however, if his semi-final win against the former world champion Karpov is any guide, will try to absorb the shock of the initial attack, and hope to take strategic control of the game during the fourth hour of play, the time when most games between well-matched grandmasters reach a crisis.

The games will start at 3.30 in the afternoon on Tuesdays, Thursdays and Saturdays: the Savoy Theatre, the match venue, will never have seen a matinee performance like it. If any game is not decided after six hours' play – as frequently is the case – then one player will 'seal' his next move, and the game will be adjourned until the following day. It is at this point that other, no less specialised, brains come into play. Both champion and candidate have analytical teams, who, if necessary, will stay up throughout the night, attempting to crack the mysteries of the adjourned position.

This is yet another facet of the game at which Kasparov, with a little help from his friends, has excelled. Originally financed by the Communist Party in his home state of Azerbaijan, and more recently by his own considerable retained earnings, Kasparov has always had at his beck and call a number of Soviet, now ex-Soviet, grandmasters – 'lackeys and slaves' Short calls them. In return for the wonderful gift of foreign currency they have given him the very best of their ideas, in the opening, in the middle game, and in the endgame. Sometimes they have been described collectively as 'Team Kasparov'.

For the world championship in London, Team Kasparov, apart from the champion himself, will consist of grandmasters Zurab Azmaiparashvili, Sergei Makarichev and Alexander Beliavsky. There might be others, but those were the only names that Short had been able to uncover before the start of the match. These three gentlemen will have spent much of their months secluded with Kasparov in Croatia separately and collectively analysing Short's games for every possible weakness and point of vulnerability.

Although Short himself has relatively small sums at his disposal and has never received a penny from the British government, an endowment from the insurance company Eagle Star has enabled him to take on as coach Lubomir Kavalek, the Czech chess champion who defected to the United States after the crushing of the Prague Spring by Soviet tanks in 1968. In 1972 Kavalek got sweet revenge as Bobby Fischer's second during the American's capture of the world chess championship from Boris Spassky, and would dearly love to make it a double. Lubomir – 'Lubosh' to his friends – regards it as a pleasure as well as a duty to humiliate the mighty ex-Soviet chess machine, and likes to point out that while Spassky, at least, was never a member of the Communist Party of the Soviet Union, Garri Kasparov most certainly was. Three weeks ago, Nigel completed his team by hiring Dr Robert Hubner, the German champion, as his chief analyst. Dr Hubner, a friend of Short, is the most thoroughbred logician in the chess world, and the last man to have defeated Kasparov in tournament play.

But, if Nigel does get into difficulties during the first game in the Savoy Theatre next Tuesday, it will not be to Kavalek or Hubner that his eyes will turn. Instead, Nigel's wife, Rea Karageorgiou, a Greek psychotherapist seven years his senior, will be seated firmly in his line of vision, as she has been throughout all his world championship eliminating matches over the past three years. And after the game, if things go badly, it will be with Rea, a woman of enormous strength and intuitive commonsense, that Nigel will exorcise his defeat.

Kasparov has, if it is possible, an even more symbiotic relationship with a woman than Nigel has with Rea. That woman is not his wife, Masha. She will remain in Moscow. The woman in question is the champion's mother, Klara Kasparova. She has been the dominant figure in Garri's life since his father died when the future world chess champion was seven. Since then she has 'devoted herself entirely to my chess career', as her only child gratefully wrote in his autobiography. And he has reciprocated with an extraordinary closeness to her. During the games she will sit in the Savoy Theatre with her strong, handsome features etched with suffering, feeling the struggle with an intensity which in turn transmits itself to her son and nourishes him in his attempt to bring the maximum mental pressure to bear upon his opponent. I have seen this happen in other of Kasparov's world championship matches. It is frightening, even from the relative safety of the dress circle.

'I can safely say,' Kasparov pronounced when Short became the official challenger for the World Chess Championship, 'that my match with Nigel Short will not be much of a contest. He is not even the second best player in the world.' But, the champion then grudgingly conceded, 'Short is the best fighter.' Indeed he is, which is why he has beaten higher-rated players than himself to get this far. I have been with Nigel Short at various times in all his world championship matches, and I have never ceased to be surprised by his appetite for the struggle. He very rarely seems to be cast down by even the most comprehensive defeat, but is only made the keener to fight his opponent on the next day. He is almost devoid of self-pity, and it is this, allied to a natural Northern toughness, which makes him a match player of rare resilience.

Nigel will need all of that toughness and resilience against Garri Kasparov. As the champion himself has said: 'In long matches – and I have already played five world championship matches – I feel if you have any weakness inside you, you are in major trouble. Even if your opponent is not experienced enough to see it, it will be shown in your moves, because your hand will not be as steady as before . . .'

In all sports, confidence is the key to success. When that goes, often for no very obvious reason, everything else collapses. The top tennis player double-faults on set point, the international cricketer bowls a series of no-balls, the golfing superstar gets the yips, the £5 million footballer misses a penalty. But in chess, a game which, unlike all the others, is entirely in the mind, with no limbs trained to take over when the brain is in crisis, a collapse of confidence is terminal. Above all, across the board the opponent can sense this mental bleeding, as clearly as a boxer can see blood oozing from his adversary's head. Ultimately, the contest between Nigel Short and Garri Kasparov, the culmination of a decade's arm's length rivalry, will be decided by the balance of confidence and fear at the time of greatest crisis. It could not be otherwise in such a battle of wills.

Fear itself is not, *pace* Roosevelt, the only thing that Nigel Short has to fear, but it is the most important. Perhaps he should take his courage from the example of a Dutchman called Max Euwe, who in 1935 became – to date – the last European to win the world championship. His opponent, Alexander Alekhine, was the greatest of all Russian world champions, with an intimidating and destructive way of playing chess which Kasparov has consciously imitated. Against all expectations, Euwe won. He wrote afterwards:

> Before tackling Alekhine I had to forget the contrast between our general records, or I should have been frightened. Earnest study of Alekhine's games had taught me that many of his most beautiful conceptions are based on his opponents' exhibiting traces of nervousness at the critical moment. So I knew already, before the match started, that only by fearlessness could I succeed . . .

I do not know if Short has managed to conquer his fear of Kasparov, but I am not afraid for Nigel. Kasparov has more than once said that 'in chess, if you beat your opponent, you destroy his ego'. This holds true for the author of the remark, whose monstrous ego could not withstand the loss of his title. Nigel, however, will be the same modest yet proud man, whether he wins or loses. That is what makes him a proper British sporting hero.

4 September 1993

DIARY

A. N. Wilson

I rather admired a friend of mine who inherited a baronetcy this summer and decided not to use his title. He and his wife both lead middle-class lives in London and felt it would be vaguely ridiculous to dub themselves Sir This and Lady That. Such things are no doubt still a little different in the country, where one would consider it affected if those with ancient or grand titles chose not to use them. There is an inevitable embarrassment factor where titles are concerned; English custom lacks the handy French habit of referring to Dukes as M. de So-

and-So. As with so many things in life, it is a matter of playing things by ear, but it is hard not to wince when the widows of knights insist on calling themselves 'Lady' This or That, or when the children of life peers deem it worthwhile to dub themselves 'Honourable'.

4 September 1993

ANOTHER VOICE

BETTER FOR THIS MAN IF HE HAD CHANGED SEX

Auberon Waugh

In a single, 20-line paragraph of his brilliant 'Diary' in last week's *Spectator*, A.N. Wilson disposed of a matter which has troubled my waking hours for as long as I can remember. It was on the subject of titles, their place in British society, the way we feel about them etc. By 'we' of course I mean chaps like me, Andrew, Angus and the rest of us – chaps who might reasonably have given a certain amount of thought to the matter. Wilson's disposal of the whole subject in 20 lines at the beginning of his 'Diary' hinted that he had other, more important things to talk about, and I confess I was most grateful to learn that the bursar of Exeter College, Commander Simon Stone, a former signals officer on the royal yacht *Britannia*, will be known as Ms Susan Marshall from the first day of next term.

But an awareness of titles is almost universal among Britons, whereas the temptation to change sex is still restricted, even among former naval officers. An Englishman who generalises on such a subject in no more than 20 lines must be either hiding something or suppressing more emotions than are usually considered healthy to suppress. Let us examine Wilson's statement line by line:

> I rather admired a friend of mine who inherited a baronetcy this summer and decided not to use his title. He and his wife both lead middle-class lives in London and felt it would be vaguely ridiculous to dub themselves Sir This and Lady That.

On the face of these two sentences, it is hard to see how Wilson's friend has done anything to be admired. Many might have admired him for inheriting the baronetcy in the first place. Despite everything said and written on this subject in recent years, it is extraordinary how many of our less sophisticated fellow countrymen continue to admire anyone with a title, just as it is extraordinary what complicated emotions titled people stir in the breasts of the more sophisticated. Again, it is a perfectly normal thing for people to take action to avoid being made to look ridiculous, even 'vaguely ridiculous'. There need be nothing shameful in that. But one does not admire someone simply because he does not wish to look ridiculous.

Nor is it true that Wilson's friend and his wife would have had to dub themselves Sir This and Lady That. They would have been invested with their new dignity and acclaimed in their titles by the social custom of their country. It would be easy to condemn Wilson's friend and his wife as traitors to their class and to the system which once distinguished Britons from lesser breeds, gave our nation its character and pre-eminence, created the culture of the English country house, which is the highest point of western civilisation, to which French, Germans, Dutch, even distant Poles and Czechs once aspired.

But perhaps it is not reasonable to accuse people of betraying a cause which is already lost. In the foolish, muddled perceptions of our time, by no means everyone is agreed that the collapse of the class system is the chief mark of our national decline. There are those who feel they have done well out of the collapse, or that they would not have been able to do so well under the previous system. I do not really wish to accuse the mysterious Mr This and Mrs That of betraying their class when they refuse to call themselves Sir This and Lady That like everyone else.

'There is an inevitable embarrassment factor where titles are concerned,' writes A.N. Wilson. No doubt it is felt by all the peers of Britain – 24 dukes, at my last count, 29 marquesses, 157 earls, 105 viscounts, 441 hereditary barons . . . what business, one asks oneself, have mere baronets, as they go about their middle-class lives in London, to feel embarrassed in this company? Last time I made an emergency call on a London dentist, I found rather to my surprise that my root canals or whatever were being attended to by a hereditary baron. The crime of which A.N. Wilson's friends might reasonably be accused is not so much that of betraying their class, but of treason to something much more sacred, an Englishman's sense of the absurd.

I wonder how many people have the faintest idea how many baronets there are. I held a sweepstake last weekend in Somerset. A local landowner (younger brother of a Shropshire earl) put it at 150. His daughter, married to an insurance executive, said 200. A daughter of mine, married to a businessman, said 100. My wife (sister of a Surrey earl) put it at 75. Her brother (the Surrey earl, himself a baronet) came through on a cellular telephone to announce confidently that the figure was 3,000. In fact, as I eventually discovered from the Home Office which keeps the Roll, there are between 1,230 and 1,330, the higher figure allowing for unclaimed baronetcies and those whose claims have not been properly established. Any group as large as that, scattered through the country, many no doubt working as vets, accountants, journalists, is part of the warp and weft or woof of society.

Perhaps one should say it is part of the woof. Undoubtedly, it is one of the more absurd ingredients in our national comic opera, and those born to it are required to play a slightly absurd role. There are some advantages to it, if not many. A Polish count to whom I put the question told me he wears his 'title' like a dinner jacket, only on those occasions which seem to demand it. But it is this enjoyment of life's rich absurdity which distinguishes the English, at least, from apes, Americans, Germans and most of the rest of the human race. We must all play our parts. To decline to do so on the grounds that you find it embarrassing or socially constricting is to renounce any meaningful participation in British life.

Of course it might turn out that A.N. Wilson's friend works for Murdoch, in which case the humour even of his renunciation is lost. We cannot throw too many stones. Even if we accept the Murdoch presence as part of an enemy occupation of our country, how many of us can be certain that we would have acted heroically as Frenchmen in occupied France? No doubt most of us would have continued editing literary journals as before. A.N. Wilson ends his famous 20 lines with a trenchant observation:

'It is hard not to wince,' he says, 'when the widows of knights insist on calling themselves "Lady" This or That, or when the children of life peers deem it worthwhile to dub themselves "Honourable".'

What one earth does he expect widows of knights to call themselves? As I say, it is extraordinary what complicated emotions titled people continue to stir in the breasts even of the most sophisticated. At least A.N. Wilson is happy to remain part of our national comic opera. As Mark Steyn observed recently, 'Britain has always been best at good middlebrow art. Gilbert and Sullivan rather than Beethoven;

P.G. Wodehouse, not Goethe.' It does *The Spectator* no harm to be edited by the child of a life peer. Even *Literary Review* might carry more weight if it were edited by a baronet.

11 September 1993

BOOKS

VARIATIONS OF A TEAM

Hugh Trevor-Roper

CODEBREAKERS: THE INSIDE
STORY OF BLETCHLEY PARK
edited by F.H. Hinsley and Alan Stripp
OUP

The wartime achievements of Bletchley Park, alias BP, alias Station X, alias GC & CS, are now generally known. Throughout the war, and for nearly 30 years after it, they were a wonderfully well-kept secret. Churchill, in his war memoirs, never mentioned them, although those already in the know could interpret his arcane allusions to 'our spies in Germany'. Then suddenly, in 1974, the story was revealed by Group-Captain Winterbotham, a former member of MI6, whose official function during the war had been to enforce the rule of absolute secrecy. Indeed, he once told me that he threatened any officer who should break that rule with instant execution. So his own pioneering breach of it has always struck me as paradoxical. To the former members of BP it was a shock; indeed, it shocks them still.

No doubt this long-preserved silence was partly psychological. Those engaged in this delicate work were so conscious of its importance, so careful of its security, and so bound together in loyalty that secrecy became second nature to them and its maintenance a point of honour. Besides, the details of their work were so complicated that it is hard to explain them, or make them interesting, to the uninitiated, as some readers of this book may find. But the book is an important record, for it is essentially their book: a series of essays and reminiscences describing life and work at the institution which, in the course

of a single year, uniformly disastrous in the field, 'raised secret intelligence to a position in the directing of war which it had never held
before', and so contributed, perhaps decisively, to final victory.

I first knew BP in January 1940. It was then in its infancy and seemed
informal, even amateur, in its organisation. The few officers worked
mainly in the hideous Victorian mansion which had been taken over
by the late head of MI6, Admiral Sinclair. But these officers were, or
included, the survivors from Admiral 'Blinker' Hall's famous 'Room
40' at the Admiralty in the war of 1914 and the institution still retained
a certain naval flavour. Its head, Alistair Denniston, had the rank of
Commander and had acquired, while teaching French at Osborne, a
very convincing nautical roll. Other professionals were Colonel
Tiltman, Nigel de Grey, Dillwyn Knox – a classical scholar who had
translated an unbelievably boring Greek writer into indescribably
mannered English, and Oliver Strachey, the elder brother of Lytton, an
Epicurean pillar of the Oriental Club. These men not only provided
continuity with the first war: they also brought in, mainly from
Cambridge, the mathematicians, linguists, papyrologists, Egyptol-
ogists, chess-players, etc, who would continue their work in the
second. Denniston had asked for 'professor-type' men. Since no one
knew that the place existed, there could be no applications to enter it,
no open competition. Recruitment was by patronage only: an excellent
system, provided that the patrons are sound.

Such were the apparently amateur beginnings of an organisation
which, by 1942, was a highly professional factory employing thousands
of persons turning out some 4,000 German signals a day (as well as
Italian and Japanese) and communicating vital intelligence extracted
from them direct to high commands in the field. The Germans, of
course, deciphered some of our secret codes, but they had nothing like
this.

The material sent out from BP was known generally as 'MSS' (Most
Secret Sources), then, once the Americans came in, 'Top Secret (U)', or
simply 'Ultra'. The most spectacular and valuable category of it was
the regular communications of the German armed forces (including
the Abwehr or Secret Sources), which used varying forms of the famous
'Enigma' machine. The Germans believed the Enigma cipher to be
quite unbreakable. Again and again, faced by evidence that their plans
and dispositions were known to the enemy, they asked themselves
whether perhaps Enigma was being read, but always they ended by
excluding such a possibility. The machine, they thought, was invulner-
able – as indeed, in theory, it was; but there are also facts of life, including especially 'the indiscipline of the German operators' which, as

Peter Twinn writes, led to this 'catastrophe for German intelligence'.

The cryptographical problem was solved in the end by a combination of luck, daring and genius. The Poles – brilliant cryptographers – had reconstructed the Enigma machine before the war, which gave us a good start, though the design was changed later; the Channel gave us time, which was denied to the Poles and French; the capture of Enigma machines on trawlers and submarines helped. The genius, the hero of Enigma, was Alan Turing. Knox, who worked on it first, was (I now learn) defeatist about it, but Gordon Welchman was convinced that success was possible and persevered. He is the second hero of Enigma. At a critical moment, when an increase of manpower had been refused, he, with Turing and some others, appealed directly, over the heads of their compliant superiors, to Churchill, and won. After the war he was 'ridiculously persecuted' by the secret establishment for revealing what had already been published by Winterbotham. The scholars of BP were not a privileged class like the clubmen of Broadway.

Of the four sections of this book, the first deals with the production of Ultra – the organisation of the factory, the distribution of the work between its units – Huts 6 and 8 assigned to cryptography, 3 and 4 to analysis and intelligence – and the changes brought about by events, including the arrival of the Americans. The second section is devoted to the actual machinery: the Enigma variations (for they varied in type and time), the mechanics of decipherment, the construction of the *bombes* which unravelled the wheel-settings of the machines and yielded the daily changing key. The third section deals with an altogether different kind of material: the non-Morse teleprinter impulses transmitted at high speed by radio and used by the German armed forces at the highest level. It was known as 'Fish' and served to supplement Enigma, or replace it when that traffic was unobtainable, being passed by land-line, as in occupied Europe. Fish was invaluable after the invasion of Europe in 1944, for it revealed the information passed between Berlin and Field-Marshal von Rundstedt, the Commander-in-Chief, West. The fourth section deals with 'Ultra's poor relations' – field ciphers and tactical codes. Finally there is a section on the codes used by the Japanese armed forces. But the greatest cryptographical triumph against Japan was not British but American: the breaking of 'Magic', the Japanese diplomatic code, which incidentally turned the Japanese ambassador in Berlin into an invaluable, if involuntary, spy for us in the heart of the Reich.

Much of this is inevitably highly technical and does not make easy reading, and some of the recollections are on a trivial level, for the regular work was monotonous and continuous, in eight-hour shifts, and the discipline strict. As one of the humbler workers puts it, the triumphs of cryptography and interpretation depended on 'the unremitting toil and endurance of almost 2,000 Wrens' who kept the machinery going – 500 of them tending the *bombes* – but had no direct part in the thrills of the chase: they were members of a chaingang. Their

> long chain began with the Y service which intercepted the cipher radio messages and finished with the SLUs (Winterbotham's threatened officers) which distributed the information to the Allied Commanders, who, in the final reckoning, either used or misused it.

Or perhaps could not use it. For battles are not won by intelligence alone. The best intelligence in the world is helpless against overwhelming force. Ultra revealed dispositions during the Norwegian and Greek campaigns, but to no avail. It gave the complete German plan for the capture of Crete but could not save the island. Though valuable against the Italians in the African desert, it was not till 1942 that it could turn the scales against Rommel, who replaced them. Then it was vital. Analysis of its use, says Sir Harry Hinsley,

> fully bears out the view which Auchinleck expressed at the time, that but for Ultra 'Rommel would certainly have got through to Cairo'.

And it ensured the final victory there. After El Alamein the analysts of Hut 3 were impatient of Montgomery's excessive caution. Why did he not press on? He had 270 tanks while Ultra showed that Rommel had only 11 left: his supply ships, again thanks to Ultra, had been regularly sunk. Now he could surely be 'annihilated'. Above all, Ultra was invaluable at sea: it not only deprived the Afrika Korps of supplies; by locating and so defeating the U-boats in the Atlantic it also saved us from starvation. To say that BP won the war would be untrue and unfair. But it certainly tipped the scales, shortened the war, and preserved us from defeat. Where would we be – what would the world now be like – without it?

18 September 1993

SALE-ROOMS

SURPLUS TO REQUIREMENTS

Alistair MacAlpine

Sotheby's are selling goods surplus to the requirements of Her Serene Highness the Princess von Thurn und Taxis, whose husband's family did not invent the postal system. That most useful of inventions appears to have originated in ancient Persia. Ruggiero de Tasso, an Italian, decided to run a postal system of his own, which he did with great skill, helped by his two brothers. One, or possibly all three, of the brothers (it is not clear from the preface of Sotheby's catalogue) became the postmaster or postmasters of Augsburg. Then, I suppose, these three Italians became Germans, changed their names to Thurn und Taxis and started to collect castles and fill them with a variety of contents.

This all happened in the 15th century, so you can well imagine how many castles and the quantity of clutter this family accumulated over 500 years. Now, times not being what they were, Europe being in the grip of a great recession, Germany's situation getting worse by the hour and castles dropping quite out of fashion, Her Serene Highness has called on Sotheby's to dispose of a few items to raise a little cash.

Gold boxes and jewels have already been sold and they went very well. The present sale is described in six catalogues and a preface. Nothing like it has been seen since the contents of Mentmore were sold some years ago. Unfortunately the contents of Mentmore were a lot more entertaining than the bits and pieces offered by Her Serene Highness. The attics of ancient families in Britain are usually treasure troves of the unusual and the curious. Harewood House's attic was a fine example of this and that sale was a triumph. I can well remember when the contents of Stonor Park were sold. They included a marvellous collection of stuffed birds. Any British family who collected for centuries was bound to have the likes of a narwhal tusk, believed to be the horn of a unicorn; fossils and seashells; penny-farthing bicycles – really interesting objects of that sort.

Her Serene Highness is offering a motley collection of European furniture, china and paintings. The preface contains a potted history of the Thurn und Taxis family, directions on how to get to the sale and directions on how to bid when you get there. I am afraid that there was nothing in the whole of volume 1, furniture, that took my fancy. Volume 2, works of art, has as its frontispiece a picture of the studio of Princess Margarethe von Thurn und Taxis, 1870-1955. The catalogue tells us that she had drawing lessons as a child and then advanced tuition from Anna Lynker and Olga Wisinger. 'After 1900,' it goes on, 'she added sculpture to her accomplishments and one of her major works was a frieze, completed in 1910, in the dining-room of the Schloss Garatshaus.'

Eagerly I searched the catalogue for this lady's work. In time I counted ten paintings in another volume of the catalogue amongst several hundred other paintings and sculptures. I should not have bothered.

Next I came across a full-page illustration of the most sumptuous buffet, complete with footmen in livery – was this to show us how these people used to live before they called in Sotheby's? After that a rather good colour photograph of 'Furst und die Furstin von Thurn und Taxis' by 'B. Weber'. Her Serene Highness is seen sitting with her late husband, both dressed for another of those banquets. I like Bruce Weber's work. The photograph is, however, not offered for sale. Then comes 'a photograph frame containing a photograph of the late Furst Johannes von Thurn und Taxis', estimate £120. This lot merits a whole page of description, yet Sotheby's do not even tell us who took the wretched thing. There follow another three pages, of eulogy about Her Serene Highness. If Sotheby's were selling the lady herself they could not have devoted more space in the catalogue to her virtues. Then there she is again for no apparent reason on the catalogue's penultimate page. I admit she does look ravishing, in a large, red hat.

At this point I gave up on this sale by a family who seem to suffer from a delusion similar to that which ended the reign of dinosaurs on earth. Bonham's recently had a very successful sale in which dinosaur eggs went for £60,000 a dozen.

25 September 1993

ANOTHER VOICE

SOME SUITABLY EMINENT CANDIDATES FOR THE POLITICAL ASYLUM

Charles Moore

'Why is it,' asks Matthew Parris in the latest *Sunday Telegraph*, 'that in the *Telegraph* and *The Spectator* we read the articles of eminent columnists who plainly hate the man's guts and whose dislike for him goes deeper than political disapproval, amounting at times to a nasty sort of public-school nose-thumbing . . . and we are prepared to allow such journalism – seemingly motivated by spite – the status of serious commentary?'

This is in the course of supporting Penny Junor's defence of the Prime Minister in her new biography of him. Mr Parris quotes her judgment of Mr Major with approval: 'He is probably the most courteous man in the House of Commons. He has not climbed up on the backs of others. He has a high and rare regard for truth. And he cares about making the world a better place.'

As one who has written unfavourably about Mr Major in columns for all three publications, I feel that Mr Parris may be applying his strictures to, among others, me. I shall not plead innocent, because I do not see how one can prove one's own motives. All I can say is that Mr Major has never done me any injury, so I have no score to settle with him, and that I am surprised by the suggestion that public-schoolism should have influenced me against him, since for many years I found myself defending Mrs Thatcher and Norman Tebbit against phalanxes of Old Etonians. The 'grocer's daughter' dismissal of her was much more widespread than the 'Brixton boy' disparagement of him.

It may be that Mr Parris is right to detect a disagreeableness of tone, though. If he is, I apologise, but can perhaps explain. The note of acerbity comes from exasperation at attacks of the kind, though seldom of the literary quality, mounted by Mr Parris. For they are beside the point. The point is that Mr Major was and is unsuitable to be leader of the Conservative Party. Consider these words written in the *Daily Telegraph* of 24 November 1990, a few days before Mr Major won the second ballot: 'One would expect the man from the extremely poor background to be the more driven of the two [the other being Mr Hurd], the more abrasive, the more determined. In fact, however, Mr Major is diffident, easily tired, not very forceful. He made surprisingly few enemies in the course of his political rise. His reputation is politically dry, but is he, personally, perhaps a little wet? Can he, and his retiring wife, really face what they are embarking upon? Doesn't all this come too early for him?'

These words were right, weren't they, though I say it who shouldn't. What we have seen since White Wednesday is a more widespread acceptance of this view.

It is no answer to this to say what Penny Junor says and Matthew Parris endorses. One might not go quite so far as they, but it is certainly true that Mr Major is polite, that he is not, by the standards of politics, treacherous, nor, by the same standards, a liar. He probably does care about making the world a better place. It is just that none of these qualities, of itself, makes him fit to be Prime Minister.

It is the sentimentality on the subject of Mr Major that has been so irritating. One can forgive it in Mr Parris, who is sticking up for a friend and former parliamentary colleague, but it is less easy to indulge in the Conservative Party collectively.

This may sound an odd thing to say in a paper sometimes thought to be High Tory, but Mr Major's entire career has been so wretchedly unmeritocratic. He did not get where he is because he ever did anything original or daring, but because he did the opposite, because he was 'nice' (how useless that concept and yet how expressive that word has become), because, if you surveyed the parapet, you never, ever saw his iron-grey hair and large spectacles protruding above it. He was appointed because Tories thought that a man of his background must be a good thing, must have a feel for what ordinary people wanted, must represent a new, modern Conservatism.

There was no 'must' about it, of course. Iain Macleod, a former editor of this paper, furiously complained that Alec Douglas-Home was made leader by a Tory 'magic circle' determined to promote one of its own, preferably Etonian, kind. A generation later, the same mentality applies in reverse. A man of the people is exalted just because he is a man of the people. For a few heady months it seemed charming to have a Prime Minister who said 'God bless' at the end of a war broadcast, but then the underlying lack of cheerfulness would keep breaking through. The aim was classlessness but the result was a lack of class.

One of the things which is supposed to distinguish sentimentality from the true feeling is its rage when disappointed. This rage has fallen upon Mr Major. It came first from those Thatcherites – the majority – who had fooled themselves that he was One of Them. Now it comes from almost everyone – the journalists who originally puffed him, the opposition parties who feared his popularity and were beguiled by his amiability, the businessmen who gave money, the voters who trusted and liked him. Next week in Blackpool we shall find out how much the rage stirs in the breasts of the party workers who choose the people who chose him. As a result, Mr Parris's anxieties are becoming more justified. People *are* being nasty and unfair and spiteful. It is not Mr Major's fault that it is raining. It is not even his fault that my car radio has been stolen ten times since Christmas. But to read all the papers which quite recently exalted 'honest John', you might think it was. It has become very hard for the Government to do anything at all, so automatic is the abuse. Mr Parris may be leading a 'sympathy backlash'.

What ought to happen? In normal life, if employers conclude that someone is bad at his job, they sack or demote him. Since that is the conclusion that Tory MPs and, particularly, Tory ministers have now reached about Mr Major, the logic is clear. But politics is not normal life, and one lesson from November 1990 is that if you get rid of a leader you must know what you mean to do next. If the Conservatives, after listening to Mr Major's oratory next week, decide to replace him with Mr Kenneth Clarke, they will have someone who can lead, but will they have any clearer idea about European and economic policy and the relation between the two? On 1 January 1994 the creation of the European Central Bank begins in earnest, even though the markets have spent the past year demonstrating that it cannot work. The Government has forced through the treaty which makes the Bank possible, but at the same time it says that the Bank's declared purpose is illusory. It is not at the mention of Sir Richard Body that one hears the flapping of white coats. It is unfair to single out Mr Major for Electro-Convulsive Therapy. The whole Government needs its head examined.

2 October 1993

GLAD RAGS AND HANDBAGS

Vicki Woods

'She doesn't need hair and she'll bring her own clothes,' said Belinda, 'so she only wants make-up. And she wants to be in and out as fast as possible, Bob says, because she's got to be somewhere by six.' Where's she got to be? 'Bob didn't say.'

It was the great regret of my life that I never met Mrs T when Mrs T was the most important woman in the world, so I waited in the EC1 studio with some excitement to watch her have her photograph taken for the current issue of *Harpers & Queen*. We were all pretty keyed up. You have to watch out when there's minders about, and the Baroness's minders play drama to the hilt.

Belinda had been on the telephone for weeks to Bob, who was very MI5 about arrangements. He had told her to be vague about timing until the last minute. Indeed, he had told her not to talk to anyone about anything, but to keep 'em guessing. 'If I say "I'm Bob and I'm ringing about Monday," you'll know it's about the Lady,' Bob had said. 'You'll get the picture.'

Belinda got the picture and began behaving like Odette around the office, keeping mum and looking mysterious. Belinda had had a ride in Bob's car, which has a flash spytrap console covered in hot-line buttons where most people keep their tape-recorder, and they'd assessed 'the location' together. They'd swept the studio. They'd poked into this and that. They'd opened doors. They'd clocked the windows. They'd narrowed their eyes and checked the sightlines. Bob had said 'Tuesday or Thursday, fine-tuning to come later'; and here we were on a Wednesday afternoon waiting for the Lady to arrive. She was due at four. At five minutes to four, two cars drew up. At four precisely, after a bit of sweeping around the life-doors, in came Bob with a leather satchel under his arm, Herself with that rolling walk and a booming voice and a woman carrying garment-bags, who seemed to serve the function of a lady's maid or dresser.

The Baroness carries presence and personality before and behind. She hit the studio on a roll and kept booming. We all snapped to attention and formed a small circle, as with royalty, and she walked round it rapidly, grasping each person's hand and pushing everyone firmly away from her at the same time, as with royalty. 'How d'ye do, how d'ye do,' she said, whirling on to the next thing and suddenly finding herself in the kitchenette amid the ruins of a studio lunch. Action! 'Now dear,' she said, 'what's all this food lying around?' Erm, that was lunch. 'Lunch! Lunch!' [Glances at watch, now showing five past four.] 'Well, it shouldn't be lying around! Should be in the fridge! Cream cakes!'

Bob wasn't worried about cream cakes. He was prowling about on the balls of his feet, as minders do, especially minders who carry little leather satchels under their arm that they never loosen their hold of, worrying about sightlines and doors and windows. 'They'll spoil!' she cried, gathering up profiteroles and piling them on a plate, tut-tutting about hygiene and salmonella and looking round vaguely for cling film. 'There! Now!' she said, beaming, as the profiteroles were safely stowed at an ambient temperature. Bob, eyes narrowed wanted to check out the room where she was going to change. He was shown it. He prowled around. He didn't like the look of it. It was a huge, bare, brick, windowless room with no cubicle or curtain. 'You'll have to stand in front of the door,' he said to Belinda, 'and don't move until she comes out.' Meanwhile, the Lady was moving towards make-up and booming about clothes. She turned to her dresser. 'Crawfie,' she said, unbelievably, 'Crawfie, we brought the green suit and the navy?'

'I've hung them up,' said Crawfie, and the Lady seized her garment-bags and hauled out the green suit and the navy, booming, 'I've brought this green, which is a good, bright colour' – as we leaned over to look – 'and it's a good suit d'ye see, AQUASCUTUM, with this very firm, good stitching just here, d'ye see, on the lapels, which is how you can tell, it's the test of a good suit, this stitching.' She grabbed Sarah, the fashion editor, who gazed at Lady Thatcher's lapels with awed fascination, as well she might, with that Spitting Image voice and its fully elocuted, almost Edwardian vowel-sounds booming away in the very flesh. 'And it's brightened near the face with this brooch I put with it, d'ye see,' she said, 'and the buttons! which we found in New York!' Let's see the navy, we said, and on we whirled through more lapels and buttons. She said she'd try both, 'and then it'll be up to you.' Very professional.

She went off to have her make-up done, to the great satisfaction of Crawfie. Crawfie – such a redolent name! Lilibet's and Margaret Rose's kiss-and-tell nanny was called Crawfie – was pleased about the make-up and articulated her pleasure in the third person plural, as nannies do. 'We had our hair done just before we got here,' said Crawfie, 'and now we'll get our make-up done and we'll be all ready for dinner with the King of Jordan.' (Can she have said the King of Jordan? Perhaps it was the Prime Minister of Saudi Arabia.)

Meanwhile, behind the camera, we were getting a tiny bit exercised by the Chair. We wanted the Baroness photographed seated on a heavy brass chair, which looked worryingly like a gold throne if you looked at it with eyes narrowed (Bob's unceasing eye-narrowing was catching) – and if she didn't like the look of the chair – or throne – it would take four men a good bit of wasteful time to lift it out of the studio and swap it for another chair. We had other chairs, but they looked like mimsy little spindle-legged things for this massive presence to sit on. Maybe she wouldn't notice the chair.

There were noises off, and she rolled in like a gun-carriage, in the sharply-cut navy suit. It had looked on the hanger like the sort of perfectly ordinary light wool suit you could buy at Aquascutum for about £600, say, but looked as she moved like ten times the price: hanging beautifully, fitted on her body like couture. Her Iron Lady hairdo gleamed like a crown, and her skin glowed. She is very conscious of the handsome figure she cuts and clearly enjoys her charisma. She saw the chair and stopped dead. Jason, the art director, said, 'It's a British chair. Very modern. Made by somebody British. It's a British shoot. For the British issue.'

Slight pause. Raised eyebrow. Then, 'If it's good for Britain,' she said, 'I'm ALL FOR IT,' springing towards the golden throne. And then she folded one hand over the other and submitted, like a real pro, to 40 minutes of snapping, turning, holding, powdering and changing into the green suit halfway through, while diffident girls fiddled with her at hem-level, and tucked rogue bits of dangling petticoat up to her surprisingly unshaven knees.

Once all the pictures were done, the whole circus whirled into leaving mode; Bob still prowling, scanning, sweeping and nursing his underarm satchel. I couldn't resist asking, 'Are you packing a piece in there, Bob?' A question you always get an answer to in America. But not here, oh no. And not at *The Spectator* party, where I asked him again.

2 October 1993

BOOKS

THE WASPISH GRANDEE

Frederic Raphael

UNITED STATES: COLLECTED ESSAYS
by Gore Vidal
Deutsch

Before we get down to cases, here is an exercise in the etiquette of reviewing. You are sent a book of essays of very many pages, which you look forward to reading over the summer months, as to a sort of pro-longed, even spicy, intellectual buffet. After starting it, you discover, buried among its mountainous 1,200 or so pages, a mousy reference to yourself. Do you consider (a) that you can still read and give a fair account of the book or (b) that honour requires you to disqualify your-self from the critical role or (c) that you will not mention the slight, but grab the opportunity to give as good (or bad) as you've got or gotten?

Now for the supplementary: if, having chosen option (a), you find that your response is, in general, one of qualified enthusiasm, should you congratulate yourself on your unfashionable fair-mindedness or suspect yourself of intimidated toadyism? That this piece has been written at all reveals my belief that I can rise above personal pique, but you should perhaps allow for a tincture of bile.

Gore Vidal's greatest merit is moral courage, which I suspect to be sustained by his having had what used to be called 'a good war'. He makes almost nothing of his service in the Pacific (unlike his close enemy Norman Mailer), but his reticence speaks in his volumes, which do not scorn to gore sacred cows, including (notoriously) his – I think – step-half-sisters, the Bouvier girls. Give or take a step, he does seem to be close to a lotta lotta famous people (Louis Auchincloss's stories get a familiar pat on the back, rightly). At times Vidal reminds one of a well-connected Alastair Forbes: a Washington DC insider right from the cradle, he lent his step-half-brother-in-law Jack Kennedy books on Byzantine economics, which – we are told – he may have read in the bath (he had less recondite things to do in bed). Gore says that he liked Jack, but eventually disapproved of his presidency (in the spirit of *ho gegrapha, gegrapha*, however, he has the nerve to reprint an early piece of drool over Camelot).

These essays are copious (an editor would be bold to approach G. V. with a comment more cutting than V. G.) and often intelligent, though some of the 'scholarly' waffle – for instance, about the *nouveau roman* – could be truncated and still be too long. On the whole, however, Vidal fights good fights; with accurate affection, he rescues the novels of Dawn Powell, which I have never read, from what sounds to be unmerited oblivion. His most enduring admiration, however, is for himself. He tells us, more than once, how famous his first novel made him and how he fell from grace with his third, which recounted the unblue adventures of a male prostitute and earned him non-person status in the *New York Times*, for which – understandably enough – he cannot forgive that solemnly sententious organ.

He was a dignified, sometimes savage, defender of a person's right to same-sex sex at a time before Gay Rights became a choral number. His defence of homosexual 'preference' is complex: he argues that adult sexual behaviour is a private matter – although it has been made 'political' – and that, if we were logical, we should favour rather than deplore it, since it avoids baby-booms (this was written pre-Aids). Secondly, he insists that homosexuality was commonplace in the ancient world, at least until Judaeo-Christianity did its stuffy stuff. To my mind, it is not really decisive whether the ancients approved or not (would we advocate torture or slavery because the Lyceum crowd said it was OK?), but it has been argued – for instance by Professor Peter Green – that homosexuality in Athens was a coterie activity, not a common dish on the sexual menu. If it had been, the comedy of Aristophanes' *Lysistrata* would not have worked, since the females' sex strike would have been rendered futile by male blacklegs. Pejorative references to catamites in the literature, and their habitual political disgrace, suggest that antique hedonism was less flexible than Vidal chooses to argue. More significantly, Laius, the father of Oedipus, was condemned by Zeus for his pederastic tastes (Zeus would not have appreciated the *tu quoque* mention of Ganymede). But then again, so what?

On American politics and politicians, Vidal is amusing and illuminating. His grandfather, he soon tells us, and soon tells us again, was a senator; his father was in FDR's 'sub-cabinet'; he himself has run unsuccessfully, but honourably, for office on a liberal-democratic ticket, sponsored by Eleanor Roosevelt in whose political faith and wisdom he still places a certain boyish credence. When it comes to Nixon, Nelson Rockerfeller and Ronald Reagan, he uses both invective and ridicule; he has his applauding *New York Review of Books* gallery and he plays to it very smartly. He also accuses Jack Kennedy of thinking that war was 'fun'. Perhaps he catches his own scent there, since polemic is available by the yard with him. I am lucky, I came to realise, to have been visited only by his teeniest gunboat (at least he hasn't called me a 'sissy', yet).

All right, I hear you, I hear you: so what *did* Gore (we're all on first-name terms with the nobs these days, are we not, Bryan?) say about me, and why? Well, in the process of sneering at Somerset Maugham, he alludes disparagingly to my little biography, which is his right. He then adds that I am the author of the obituary of Vidal, Gore, which he alleges may, unless he is assumed bodily into heaven like Elijah, one day appear in the London *Times*. As it happens, he has his leaked facts pettily wrong; it was for the *Sunday Times* that I was asked, one dark afternoon some years ago, to file a piece about him. Why me? Why not? Since I have admired his work (in particular *Kalki* and a number of the essays reprinted here), I agreed to write a paltry thousand words on Vidal's literary story so far, without in the least wishing that it go no further: I remember asking tenderly after his health.

However, Vidal clearly imagines himself the victim of a buried hatchet job (a fear which, sweetly enough, echoes one of Mr Maugham's own). Since he himself is said – truthfully, I trust – to have greeted word of Truman Capote's death with the verdict, 'Good career move', one can understand a certain (unnecessary) apprehension, which seems to have led him first to abuse my modest book – modesty being a charge unlikely to be brought against any of his own – and then, by way of a one-two, to go on to allege that I am someone who claims to have read books which I have not.

This witless charge passes a little beyond the genial malice with which citizens of the Republic of Letters must learn to live. It is, however, quite shrewd, in a silly way, since – like the chant of 'The referee's a wanker' – it is almost certain to have *some* truth in it (Gore's gospel, the Kinsey Report, having established that not only referees but nearly all those who abuse them have probably indulged in one or more handjobs during their lives). In much the same way, it is statistically improbable that anyone who has been subject to the English higher educational system can swear that he or she never referred to a text or author who had not been conned from cover to cover. Though few have the nerve to claim, as did Lawrence of Arabia, to have read all the books in the Bodleian, less flagrant lies are almost *de rigueur* among those seeking to gain academic applause or preferment (bluff is part of intellectual poker). Perhaps it has even been true of Vidal, though the last thing I should like to assert, without evidence, is that he is a man like any other.

In the style of a saint unsure that others will speak well enough of him, he asserts elsewhere that he esteems himself more or less unique in always reading every word of the books he reviews. Although *United States* supplies a demanding test of critical integrity, I have now read every word; but has the author? I hesitate to say that the repetitions, misprints and venial howlers suggest that self-criticism is not among his priorities, if only to avoid another outbreak of hostilities, but truth will be served, in due course.

As for the original *casus belli* (his literary luggage is swanky with Latin tags), would anyone be utterly astounded to hear that it is now 25 years since I observed, apropos *Myra Breckinridge*, that 'Gore Vidal has announced that the novel is dead, and now he has sent M. B. to the funeral'? Subsequently, I commented amiably on his work, but if you want your words to remain unremembered among book-chatters, you have to say only nice things about them. In the trudging pursuit of his long grievance (he has many, many more against other people), Vidal goes ironically italic over the use – in my 'twee' Maugham book – of 'constipated' to describe Theodore Dreiser's fiction. Perhaps, despite his etymological affectations, Vidal is not clear that the word means, literally, stuck together or coagulated in a lump; it says nothing of the quality of the mass, only that it is pressed together. Maybe *An American Tragedy* strikes Vidal, whose wit knows little brevity, as a model of airy elegance, but one is not obliged to go to the pillory for failing to join him in his tastes.

Vidal is a great one for great ones. As befits a man whose grandfather – you will remember – was a US senator (albeit from hicky-sticky Oklahoma, where the waving wheat etc), he is at ease in lofty company, where his horse can be relied on to be at least as high as the next man's. He writes persuasively well on Henry James, as of a classmate, and he jeers at bestsellers with condescending fairness (finding reluctant skill in Herman Wouk, whose orthodox, marriage-orientated Jewishness does not, *prima facie*, recommend him to the waspish grandee).

Although our author has too much *morgue* for Ezra Pound's 'suburban prejudice', he does not conceal his disdain for Ikey-come-lately presumption in the US socio-literary scene. Well, we can all wince together at the smugnesses of the late Alfred Kazin and Irving Howe and some of the *Commentary* crowd (Midge Decter's queer-bashing gets a deserved bash in response). Why, on the other hand, Vidal insists so querulously on the illiteracy of alluding to 'homosexuals' (he would

'You have the right to remain inarticulate'

like us to say 'homosexualists'), I am not clear. He objects to the use of
adjectives as nouns, but how seriously deplorable is it? Does he refer
to himself as an Americanist?

It is very much Vidal's style to adopt the haughtiness, if not always
the charm, of his betters: for instance, he preens himself on honouring
the Nabokovian distinction between criticism of his art (which he
affects to take in good part) and that of his scholarship. In the latter
case, the 'Black Swan of Lake Leman' – hardly an apt designation, since
black swans are found only in Australia, which VN never was –
announced that he always 'reached for his dictionary'. He did so to
better effect than Gore, who – had he reached for Liddell and Scott in
due time – might have avoided explaining the etymology of 'pornography' by reference to the putative Greek words *'pornos'* and
'graphos'. He would have discovered that *'pornos'* does not exist;
although *pornee*, the word for whore, had a number of derivatives, none
was masculine. As for *graphos*, my Liddell and Scott tells me that the
noun was used once in the sixth and once in the fourth century, both
in inscriptions and never in extant literature. Does it matter that
'pornography in fact derives from *porne(ia)-graphein* (to write about
whores or whorish matters)? Not really, but if one chooses to parade
one's scorn and irony, with regard both to Academe and to Hackademe
(a twee locution which I offer Mr Vidal without ascriptive obligation),

one had better get things – preferably everything – right, had one not?

Although he has given us improving entertainment with his recensions of the ancient world (the sideshow nature of Xerxes' Greek expedition was splendidly caught in *Creation*) and his *Julian* was a fine, if extensive, gloss on Ammianus Marcellinus, Vidal should beware of speaking in dead tongues. His *oeuvre* is heavy with play on the phrase *'e pluribus unum'*, but his coinage *'e pluribus meum'* is Latin which not even the dog (*canis*) would swallow or cough up. He admits to speaking French with André Gide, in his post-war youth, but he pays too bold a homage to the old master when he attributes to him the invention of the *'acte gratuite'* (sic). Even when propounding extremely silly notions of freedom, no mandarin Frenchman, however heterodox, would take it upon himself to change the gender of words.

Although its princely author may never believe me, and it is unlikely to deter him from another prolix display of Charlus-like *hauteur*, I did not solicit this volume, nor did I have advance knowledge of its reference to me. If I should not have reviewed it, *meum culpa*, as our author might say. After taking a good deal of pleasure in its *aigre-doux* flavour, I conclude that some people are born bloody-minded; others have Gore thrust upon them.

9 October 1993

POLITICS

MR MAJOR NEEDS TO WATCH OUT FOR HIS FRIENDS, NOT HIS ENEMIES

Matthew Parris

When there was madness outside the gates it was easier to postpone casting out the devils within. But down in Brighton the Labour Party pulled themselves together, and in Torquay the Liberals looked ready for business. The competition is back on the road. Here in our own travelling lunatic asylum encamped at Blackpool, Conservatives realise that some kind of internal exorcism is overdue. You pays your money and you takes your choice, but one devil or the other will have to go.

It will not happen this week. Nothing will happen this week. We needed something to talk about all summer, so we wrote that the coming Party Conference would be the test. That was never likely. Tory conferences are designed to give support and can do little else. If it were left to a conference to dispatch a leader, or an ex-leader, the parliamentary party would have failed in its duty – like asking the shareholders to oust a managing director or an elderly chairman. These things are a matter for the Board.

So it is the behaviour and demeanour of the directors that we must scrutinise this week. But this is not the place where they would act – they are here among shareholders to smile, hand around the canapés and gossip among themselves. Later they will meet behind closed doors. How are Members of Parliament, junior and senior, looking, feeling and talking? For John Major's supporters, there is a distressing, but not yet fatal, sign. The . . . here your columnist encounters a problem he has never met before. I want to use a word for Tory MPs which is hardly acceptable in a polite journal but which is quite central to something I need to explain: a word for which no substitute in our language will really serve. I think the Norwegian is *dritt*. Of course one could write 'rat' or 'cad' but neither captures the essence . . . Ah well, I shall write it and leave the editor to take the risk, or insert liberal dashes in place of letters . . .

The shits are on the turn.

The majority of Conservative MPs are not shits, but a good many are, and I am not sure whether Mr Major realises how many. Generally speaking, a parliamentary party well reflects the variety of its electorate. Tories these days are drawn from different classes, boast representatives of most trades and professions, draw upon a range of intellect and education which varies from the most polished to the sub-Neanderthal, and include at least as large a quotient of lunatics as are found in the population at large.

But two groups, I find, are hugely over-represented in parliament: lawyers and shits.

The lawyers are a problem but one we can deal with. They are extremely visible – it being hard to pretend that you are not a lawyer when you are – and so we learn to discount their oratory, take their opinions with a pinch of salt, and employ them in the tasks at which they excel: Chancellor, Home Secretary, etc., the jobs which are mostly a matter of reading other people's briefs.

But it is the shits who could cause Mr Major immense difficulty. About one in six Tory MPs is a shit. There are roughly 50 of them. We can mostly guess who they are and you would find surprisingly little disagreement among their own colleagues as to their identities: for, surprisingly, the quality is not variable but tends to be present – or absent – in a man. They are all men; this is not a female attribute. A man is or he isn't.

This is the element in the party which gives it its inherent instability. They will wash to one side or the other of their tanker, depending upon which way it is already beginning to lean. A well-designed oil-tanker is a honeycomb of many small internal compartments so that, as the ship rolls, its cargo does not all swill over in the direction of each roll, accentuating the aberration. A well-built political party should do the same, but, alas, the Conservative Party fails to meet this designed specification. It does, it is true, contain a few sealed internal compartments. Your proper wet remains a wet – and did, even when it was uncomfortable to be so, in the early Eighties. Your proper bastard (Lilley, Forsyth, Redwood) was a bastard before this suited his career, and would remain so should it again cease to be convenient.

Your genuine Federalist has been honest about it from the start and will not change. We know who they are. Your real Euro-sceptic is a brave man or woman and nothing – no stick, no carrot, no hankering to join the crowd – will alter his opinion. You cannot whip him. These people, all of them, give both transparency and stability to the broad coalition which our Tory party must always essentially be.

But your proper shit is different. You can whip a shit. You can bribe him. You can blackmail him. You may find him among the Euro-sceptics – or not. He may vote with the wets, or with the bastards. He may have been a great supporter, once, of Mrs Thatcher; then a keen fan of Mr Major's. And now . . .

Now the shits are turning. I see it in a score of raised eyebrows, I hear it in 100 little sighs, a dozen clucks of disapproval, many sneers and much sniggering about Mr Major's voice.

And so I say to Charles Moore, who complained on these pages last week that I mistake his motives in opposing Major, that I do not. They're noble if mistaken. Mr Moore is not a shit and never could be. But Mr Moore is not the problem; Mr Budgen is not the problem. Teddy Taylor, Teresa Gorman, Richard Body, none of these is the problem. These are the enemy, they are visible, they are honest and they are remarkably few. Mr Major's enemies are not his problem. His problem is with some of his friends.

Mr Moore will laugh at me for saying this, but I do believe it: the only question to be settled now is whether a party like the Conservative Party in its present mood deserves a leader as sensible and capable as John Major.

9 October 1993

BOOKS

HIS REVELS NOW ARE ENDED

John Mortimer

LONG DISTANCE RUNNER: A MEMOIR
by Tony Richardson
Faber

Tony Richardson was at the forefront of the most significant theatrical movement since the war. He made British films important, when there was a British film industry. From *Tom Jones* he made himself a millionaire, and was prepared to lose as much of his own money when he sacked Richard Burton from *Laughter in the Dark*. He was a director of great brilliance with an unsure sense of narrative. He was a man of uncertain sexuality who loved his daughters and they, ungrudgingly, returned his love. His high, nasal tones and disconcerting laughter were widely imitated; only Nöel Coward and Ralph Richardson have had as many impersonators. I found him a loyal friend and countless friends found him a host of amazing generosity. Of all his theatrical creations his home in the South of France was perhaps the most fascinating. He ruled that beautiful and isolated place as Prospero ruled his island; and like Prospero he could think of a thousand magical ways of causing trouble.

Le Nid du Duc isn't just a house but a small hamlet surrounded by cork trees and looking out over a long, empty valley, half an hour's drive inland from St Tropez. The main house smelt of log fires and coffee, cooking and lavender; the cushions had been eaten by Tony's whippets and his parrots screamed in imitation of his laughter. There never seemed to be fewer than 20 guests at lunch at the long table in the sunshine by the back door; cleaning ladies, children, John Gielgud perhaps, or Nureyev sat down to lunch together. In this household Tony was the impresario, the observer, sometimes, it seemed, the instigator of shifting relationships, a role which saved him from boredom, his great enemy. If things got a little slow there was his majordomo, his steward, his small, good-looking Caliban, an ex-pavement artist, who could be relied on to sleep with anyone of either sex to complicate the situation. There were wonderful diversions at Le Nid du Duc, huge

Easter treasure hunts for which we would compose clues in verse and
Tony and I would sit in front of the house watching countless guests
stumble round the valley as confused as the characters shipwrecked in
The Tempest. We also did ambitious stage productions, mainly musicals, for which Tony acted as the lighting director and the audience. In
this book he describes Joely Richardson, then a child, making her
entrance, a mixture of beauty and fear, delicately removing long black
gloves in our production of *Gypsy*. Those days at Le Nid du Duc have
gone; Tony is dead, Jean-Pierre, the omnipresent majordomo, shot
himself and wounded his girlfriend. A way of life has ended, as it did
when the sound of axes was heard in the cherry orchard. I found it most
moving when he wrote of it in this memoir as a place he loved more
than anywhere else on earth. As Ellie says in Shaw's play:

> This silly house, this strangely happy house, this agonising house, this
> house without foundations. I shall call it Heartbreak House.

And in heartbreak house, it has to be said, Tony did something to
encourage the heartbreaks. When I left it once to fly to Hollywood,
leaving my wife in Le Nid du Duc, Tony said to her, 'I'll bet you hope
John dies in a plane crash, leaving you a nice, rich little widow.' I
suppose he meant it as a strange joke, but my wife didn't laugh at it. I
also remember one dinner party when a French movie star, whose
beauty I had always admired, was one of the guests. The evening was
uneventful, the conversation dull and Tony was discontented. We went
to bed early, but in the morning he was in the best of spirits. After we
had left the actress had thrown an extremely heavy glass ash tray at her
boyfriend. He had to be rushed to the outpatients in St Tropez. 'Six
stitches!' Tony was braying with laughter and massaging his thin
thighs in the way he had when he was particularly delighted. To do him
justice, it wasn't the pain he was enjoying, it was the drama. He wasn't
only capable of mischief, of course, he could be hugely kind. But he was
an enigma, a mystery. He drank champagne but seemed to care little
for his own comfort. It was impossible to tell which of the many bedrooms he slept in, or with whom. He moved in his magical and
mysterious way and left few clues behind him.

Natasha Richardson, his eldest daughter, a person in that household
with much-needed common sense, who from the age of ten used to sort
out the guests and organise rehearsals, found her father, at the beginning of his illness, lying on a sofa in his Los Angeles home (a not
entirely convincing reproduction of Le Nid du Duc) scribbling on
yellow pads. When he died of Aids she discovered the manuscript in

the back of a dusty cupboard where he kept his Oscars. She organised the publication of a book of great interest, many funny stories and some wisdom. But what I found surprising was the absence of so much of the Tony I love to remember. He has not, it seems and quite uncharacteristically, 'set down aught in malice', and this is disappointing. His comments on everyone are generally kind, even forgiving. I can't quite hear again the high laughter, which went with the thigh massaging, at all the great disasters. It's as though the approach of an appalling death, coupled with the love of his three daughters and their mothers who came to be with him, had produced moments of sunshine and reconciliation. It was a time when he could even bear parting forever with Le Nid du Duc.

> I know I will pass one day [he wrote]. As the peasants have passed, as the fires have passed, as all the dramas have subsided; but the crumbling house of stone and plaster and the hills and the cork-oaks and the winds will endure.

There are happily some actors he doesn't treat with complete forgiveness, Richard Burton and Ian Bannen among them. Burton was drunk and refused to come to the location, Bannen also failed to turn up and closed his briefcase on the mouth of an ancient lion brought to meet the English film unit in a ministerial ceremony at Addis Abbaba airport. It was also Bannen who caused a driver to skid off the road by seizing his genitals whilst he was driving at speed. Otherwise the past seems golden, even the long quarrel with John Osborne happily concluded.

But you must also look at the photographs of Tony. The eyes are piercing, hypnotic; the mouth, except in laughter, often turned down and disdainful. He was a very brave man as well as a generous one. He didn't really fear anything, and that was the secret of his uneven success. I suspect he met death with similar bravado. Above all he didn't fear failure. At the end of the book he tells a story of importance to all of us who live our lives as entertainers. An actor rehearsing a play by Beckett at the Royal Court moaned, 'I can't do it. I'm failing, I'm failing.' 'That's all right,' Sam Beckett reassured him. 'Go on failing. Only next time try to fail better.'

16 October 1993

ONE LETS IT ALL HANG OUT

William Cash

Los Angeles

It took a while before the blue-eyed, Oxford-educated Lord Alexander Rufus Isaacs – a highly-successful 36-year-old LA lawyer who trained at the Bar – worked out why so often he could not get a table in smart LA restaurants.

'Hi,' he would say down the phone. 'I'd like to make a reservation for dinner.'

'The name, sir?'

'Rufus Isaacs.'

'Hold the line, please.'

Pause. Hushed murmurings in the background.

'I'm sorry, Mr Isaacs,' a voice would reply, 'we seem to be fully booked.'

'What about tomorrow?'

'I'm real sorry, sir – we're booked up all month.'

Click.

As has been delicately pointed out to Xan, the only problem with modestly styling himself 'Rufus Isaacs' – from his Wells Fargo cheque-books to his law office voice-mail – is that Americans invariably assume he is black. They think his Christian name is 'Rufus' – being to south-central LA what Rupert is to the English shires. Nothing wrong with that, of course – although his great-grandfather, the 1st Marquess of Reading, was Lord Chancellor and Viceroy of India. 'It's a bit annoying not being able to get into decent restaurants,' he told me. 'But I don't like using my title out here because you find people always take it the wrong way.'

Like the 'middle-class' friend of A.N. Wilson, whose choosing not to use his newly inherited baronetcy has caused Auberon Waugh and Charles Moore some angst in these pages, Xan Rufus Isaacs is but one example of the burgeoning army of British toffs who have descended in droves upon America – and especially LA – in the hope of turning class-less.

In fact, Rufus Isaacs represents the reversal of a trend. In his famous Sixties essay, *The Mid-Atlantic Man*, Tom Wolfe savagely mocked the new breed of chippy, usually comprehensive or grammar-school educated Englishmen who embraced and imitated the executive lifestyle of the 'modern successful, powerful American' as a way of escaping the fetters of the English class system. Mid-Atlantic Man, he wrote, would probably be in a new industry like advertising, media, PR, banking, consulting and, above all, anything to do with the movies, television, the music business, creative agenting or management.

Traditional Mid-Atlantic Man would be say, Dudley Moore or Andrew Neil. When I used to work in Wapping, Neil's shiny black Jaguar was always parked in its special parking spot (Mid-Atlantic Man must have a designated parking space) outside the concrete steps of the *Sunday Times*. Rather absurdly, I seem to remember his having a Rand McNally road atlas of America exhibited on his rear parcel shelf. Casually lying on the leather back seat would be the American edition of books like Paul Kennedy's *Decline and Fall of Great Powers*.

As Wolfe put it, 'He wants to get out from under the domination of the English upper classes . . . He is vaguely aware – he may try to keep it out of his mind – that his background in England is irrevocably middle-class and that everybody in England is immediately aware of it and that this has held him back. This may even be why he has gravitated into one of the newer fields, but still the ancient drag of class in England drags him, drags him, drags him . . . '

Today, the very opposite is happening. In John Major's 'classless' Britain, where a disturbing virus of reverse discrimination now seems to work against anyone from a privileged background, droves of English nobs are effusively embracing the New World because they feel they are being held back in Britain by their irrevocably upper- or upper-middle-class backgrounds. There are an estimated 400,000 British living in southern California. A hugely disproportionate number are the rapidly growing new breed of Mid-Atlantic Toff.

Probably the most glaring example of Mid-Atlantic Toff in LA is 27-year-old Henry Dent-Brocklehurst. The energetic and ever sun-tanned Henry is the heir to Sudeley Castle in Gloucestershire – the royalist stronghold in the English Civil War which later became the family seat of the Dent glove fortune. Henry was meant to follow in the family tradition by going to Sandhurst.

'If you are upper class in England, you are discriminated against in the workplace,' he frankly admitted. 'It's one thing to go into the City, but if you want to do anything outside the traditional realms, especially anything like commercials, you are immediately called a "spoon". If you're considered a "spoon" by your bosses and colleagues – who are probably quite middle class – you always hit this false glass ceiling which you cannot rise above.'

In LA, Henry runs a television commercial company he has co-founded called Sudeley Productions – notable successes so far include a series of cat-food commercials. Having recently persuaded some Middle Eastern tycoons whom he met on a luxury yacht in Spain to invest heavily in his company – 'I told them that the best way to meet beautiful American girls was to own part of a film company' – he is in the process of expanding his business, with plans for a swanky new office on the Sunset Strip.

Henry lives in a regal four-bedroomed mini-castle off Mulholland Drive. The ivy-clad bungalow boasts a moated swimming pool, beside which Henry makes his transatlantic calls, and an electronic portcullis gate. Parked outside is a gleaming navy-blue Porsche 911 convertible and a dark green Cherokee 4 x 4 jeep. He is currently looking to swap his jeep for a Range-Rover. He's worried it could be getting a little *déclassé* in LA.

'You have to play the Yanks at their own game,' he explained over breakfast. 'You can't just walk into a restaurant with a Constable or a Turner (naturally, both of which he has) under your arm – so you have a car which says you are successful and have style. A car "combo" is very important because it means you haven't invested everything in your car.'

Henry Dent-Brocklehurst's five years in America is a peculiar story of ever decreasing syllables. Shortly after arriving, he dropped the 'Dent' and became Mr Brocklehurst. Now he simply styles himself Henry Brock on his business card. 'I just got fed up with wasting half my day spelling my name to dumb secretaries.'

As Henry admits, Mr Brock and Henry Dent-Brocklehurst are two separate people. The classless Mr Brock likes to read self-help books on power-executive 'assertiveness training'. He has taught himself American executive 'dialogue techniques'. Sliding into a Californian drawl, Henry gives me an example of how he might go about cutting a deal in LA. He will say, 'I really love you, I think your family's great, I respect you as a person, and I like you as a friend – but putting that aside, let's talk business . . .

'And in here . . .' he says, leading me into a dressing-room which looks not unlike a costume room for *Miami Vice*, 'this is what I have to subject myself to in order to pay for the old pile of bricks.'

Henry Brock's Mid-Atlantic wardrobe comprises at least 20 designer-suits, most in pastel colours; seven pairs of shiny cowboy boots – including one in green lizard skin; dozens of suede loafers, even a pair of Doc Marten's – not a pair of brogues in sight; four leather jackets; seven different pairs of training shoes – jogging, tennis, cross-trainers, for pumping iron, and so on. He has 30 pairs of jeans – in every colour you can buy.

Another Mid-Atlantic Toff in LA is 30 year-old screen-writer Alex Cary, whose father, Viscount Falkland, is Scotland's premier viscount – a former journalist, theatrical agent, and shipbroker who sits in the Lords as a Liberal Democrat, and lists his interests as 'golf, cinema, motorcycling'. The family title was created in 1620. Alex – whose title is Master of Falkland – has recently married an American actress, and lives in Beverly Hills. He turns up to play tennis on his Harley or in a two-tone Ford pick-up. 'Out here I am anonymous,' he says. 'The principal reason I like America is because of its size. The idea of escape is very attractive to me.'

A rugged and swarthy figure in his sky-blue 'sweat-pants', with dark-brown eyes and tousled hair, it is difficult to imagine him as one of the youngest acting majors – Scots Guards – in the British army in the Gulf war. He certainly doesn't wear his Brigade of Guards tie in LA. 'I came out here to really break away from England,' he admitted. 'In England, I found myself bracketed, required to behave in a certain manner – to do certain things.'

Out in LA, he doesn't use his title. In the Guards, his regiment had 'insisted' upon it. 'In this day and age, and especially in America, an English title doesn't bear much relevance. It can be embarrassing. Americans think that it is an advantage, which is something I don't play at all.'

He gave the example of how, shortly after he inherited his courtesy title, he went along to the British Embassy in New York to get his passport changed. When he informed the official that his name was now the Master of Falkland, she looked up at him and said, without a trace of humour, 'Oh, yes – we had the Master of the Universe in here the other day.'

Other LA toffs include the Hon. Jack Ashton, son of Lord Ashton of Hyde, who drives a Harley and has recently completed a masseur's course at UCLA, and Old Etonian actor 'Baron' Clement von Franckenstein, whose father was Austrian ambassador to London between the wars. In his latest movie, *Fatal Instinct*, he plays a spoof upper-class English buffoon called Ambrose Arbuthnot-D'Avignon-Smythe-Jones. 'I made that name up,' says Clem. 'I'm kind of taking the piss out of myself.'

Some English nobs in LA have gone to comically absurd lengths to go classless. The most bizarre example I have come across is 24-year-old Mike Strutt, who went to Eton and read classics at Wadham College, Oxford. Although in line to become the 6th Baron

Belper, he is now happily living in sub-squatting conditions in the
basement of a rickety old house in Beachwood Canyon that doubles
up as the home/office/rehearsal studios of an up-and-coming young
rock band called Zebra Crossing. The super-swarthy Mike, who
manages the band, wears Indian hippie clothes, and carries around
demo-tapes in a smart leather briefcase given to him for his 21st
birthday by an uncle. He has been dubbed Lord Grunge of Grunge
Manor.

Mike wears a baseball cap the wrong way round when he plays
cricket under the Hollywood sign on Saturday afternoons. He drives
around LA in an old van which he bought for $1,000. Fitted with luxury
wall-to-wall carpeting, the vehicle came in handy in furnishing his
house. Whenever one of his band members – educated at Eton, Stowe
and Harrow respectively – saw an abandoned piece of furniture sticking out of a skip or lying on the side of the road, they would rescue it
and pop it in the back of the van. Lord Grunge's bedroom ('the shed') at
Grunge Manor comprises a cramped cubicle he has built for himself on
the corridor – just large enough to lay an old mattress on the floor. He
says he is very happy there.

Although the day that 24-year-old Lord Grunge sits in the House of
Lords remains decades away, he says of his future title, 'I doubt I would
ever use it over here, or bring it up in conversation. The enticement of
girls who fawn over the aristocracy doesn't appeal to me.' Mike stresses
that he is not a 'class drop-out'.

But it is not just the aristocracy who have been flocking over to LA.
The real invasion has been from the upper-middle classes who would
traditionally have gone directly from university into the professions.
Whereas in the past most types who sought refuge in America tended
to be looking for a fresh start after some personal or career foul-up in
London, often drink-, drug-, or divorce-related, today is seeing a whole
new breed of British bourgeois class-exiles escaping to America
immediately after leaving university. They simply feel that if they
want a career in new industries like film, television, PR, creative management etc., any sort of privileged background is a disadvantage in
Britain today.

Everyone I have spoken to in LA has given me the same story – for
example, 25-year-old Harrovian George Ward – a graduate in fine art
from University College, Oxford. George now works for Channel
Productions on the Sony Lot as a 'creative assistant'. Following a job at
Warburg's after Oxford, he came out to LA after trying for a year to
work in film in London – and finding his background held him back.
'It works against you,' he said. 'You don't bring it up. There's a very

strong pay-your-dues thing in England, they don't want public school-boys coming in.'

One incident he remembers well. He trudged around to Jonathan Ross's Channel X company in London to leave them a copy of his CV. After walking out, he realised he had left his *London A-Z* on the counter. When he went back inside 30 seconds later, his CV was already in the bin.

Twenty-four-year-old Andre Burgess went to Eton and Balliol College, Oxford. He is now earning $265 a week working as a prestigious graduate-trainee agent at the United Talent Agency (UTA) in Beverly Hills. Before coming out to LA he spent a year in London, trying to work in films, and having a 'shit time'. During his interview at UTA, 35-year-old Jeremy Zimmer, one of Hollywood's top agents, glanced down his CV.

'What's this Oppidan Scholar thing at Eton?' he asked.

After Andre told him, Zimmer offered him the job on the spot.

16 October 1993

DIARY

David English

Diary writing is a new journalistic excursion for me. I have never worked on a newspaper diary nor kept a personal one. Indeed, I feel we should always be wary of obsessive diary writers, as the following conversation, which occurred at a recent party, illustrates. Andrew Knight, chairman of News International, greets Paul Johnson, who needs no introduction. Knight: 'Hallo, Paul. How nice to see you.' Johnson: 'Well, it's not so nice to see you.' Knight (taken aback): 'What do you mean?' Johnson: 'You told me that you were going to fire X' (he names a News International editor). Knight: 'I did not.' Johnson: 'You did and you have failed to do so. That is shameful. X is a vulgarian, a guttersnipe and a disgrace to the profession.' Knight (nervously): 'I assure you I never said I was going to fire anyone.' Johnson (triumphantly): 'Yes, you did and I can prove it. It is in my diary. I write down everything, every night. And that promise to fire X is written down on the day that you said it.' Knight (desperately): 'I am sure I said no such thing. I can't believe that I said anything of the sort.' Johnson: 'You said it! It is written down! I will show you the entry if you like. Not that it's important. What is important is that you haven't done it. You haven't sacked X and you should have done so.' Who is X? Nothing will induce me to say. We shall have to wait for the publication of the *Paul Johnson Diaries*, or, life being what it is, the serialised version which will undoubtedly appear first in the *Sunday Times*.

Meanwhile, Rupert Murdoch continues to construct his digital highway in the sky. The Government (and no doubt others) mutters under its breath about his increasing power. But surely Rupert is just a man who falls in love with new ideas and the fun of developing them first. Having said that, I must admit he can be somewhat unnerving even in jest. Some weeks ago, he asked if we were interested in the *Independent*. I said that as the *Daily Mail* no longer regarded the *Express* as a major rival and a reinvigorated *Independent* could usefully divert our real competition, the *Daily Telegraph*, I hoped that it would survive. I added that I couldn't see anyone buying it except for a musical price (and that was not on offer) because the cost of making it viable would be vast. 'Much more than vast,' Murdoch replied. 'And I'll tell you why.' He proceeded to let me into his plans to drop the price of the *Times*. Then, seeing my face, he touched my arm solicitously and added, 'Don't worry about the *Telegraph*. Leave them to me. I'll put them out of business for you.'

I invited John Smith to lunch and he was fun. Unlike his predecessor, Neil Kinnock, who refused to enter our headquarters, Smith thoroughly enjoys a knock-down-and-drag-out meal with the capitalist press. He has decided to press the cause of single mothers in opposition to the Tory tactics of denouncing them. He refused to accept the findings that the children of single parents (nearly always mothers) fare more badly in school and are more likely to be involved in criminal activity. Such surveys, he said, were warped because these children were victims of poverty not one-parent families. He seemed not to know about research conducted amongst the poorest part of the population, like for like, which shows children with two parents perform better in school and are more law-abiding than those with just one. He must read the conclusions, we said, of King and Elliot in the soon-to-be-published *Oxford Text Book of Medicine*. That brought about a change of subject and we talked about his heart attack. Going back to work, he explained, had speeded and completed his recovery, so he was pleased to see Michael Heseltine returning. 'It's the best way to get better,' he said. 'I know. And, anyway, what else would Michael be doing if he wasn't back in the House?' It was a good question, for Heseltine has not been enjoying his enforced convalescence. He told me in Blackpool that he had done something he had never had time to do before. He had watched a great deal of television. And? It had disgusted him. The 'transatlantic rubbish' was mindless and appalling. He just couldn't stand it. The violence and the gore of television was one of the reasons for the increase in crime in Britain. Could nothing be done about it then? 'I don't know,' replied the great interventionist. 'But I dread to think where society is going with it.'

When Margaret Thatcher heard that the friends of Larry Lamb were giving a private dinner for him, she re-arranged her diary so that she could come. 'Larry did so much for me and our party,' she said. The once formidable editor of the *Sun* has spent months recovering from a massive heart attack and, as he himself says, 'Don't get around much any more,' so Margaret's presence meant a lot. She was immensely solicitous, listening to his views, gently asking how he spent his days, talking about the old times, showing quite the opposite face to the one she had turned on Sir Robin Day the week before. Day (who seems heartily fit) tried his regular line of chat with her. 'I'm getting so old,' he wailed, 'I don't know what will become of me.' 'Don't talk such nonsense,' she answered briskly. 'But I'm nearly *seventy!*' he quavered, gazing at her expectantly. 'What am I supposed to do?' I have seen the old fraud try this technique on a number of comely young women at parties. It invariably brings out their maternal instincts and they often drop everything to go to dinner with Robin in order to see he gets proper nourishment. (They have of course inferred that he's too shy to enter restaurants alone and, unless he has a companion, it's home to an empty flat and beans on toast.) It's his personal Meals on Wails programme and it normally works a treat. But not with Lady T. 'Think positive, Robin. And do not give in! Look at Denis, he smokes and he drinks and he's seventy-nine. He doesn't give in.' He certainly doesn't, especially on the one-liners. When Margaret was telling Larry about the magnificent food and service in an oriental hotel the Thatchers had recently visited, he interrupted her to bark, 'So it damn well should have been. You may not have noticed, my dear, but they were charging like the bloody Light Brigade.' *Charging like the Light Brigade!* How does he do it? I intend to use this marvellous Denis phrase at every opportunity and I pray it goes into the vernacular.

23 October 1993

THE TRICK OF THAT VOICE

J. Enoch Powell

An individual by the name of William Shakespeare (variously spelt) was baptised on 26 April 1564 in the parish church at Stratford-upon-Avon, Warwickshire, and there buried in April 1616. We happen to have his will, dated also in 1616. At the end of 1623 or the beginning of 1624 ('1623' then ran to 31 March 1624), a sumptuous folio volume was published containing 36 plays, including some of the greatest pieces of English literature, as having been written by William Shakespeare. The prefatory matter to that Folio contained the earliest hint of any connection between the plays and Stratford-upon-Avon.

Are the two William Shakespeares the same? Indeed, do they have anything to do with one another? The world says yes, and has tended to go on saying yes. But is the world mistaken? There are some mightily curious facts which keep intruding.

In 1593 and 1594 respectively were published the poems *Venus and Adonis* and the *Rape of Lucrece*, dedicated by 'William Shakespeare' to the Earl of Southampton. After that, the name did not appear in print again until 1598. In the autumn of that year of 1598 a schoolmaster, one Francis Meres, published a pedantic work under the title *Palladis Tamia* or 'Wit's Treasury'. It is arranged on a repetitive scheme, citing in each compartment equal numbers of Greek, Latin and English authors, to illustrate and prove England's competitiveness with the ancients.

Suddenly, however, Meres throws his own framework over, with an astonishing outburst which has to be savoured in detail. The outburst is a kind of cuckoo in the nest, quite out of harmony with the rest of the book into which it is foisted. I will quote it in the original form in full and then comment:

> As the soule of *Euphorbus* was thought to liue in *Pythagoras*: so the sweete wittie soule of *Ouid* liues in mellifluous & hony-tongued *Shakespeare*, witnes his *Venus and Adonis*, his *Lucrece* his sugred Sonnets among his priuate friends, &c.

> As *Plautus* and *Seneca* are accounted the best for Comedy and Tragedy among the Latines: so Shakespeare among ye English is the most excel-

lent in both kinds for the stage; for Comedy, witnes his *Getleme of Verona*, his *Errors*, his *Loue labors lost*, his *Loue labours wonne*, his *Midsummers night/dreame*, & his *Merchant of Venice*: for Tragedy, his *Richard the 2. Richard the 3. Henry the 4. King John, Titus Andronicus* and his *Romeo and Juliet*.

It was manifestly fatuous for Meres to refer his readers not only to *Venus and Adonis* and the *Rape of Lucrece*, already published with the dedication by 'William Shakespeare', but also to the Sonnets which are tantalisingly described as only available to the poet's 'private friends'. Nor is that all.

The six comedies and six tragedies which Meres calls in evidence for Shakespeare being 'the most excellent in both kinds for the stage' are a remarkable list. One of the items, *Love Labour's Won*, is neither known under that title nor securely identifiable with any play known under any other title. Three items in the list, *Love Labour's Lost*, *Richard II* and *Richard III* were published or republished in 1598 (the year of Meres' book) as 'by William Shakespeare' or 'newly corrected and augmented by W. Shakespeare'. *Henry IV*, first published in 1598, was re-issued in 1599 as 'newly corrected by W. Shakespeare', *The Merchant of Venice*, entered at Stationers' Hall in 1598, was published in 1600 as 'written by William Shakespeare'; and *Midsummer Night's Dream* was first published also in 1600, with that attribution.

Two more plays in Meres' lists, though already in print, were not to be attributed to Shakespeare until much later. *Romeo and Juliet*, published in 1597, was attributed to Shakespeare in some copies of a quarto reprint issued in or after 1612. *Titus Andronicus*, published in 1594, was not attributed to Shakespeare until the Folio. That leaves three plays still not accounted for. *King John*, if that is 'our' *King John* and not *The Troublesome Reign*, was first published in 1622 as 'written by W. Shakespeare'; *Errors* (that is, presumably, the *Comedy of Errors*) is known to have been performed in 1594 but was first printed in the Folio; and *Gentlemen of Verona* (that is, *Two Gentlemen of Verona*) was first published in the Folio and no record is known of any performance of it.

It was thus not only in respect of the Sonnets that Meres was flaunting knowledge restricted to the poet's 'private friends'. He was also aware of the authorship of unpublished plays and plays published with no name of author which were to appear in the same year or immediately succeeding years as 'written etc. by William Shakespeare'.

The flow of such plays soon ended. After 1600 the only 'new' appearances, apart from the Sonnets themselves in 1609, were *King Lear* in 1608 and the pirated edition of *Troilus and Cressida* in 1609. I use the word 'pirated' boldly because that is what the publisher's preface says, cocking a snook at mysterious 'grand possessors', who would have prevented publication if they had had their way.

So where does all this leave us? In a situation which imperiously demands explanation. From the beginning of the 17th century a huge and glittering treasury of plays existed unpublished in the control of persons called 'the grand possessors'. In the years around 1598 to 1600 the author or various 'private friends' evidently expected imminent disclosure and were making preparations for it, if not actually making a start. But whoever expected that would have been doomed to disappointment. Not until somewhere around 1620 did the property become 'too hot to hold', and was publication of the plays not merely permitted but organised.

The problem was to account for their sudden appearance. The playwright Ben Jonson wrote a preface for the Folio explaining they had been issued by fellow actors, Hemmings and Condell, from the author's original manuscripts – a lie, if ever there was one, because (so it is generally agreed) the Folio used an already published text wherever one was available. And the author was – ? Why, Master William Shakespeare of Stratford-upon-Avon, now several years dead – his widow too having died in 1622. In case anyone asked to see the evidence of Stratford's recognition of its illustrious son, a memorial was erected in the parish church, complete with his bust* correspondent to the portrait engraved as frontispiece for the Folio edition. Someone not very well briefed produced for the memorial a copy of laudatory verses in Latin, setting the playwright on a level with (of all people) Nestor, Socrates and Virgil.

There existed, then, from early in the 17th century a mass of theatrical material, the source of which – indeed the ownership of which – it was necessary to conceal if profit were to be made by publishing it. We are moving in high circles, perhaps in the highest of all. Somebody of overwhelming genius had not merely created it but continued creating after current use was no longer being made of the material. Who was it? The secret was well kept – presumably because it had to be kept. That points to a group of courtiers who supplied the

---

I am unalarmed by the fact that William Dugdale's illustration of the monument (in Antiquities of Warwickshire, 1656) shows an altogether different bust in place: Dugdale's illustrations were often based on sketchy written descriptions.

court with plays, and to one person among that group whose identity has been industriously concealed.

I refer advisedly to 'a group', as the natural means of accounting for the notorious and phenomenal polymathy of the works attributed to Shakespeare. From inner knowledge of the politics of Italy and France to familiarity with professional vocabularies like those of the law and the Church, the spread of experience which even the earlier plays exhibit exceeds the scope of a single individual; and we too easily underestimate the potentialities of intimate co-operation between the members of such a group of literati as the court included in the closing years of Elizabeth I.

One would need to be abnormally credulous to believe that William Shakespeare of Stratford-upon-Avon wrote poetry and plays but left behind – not bequeathed! – when he died a massive further opus of at least equal volume and quality which had remained unused and (except piratically) unpublished.

It was an astonishing cornucopia, this treasure which 'the grand possessors', after complicated precautions, resolved in 1623 to pour out before the public. The power and philosophy of this 'new' work – it cannot be entirely fanciful to feel – represents an advance upon that of the plays of the 1590s. If so, composition must have been proceeding for all or much of the intervening time. So comes the acid question – the heart of the mystery of William Shakespeare – what sort of person was it, or what sort of group could they be, who created and accumulated with no visible outlet work of the fecundity and quality finally produced to the light of day in 1623 and who in addition were under some strict obligation of self-concealment? If we could answer that question convincingly, we should have banished forever the masked figure called William Shakespeare of Stratford-upon-Avon, playwright, who was invented to solve the dilemma. The deepest of all the mysteries, the nagging question which refuses to go away, is not 'who wrote those plays?' but 'what happened to create the black hole between *Hamlet* (printed in quarto in 1603) and the sending of the copy for the first Folio of 1623 to the printer?'

30 October 1993

TIME FOR FRATERNISATION

Timothy Garton Ash

One could recount the history of Anglo-German relations over the last few years in *Spectator* covers. First, there's Nick Garland's wonderful cover of 1988, showing a red-faced Margaret Thatcher sitting out the dance, while a cartoon Fritz and Madame Liberté whirl off to European Union in a Franco-German waltz. Then there's Peter Brookes' ingenious drawing of 1990, at the time of German unification, showing the shape of West Germany on the map as the face of Helmut Kohl, devouring little East Germany for lunch. *Der Spiegel* recently reproduced that one, to illustrate their extracts from Lady Thatcher's memoirs.

From the same year there is the Garland cartoon showing Nicholas Ridley daubing a Hitler moustache on a poster of Helmut Kohl. Subsequently, there is the short-lived period in which John Major seriously seems to believe that Britain now has a special relationship with Germany. So in August 1992 Garland depicts John Major with a huge portrait photo of Helmut Kohl dominating his desk, while on the inside illustration we see Helmut Kohl with a tiny portrait photo of John Major tucked away at a far corner of his desk-top. How true, how very true. Just six weeks later, the pound sterling is catapulted out of the exchange rate mechanism of the EMS.

And now? Lady Thatcher has, with her memoirs and with an outspoken interview in this week's *Der Spiegel*, once again thrown an outsize spanner into the Anglo-German works. In her memoirs, she says with remarkable frankness that she was opposed to German unification in 1990 but unfortunately failed to prevent it, because President Mitterrand decided after all to stick to Chancellor Kohl, and so did President Bush. 'You Germans,' she says in the interview, 'don't want to anchor Germany in Europe. You want the rest of Europe to be anchored in Germany.' The remark is rather outrageously abridged by *Der Spiegel* into the headline: 'You want the rest of Europe'.

It would be wrong to underestimate the hurt which such remarks, or reported remarks, can cause in Germany. For Germany, in sharp contrast to Britain, is still enormously sensitive to what the outside world says about it – and above all to the opinions of the former victims and the former victors of the second world war. To this day, when I go to Germany I still find myself being asked about the views of a certain

Herr Ridley, as given in Dominic Lawson's famous *Spectator* interview. And someone is always sure to mention the 'Chequers affair' – that is, the leaked memorandum by Charles Powell rather colourfully reporting a discussion with German specialists, including myself, at Chequers in March 1990.

The whole business has been forgotten in this country. Lady Thatcher quite rightly does not even mention it in her memoirs. Heaven knows, there were far more important conversations going on at that time. Yet again and again people in Germany still raise the subject – the word 'Chequers' in German having now almost the inverse symbolic connotations of 'Munich' in English. Of course we really didn't mind, they say; and then talk about it for half an hour.

Meanwhile, for as long as I can remember British diplomats and officials have gone around saying that the Anglo-German relationship is much better than it seems. In fact, they say, it is really more solid and substantial than the Franco-German relationship. It's just that the French and Germans haven't *noticed*, poor things. There is a touch of whistling in the dark about this, but there is also some truth in it.

In fact, one can make a strong case that there is actually an even greater overlap between British and German interests now than there was before German unification. But this large area of common or complementary interests has been obscured by the shadows of history, inherited misunderstandings and, in the case of Margaret Thatcher and Helmut Kohl, a straight clash of personalities.

Let's start with the shadows of history. These are actually not half as long as in German relations with France, let alone those with their Slav neighbours to the east. There is no great mediaeval or early modern conflict between our peoples. In the 18th century, when, as Linda Colley shows in her book *Britons*, the British national identity was forged in war and conflict with France, our kings were Germans. Whether or not Lady Thatcher's fighting spirit comes originally from some Saxon (i.e. German) warrior forebears, our monarchs certainly come from the houses of Hanover and Saxe-Coburg-Gotha.

No, what Paul Kennedy called 'The Rise of the Anglo-German Antagonism' is of comparatively recent origin. In his splendid book of that title, Kennedy traces it from 1860 to 1914. In the 1860s, Kennedy notes, *The Spectator* was in favour of German unification. By 1900, this journal was describing Germany as 'England's Real Enemy'. One of the main explanations Kennedy gives – the shift in relative economic power – seems somehow familiar.

Of course, it would be absurd to underestimate the importance of the subsequent, tragic experience of two world wars. But there is some

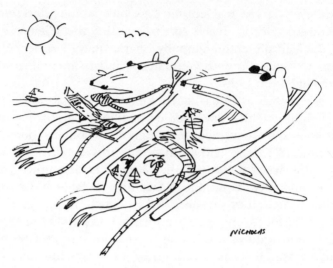

'It's great to get away from the human race'

real mutual incomprehension here. People in Germany are understandably offended by tabloid comparisons of, say, the Bundesbank with the Reichswehr. Yet they also, in my experience, often find it hard to grasp how far the British memory of war has nothing whatsoever to do with the Germans. For in harking back to the 'finest hour', affectionately or ironically, we are essentially talking to ourselves and about ourselves. *Dad's Army* is really no more about Germany than is *Coronation Street*.

Der Spiegel also illustrated its extracts from the Thatcher memoirs with a Mac cartoon of Mrs Thatcher pushing model battleships across a war-chart of Europe, while Denis advises her to have a nice cup of tea before declaring war on Germany. I wonder how many *Spiegel* readers really appreciated that this was a joke not against Germany but against Mrs Thatcher – and on ourselves. So all British war-related humour is liable to be misinterpreted unless stamped in large letters: *Britische Selbstironie*. (Peter Brookes' illustration to this article may furnish another case in point!)

This said, British attitudes to Germany surely do have an undertow of resentment which derives from the feeling that 'we won the war but they won the peace'. Unification, and the resulting further shift in political as well as economic power, at least temporarily sharpened the edge of that resentment. When the federal state of Bavaria had some difficulty adapting to German unification, the diagnosis ran: 'Germany has got bigger, Bavaria has not.' Well, nor has Britain.

This is further reinforced by the sense that Germany will always side with France, and that America is most likely to side with Germany. Those are the special relationships now.

It is often forgotten that Britain actually played a larger and more constructive part in the post-war reconstruction of West Germany than France, up to and including the unprecedented treaty commitment in 1954 of a British army to defend West Germany. But after Churchill declined Adenauer's invitation to take the lead in the integration of western Europe, after Britain declined to join in the process leading to the founding of the EEC, after de Gaulle made his grand, calculated reconciliation with Adenauer and signed with him the Elysée Treaty, then a course was set which Chancellor Kohl once again reaffirmed in the French Senate a fortnight ago.

Moreover, the United States has generally, if inconsistently, seemed to like and encourage this course. A Vicky cartoon of 1962 shows John F. Kennedy wooing the ugly sisters Adenauer and de Gaulle, while Harold Macmillan as Cinderella complains, 'But in the story I have a special relationship with Prince Charming.' When President Bush declared in spring 1989 that America and Germany should be 'partners in leadership', and consequently backed Chancellor Kohl in his rush both to German and to (West) European unification, Lady Thatcher obviously felt rather the same way.

And as John Major has discovered to his cost, Garland's 1992 cartoon with the portrait photos brilliantly captured an essential truth. Whatever may be said in diplomatic speeches, whatever his own officials may tell him, intellectually, emotionally and politically Chancellor Kohl simply does not regard the relationship with Britain as being on the same plane as those with France and America.

This – in, so to speak, cartoon history – is where we come from. But it is not precisely where we are at. Such a sketch neglects the deep ties that have been built up over 45 years, in business, in the military, in politics, in intellectual life, in all the élites represented at the annual Anglo-German Konigswinter conferences. It understates the degree of western and European integration already achieved, the habits of day-to-day co-operation. But more importantly, it overlooks the actual and even more the potential common interests.

The point here is that, while every state in Europe, including Britain, has to re-examine its vital national interests after the end of the Cold War, no state has a more fundamental re-examination to make than Germany. This is somehow obscured by the massive bulk of Helmut Kohl, who is profoundly committed to continuing on his old course of building a 'European Union' around a Franco-German core. But even if he emerges as victor from Germany's 'year of elections' (19 of them) in 1994, even if he carries on for a year or two after that, he is most unlikely to achieve that result.

There are too many streams flowing too strongly against it. In Germany, as elsewhere in Europe, Maastricht, intended by Kohl and Mitterrand as a European response to German unification, has proved a treaty too far. In Germany, as elsewhere, there is a strong reaction against the technocratic building of Europe from above. The Federal Constitutional Court has just hedged about the German accession to Maastricht with some quite significant reservations.

The federal states, the *Länder*, are worried about their own powers and authority being diminished. The German business and banking communities are delighted with the single European market, but generally in no hurry at all to move on to a single European currency. They, too, see the importance of a Gatt agreement for their other export markets. The German government itself, struggling under the colossal financial burden of unification, is no longer half so willing to bankroll large transfers to the Community's poorer states, in the interests of 'cohesion'.

More broadly, Germany has the challenge of post-communist Europe at its front door. When the German government has moved to Berlin, which it has now firmly resolved to do by the year 2000, Poland will be less than an hour's drive away. In the circumstances, many are asking whether it is really more important to deepen the EEC to Germany's west than it is to bring at least her immediate eastern neighbours into the Community at the present level of integration. Adapting the current Eurojargon, Lord Dahrendorf, once described as Britain's most famous German and Germany's most famous Briton, has argued that 'widening *is* deepening'. His argument finds echoes in Germany as well as Britain.

Beyond this, Germany is very directly affected by the civil disorders and wars in the former Soviet Union and former Yugoslavia. Faced with these challenges, it looks more than ever for the firm alliance and support of the most militarily experienced and self-confident western powers, which means above all the United States, but also Britain. Certainly this seems to be the case with the country's fluently Anglophone (and, one trusts, still mildly Anglophile) defence minister, Volker Rühe.

I don't suggest that in the mid-1990s we will see a *special* relationship developing between, say, the government of a Chancellor Rühe or Schauble and that of Mr John Major or his successor. (Or, for that matter, between the governments of a Chancellor Scharping and a Mr

Smith.) That would be to nourish yet another British illusion. But a sober analysis of common and complementary interests in Europe after 'Yalta' may indeed point to a somewhat stronger, closer relationship. And there is quite simply no other country in the world which is more important to the economic future of Britain.

However, such relationships are not just built on sober analysis. Historical baggage, personalities, emotions and legacies all play their part. Plain speaking about national and European interests can only be to the good. But, especially in this case, plain speaking, or just humorous speaking, can also wound quite deeply, even if it is only meant to tickle or stimulate.

To adapt a famous wartime warning: careless talk costs jobs.

30 October 1993

YOUR PROBLEMS SOLVED

DEAR MARY

Mary Killen

Q. My husband is an ambassador and fond of telling anecdotes at the dinner table, but his declamatory style is more suited to ancient Greece than to a typical social audience of people with diminished attention spans. How can I curtail his love of oratory and embellishments and remind him discreetly to get to the point?

Name and address withheld

A. A traditional egg-timer could be a useful aid to your husband as four to five minutes is the maximum concentration span which can be expected of people today. Set it up within his field of vision by prior arrangement and set the sands a-running as he begins his anecdote.

Q. As the husband of a famous actress I am expected to join my wife at a plethora of social events. These might be enjoyable if it were not for the fact that my regal mother-in-law sees her presence at these occasions as her maternal prerogative. The problem is exacerbated by my wife's encouragement of her mother's expectations. How can I tactfully prevent my mother-in-law from joining my wife and me at these events without hurting her feelings and incurring my wife's displeasure?

Name, sadly, withheld

A. As you already know many members of the acting profession it should not be too difficult for you to arrange for one of them to telephone your wife or your mother-in-law posing as a tabloid journalist and ask for an interview . . . 'for a piece about mother and daughter teams – you know, like Mandy Smith and her mother, or Naomi Campbell and hers . . . Basically it's a story about how the mother gets in on the act.' Naturally they will refuse the invitation but should it be insufficient as a deterrent, you will have to take the more serious step of pretending to your wife that you have started to find her mother physically attractive.

Q. I am trapped in the routine of giving a lift in my car every morning to a plump, moody colleague. Her personal hygiene and time-keeping are disappointing and I have tired of circling a well-known West London roundabout waiting for her waddling bulk to appear. How can I discontinue this unsatisfactory arrangement?

A. J., London W1

A. Tell your colleague that you have a new schedule of duties in the mornings as you have agreed to do a school run to help out a neighbour. This will involve you leaving half an hour earlier than before and going to the office via a circuitous route. Sadly this will mean you will no longer be able to offer her a lift as she will no doubt be unable to meet the new earlier deadline.

6 November 1993

LOW LIFE

DOWN THE SLIPPERY SLOPE

Jeffrey Bernard

Sometimes, in the middle of the night, usually at 3.30 a.m., I am woken up by the noise of the dust-cart clearing up Berwick Street market beneath me. Then I get up, go to the sitting-room, pour myself a drink and find myself wondering where and when it all started to go wrong. A psychiatrist at a dreaded drying-out clinic like the well-named but badly pronounced St Bernard's in Ealing would most likely say, when the booze first interfered with your work.

Well, that was in 1958. It was then that I got the sack from the Old Vic where I had been working as a stagehand. We worked in the mornings, matinees and evenings, but we usually had the afternoons off and it was a habit then to go and get drunk with Francis Bacon in the Colony Room Club. I did just that once too often and one night from the flies I put in the backdrop of a churchyard from *Much Ado About Nothing* into the Rialto scene from *The Merchant of Venice*. So that was that.

I went on to six of the most boring months of my life working on *My Fair Lady* at the Theatre Royal, Drury Lane, and then had some fun with the Folies Bergère at the Winter Garden, where the dancing girls were very good to me. I kept my nose, at least, clean then until 1971 when I had broken into this lark and got the sack from the *Sporting Life*. But it was somewhere between Francis Bacon and the *Life* that things got out of hand. Somewhere around then I began drinking at home. Up until then the licensing laws had acted as a sort of brake and I passed the hours in Suffolk cleaning my shotgun in readiness to shoot my wife with the left barrel and my landlady with the right.

In those days I could hardly do anything at all without the aid of a drink but then it had to wait until opening time. But there were things I did do voluntarily but I certainly couldn't do now and not because I am simply physically incapable. There was an enormous oak tree in my village of Chelsworth that fell down one night and I daftly (looking back on it, daftly) offered the rector my services to saw it up and cut it up with a felling axe. I found it hard to believe that I sweated for hours over that tree. Today, I would have gone on staring at it through the windows of the Peacock inn while sipping at vodkas.

The lack of a drink has men doing strange things, such as preaching sermons, walking across the Antarctic and extracting other people's teeth. Some of them even take to editing weekly journals. But it was drinking at home, as I have said, that was the top of the slippery slope, and it was kissing Norma King in the rhododendrons when I was 12 that was the top of another slippery slope, not so physically ruining as Smirnoff but certainly psychologically disastrous.

Anyway, I have known about where and when this disaster started but perhaps it wasn't a disaster, otherwise I wouldn't be writing this wretched column in the first place. My mother sometimes gave me looks that signified that she was fairly sure that I was bound for hell. What she never guessed obviously was much worse, and that was that one day I would own a cocktail cabinet. Actually, I haven't got a cock-tail cabinet. What I have got is a table and a kitchen and a bedside table and this flat sometimes looks like a pub in readiness at five minutes to 11 on a Saturday morning. It is only sad that the aforementioned Francis Bacon isn't here to be the catalyst for my getting the sack yet again.

6 November 1993

ARTS

MEMO TO THE CONTROLLER

Alan Brownjohn

A recent concert programme advertisement for Radio 3 plugged the 'breakfast mix of news, music and information' (in that order) to be heard on the early morning *On Air* programme and the 'varied diet' of the same thing available on the early evening *In Tune*. Ranged round the bland printed text were the faces of 14 smiling presenters, includ-ing Andrew Green, Natalie Wheen, Richard Baker, David Owen Norris (in a musical pullover) and Michael Berkeley (in a baseball cap). Nothing suggested that the network might be exciting, stimulating, a voyage of discovery for the open-minded. Tony Scotland wrote eloquently in *The Spectator* of 21 August about the network's role as an invaluable cultural asset, a flagship of the nation's sensibility. Nowadays, the cheery confidence of 'our regular presenters' seems increasingly to be what the new, approachable Radio 3 FM is all about.

Large chunks of air-time on Radios 1 and 2, on BBC local radio and on all the commercial networks are fixedly associated with presenters' names and often identified by a name and nothing else. It has long been the standard way of cutting up yards of musical wallpaper into sections tinted with personality: you switch on or off according to whether you relish the wit and wisdom of Richard Skinner or Jakki Brambles or the Emperor Rosko. To install this device of personality presentation on Radio 3 last autumn involved surrendering the content of around 20 per cent of broadcast time to easy listening, a percentage now set to rise when non-stop news – the juggernaut nobody ever wanted – rolls over Radio 5, leaving Radio 3 to adopt what remains of school broadcasting. That policy was a vulgar blunder, with wider implications which become clearer as this September's second batch of innovations ('extending choice', of course) takes effect.

On Air and *In Tune* are 'drive-time' shows for listeners snatching a rapid breakfast or heading home through the rush hour. Since September one regular presenter, Andrew McGregor, has commanded every weekday morning and three others share the five weekday teatimes with two regional voices. Personality presentation requires them (between playing discs) to conduct interviews rather less revealing than those on *Desert Island Discs*, introduce news headlines and traffic information, provide gobbets of music publicity and give frequent time-checks. Memo to the Controller of Radio 3: don't a lot of homes and cars have *clocks*?

Here are some impressions of the tone of the drive-time shows as one listener has registered them. You can tune in to Andrew Green (Mondays) if you enjoy heavy jocularity with your musical snippets: 'And now the John Barry music from the film *Out of Africa* – pity about Robert Redford (did I say that?)'. Natalie Wheen on Wednesdays may be recommended if you want chatterbox enthusiasm for absolutely everything: 'Mischa Maisky, having a whale of a time with Tchaikovsky's *Variations on a Rococo Theme*'. On Fridays, Richard Baker is gently magisterial, as ever; but wasn't he born for Radio 4? It is deplorable that Radio 3, of all places, should require Mr Baker to play Thomas Allen's rendering of 'The Heather on the Hills' from *Brigadoon*, thereby pitching him at a lower level than his admirable *Taking Notes* programme on the other network.

Since September too (in one tiny concession to the critics) drive-time presenters have passed on the news and the traffic to handy colleagues, who present them less woodenly. But many listeners (exercising choice) will surely have switched over, cleverly, to Radio 3 after having heard all of that more fully on Radio 4's *Today* or *PM*. Memo to the Controller: Isn't this just clumsy planning? Why have tiresomely repeated half-hourly bulletins on Radio 3 at all? And exactly how many quick-thinking, map-reading motorists not already stuck in it will be warned off the tailback on the A684 by hearing about it (again!) from Penny Gore?

The truth is that these flagship programmes are an embarrassing, condescending hotchpotch, and it would be good if their style was at least confined to drivetimes. But as the formula becomes entrenched, it seems to be spreading a kind of populist blight across the schedules. The bittiness and the trivialising mannerisms are creeping into other places. Newsy chat crops up in intervals between programmes. New presenters of operas, concerts and recitals feel obliged (by instinct, or on instruction?) to copy the chummy, jokey manner of the peak-hour trend-setters. The BBC now seems to be terrified of élitism (meaning 'the enjoyment of things I don't understand'), and instead of considering how presentation might advocate and enhance quality has gone shamelessly downmarket to find ways of cheapening it.

Do snappy programme titles – *Vintage Years, Midnight Oil, Making Waves, Night Waves* – really catch the eye in the listings? The last two programmes, both arts magazines, certainly contrive to frustrate or irritate the ear. The idea that a group of informed critics might thrash out the value and interest of something in sustained, intelligent conversation (as in *Critics' Forum*) has been banished. We now have further breezy, self-absorbed presenters leading unedited studio prattle, often in the presence of the author of the book or play in question: Michele Roberts on *Night Waves* asking Paul Theroux to 'Throw us a titbit, please!' from his latest fiction.

Night Waves in particular seems to be modelled on Radio 4's increasingly bizarre *Kaleidoscope*, as if there were no other arts magazine format: brassy personalities, bits of stage dialogue leadenly taped for the broadcast, musicians imported to perform from cold in the studio. The wonderful Tamsin Little recently played Sarasate's arrangement of a *Carmen* tune 'to create the Spanish atmosphere' before historians discussed a biography of General Franco. Memo to the Controller: wouldn't you call this 'coarse culture'?

Does this dismal, patronising stuff widen the audience (including the younger audience) for Radio 3, as intended? If it does, what is it widening it for that other networks cannot provide? On the face of it, the

changes would look to be narrowing the intellectual appeal: less drama
(particularly new drama); merely token amounts of new poetry; the
loss of most straightforward talks and symposia. Why should Radio 3,
the network where Bertrand Russell and Father Frederick Copleston
once locked horns for 90 minutes about the existence of God, now
boast no regular discussion content even as substantial as *The Moral
Maze* on Radio 4?

The network occupies over 17 hours a day. William Haley's Third
Programme of the late 1940s and 1950s, bustling with creative fervour
and originality, accomplished so much more, had so much greater
diversity and breadth, with only six hours a night. In those days, classical music retained a place on the Home Service, and even on the
Light Programme. Here is a thought: is the BBC itself to blame if its
rigid demarcation of Radios 1 to 4 – pop, light, high classical and speech
– simply left out the classics from its mass appeal networks, leaving a
gap which Classic FM eagerly filled with fast-food music?

If the nub of this question is the BBC's hope of drawing in the young,
it could do worse than to talk with some of them direct – like the
people in two socially diverse sixth forms I visited not long ago. A few
of them listened to 'the classics'; nearly all used radio for 'pop' or 'background'. (None, incidentally, read the ineffable rock columns in the
broadsheet dailies, confirming my impression that those are written by
and for middle-ageing children of the Sixties.) To my question, 'Would
you listen to Radio 3 more often if the classics were presented more
like light music or pop on the other networks?', the general answer was
a puzzled 'No'. One 17-year-old performing arts student, very much
the kind of listener the Controller of Radio 3 would want, put it
bluntly: 'Rubbish! Who would they be kidding? Different types of
announcer go with different types of music'. He liked, he said, 'some
of all types'. But presentation alone was not going to make him like
one type more.

Outside the widening patches of populist blight, the fabric of
daytime and evening listening even now remains remarkably sound,
not beyond rescue. It is still capable of throwing up enthralling surprises: in recent weeks, the drama of Tirso de Molina, the music of
Howard Ferguson, a dialogue between Miroslav Holub and Oliver
Sacks on (yes) *Night Waves*. This is because some imaginative and
venturesome producers are still there, and some excellent programmes
with long-tested formats and uncondescending presenters have survived: *Record Review*, *Jazz Record Requests*, most *Composers of the
Week*. But also, an unobtrusive manner of presentation crafted over
half a century of unequalled quality broadcasting still seems the

instinctively appropriate way of doing things on Radio 3, and dies hard. Not all the dignity and intelligence has dissolved in chat.

So it may not be too late to change course, provided there still exists among the planners sufficient humility to listen to the unprecedented volume of complaint and pleading from Radio 3's most loyal and passionate listeners. My guess is that, almost to a man and woman, those listeners would back the following, final memo to the Controller: Forget the populist cant; check the presentational deterioration; use the money lavished on your marketing consultants to improve your output; and start to build again on the long-term strengths of your network by trusting the talents of the dedicated producers and broadcasters you are still fortunate to employ.

6 November 1993

BOOKS

CHAIRING FROM THE FRONT

Douglas Hurd

THE DOWNING STREET YEARS
by Margaret Thatcher
HarperCollins

'I know that I can save this country and that no one else can.' The words of Chatham are borrowed, with a word of apology, near the beginning of Margaret Thatcher's book, and the thought runs through every chapter. Because she was indeed a remarkable Prime Minister it is a remarkable book – well written, cogent in argument, sometimes vivid in description, rising to moments of memorable climax. But it would have been a great book if she had waited for five years. The bruises would have healed, and time would have brought a wiser perspective.

British Government, under Margaret Thatcher as under anyone else, is a matter of endless meetings, compromises, decisions, concluded not mainly by the Prime Minister, but by those whom she appoints and by officials. The Prime Minister supervises, but cannot be everywhere doing everything. Margaret Thatcher was a more active and intrusive Prime Minister than most. But her reputation in this respect soared beyond the facts. 'Maggie Acts' became the most familiar newspaper billboard. 'Maggie Acts' could have been a subtitle for this book.

I give a stray example of how this misleads. In 1990 it became important that a united Germany should settle in a new treaty its eastern border with Poland. Many meetings and much paper were devoted by many people in many countries to this task, which was successful. The Prime Minister was interested, and supported this work. But the episode is described here as if she were the sole begetter of the Polish-German Treaty. She was indeed the driving and decisive force in many great matters. That truth would have emerged more convincingly if it had not been presented as universal.

Margaret Thatcher describes fairly her own technique of leadership as 'chairing from the front':

> I like to say what I think quite early on and see whether arguments are addressed which show me to be wrong, in which case I have no difficulty in changing my line.

She is scathing about the failure of men around her to respond to this technique with frank and forceful argument. It is perfectly true that she was willing to listen to counter-argument clearly based on knowledge. The difficulty was that many people, confronted with unequivocal statements of opinion from a woman Prime Minister did not realise this. The result was mumbled dissent, or dissent expressed behind her back. Neither of these could she abide.

The main reason for Margaret Thatcher's loss of the leadership was, I believe, her failure over the years to make the best of the cabinet system. This depends on mutual tolerance and mutual support, which in turn depends on knowledge of each other. The Prime Minister was amazingly thoughtful about the personal well-being of her colleagues. No trouble was too great if someone was ill or in private difficulty. But she did not always understand that colleagues too had knowledge and views. She relied on her individual powers excessively. Antagonisms and mutual suspicions built up, one after the other, until they became too strong even for her strength.

This is a masculine book about individual, old-fashioned leadership. It does not reflect the extraordinary combination of masculine and feminine qualities which gave Margaret Thatcher such a unique armoury. I remember taking to see her a senior police officer who had a plan for reorganising part of his command which had come to her notice and with which she disagreed. It was a matter entirely within his jurisdiction.

He made his case competently. She tore into him mercilessly. He held his ground knowing its strength. She said that he must act as he thought right, but she would never be convinced. He crumbled, and said that in those circumstances he would not proceed. She immediately changed her approach, leaning forward in her chair and softening her voice. She hoped he wasn't angry. She had such a high opinion of him and his professionalism that she would hate to feel there was disagreement between them. The poor man departed blissfully happy, having lost not only his plan, but the right to be angry at the loss.

Margaret Thatcher deals cursorily with a number of subjects which she found less than tractable. The sourest note is reserved for the Scots. Her own divisive manoeuvres inside the Scottish Conservative Party are presented as part of a missionary campaign to convert the country to Thatcherism, a campaign which she admits did not succeed. Her treatment of broadcasting is also unsatisfactory. In my limited experience this was one of the least successful reforms of these years. Fortified by two radical Ministers (Nigel Lawson and Nick Ridley), by a slightly bizarre range of advisers, and by her own dislike of most of the broadcasting establishment, she struck out boldly into a thicket which proved impenetrable. We in the Home Office, bewildered by the enterprise, tried to produce some maps, walking sticks and cautionary advice, but the expedition struggled on regardless. Eventually there were compromises. The BBC licence fee was not abolished. Channel 4 was not entirely privatised. The constantly shifting compromise on the way in which ITV franchises are allocated satisfied no one.

But the set pieces of the book are compelling. Although I was not involved at the time, the account of the Hong Kong negotiations strikes me as entirely fair, and justly generous to Geoffrey Howe. The story of the Scargill strike is told with complete authority. But above all the superb story of the Falklands War holds the imagination, precisely because for the Prime Minister it was the high moment. The conviction which sustained her through the weeks of doubt and bad news was based on fundamental and sound emotions which she manages to convey to the printed page.

And so, inevitably, to Europe and the end. Here the jury is out, and she would have been wise to wait until it returned. Just as Margaret Thatcher is scathing about the Foreign Office but praises individual diplomats, so she is scathing about the European Community, but perceptive about and on reasonable terms with all its leaders, in particular Chancellor Kohl and President Mitterrand. She now builds up a fashionable impression of principled opposition to anything which smacks of European integration. But that is not what the record of her premiership shows. Her tactic, rightly though reluctantly, was to argue and sign – once she was convinced she had the best available deal. The narrative, even as told here, of the negotiations for the British rebate, and for the Single European Act prove the point. If Margaret Thatcher had been Prime Minister, there would have been no Treaty of Maastricht. There would, I think, have been a great row at Maastricht, and a Treaty agreed by Britain at Lisbon six months later. That is the track record. Whether the Treaty which she would have agreed at Lisbon would have been as favourable to Britain as arrangements which the Prime Minister achieved at Maastricht is a matter for speculation – and doubt.

Margaret Thatcher makes out a strong case for her Bruges speech, which has indeed worn well. The main themes of the speech were the folly of seeking to build Europe on the suppression of the nation states, and the need to open the Community to the East. Both ideas are clearly right, and more widely accepted on the continent than when she spoke. In her book she restates her views firmly but with moderation. If she had always spoken thus in public and in private all might have been well. But of course she did not. The pleasure of playing to the domestic gallery too often prevailed. Those with whom she dealt in Europe saw plainly that her particular brand of Gaulism was rooted in a reluctance to understand the purposes of the founders of the Community. They in turn failed to see that by pressing too dogmatically down the path set by the founders to integration they were bound to arouse the resentments to which Margaret Thatcher gave utterance.

The misunderstandings about the nature of modern Europe reached their climax, so far as Margaret Thatcher was concerned, in the drama of German unification. The book shows how she took seriously the possibility that with the French and the Russians she could block the process. Presidents Gorbachev and Mitterrand were perfectly happy to join with her in gloomy fireside chats about the defects of German history and the German character. But it was clear even then that they had no intention whatsoever of joining in some blocking manoeuvre. Nor would there have been any sense or long-term purpose in doing so.

I shall not forget the last hours of Margaret Thatcher's premiership, and in particular the hours in Paris after the unsatisfactory results of the first ballot came through. I do not fault her description. She carried herself magnificently at the great dinner at Versailles that evening. All eyes were upon her as dinner followed ballet, and course followed course at the immense table in the Galerie des Glaces. They looked on her as on some great wounded eagle, who had herself wounded many in the past, but whom no one wished to see brought down, unable to soar again. Thanks to her own style and courage she was not humiliated. During the 11 years in which I served in her Governments I felt many emotions towards our Prime Minister. Admiration was rarely far away. But I never felt so admiring as on that last night in Paris in November 1990.

6 November 1993

AND ANOTHER THING

THOUGHTS ON LIFTING THE SPIRITS OF A SUPERANNUATED MAN

Paul Johnson

Paradoxically, the wet, sunless summer has produced autumn colours of exceptional glory. And, wandering round the Quantock beechwoods last weekend, I found myself in elegiac mood: how many more would I see? For I have just turned 65. A polite Scotswoman from the Ministry phoned to say that I would now receive weekly from the Government the handsome sum of £62.34. So I have passed the watershed into old age and hereafter it is downhill all the way. What have I missed, or contrived to avoid?

Well: I have never attended a pop concert or a soccer match, watched *Coronation Street* (or *EastEnders* or *Neighbours*), seen *The Mousetrap* or *Gone with the Wind*, picked up a Jeffrey Archer or a Martin Arnis, sat through *The Ring* or finished *A la Recherche*, read the *Economist* or *Time Out*, owned a car, run an overdraft, bounced a cheque or appeared in court. I have never cooked a joint, used a launderette, changed a nappy, been to Annabel's, stayed at the Cipriani, supped at Maxim's, killed a fish, hunted a fox, stalked a stag or even squashed a spider – though I once threatened a tarantula in Recife. No one has ever offered me drugs, invited me to an orgy or even sold me a contraceptive. Golf, bridge, night-clubs and gambling are anathema to me. I have never had the slightest wish to possess a Picasso or a Ferrari, to be dressed by Armani or housed in Aspen. I have always given Oxfam, the RSPCA, Save the Whales and all forms of organised dogoodery a wide berth.

On the other hand, I have delivered a baby, climbed the Matterhorn, asked Kerensky why he didn't have Lenin shot ('Because I didn't t'ink him important'), smoked cigars with Sibelius – and Castro – swum in the Caspian and Lake Titicaca, made de Gaulle cross, Churchill weepy and the Pope laugh, chatted up Ava Gardner, slaughtered a bear, published 28 books and written thousands of articles. I have stood on the spot from which the Archduke Franz Ferdinand was shot, lectured from the stage where Herzl founded Zionism and held Domesday Book in my hands. I think of myself as a typical, down-to-earth, unromantic Englishman of my day, class and age, whose views, likes and dislikes are shared by multitudes. But I may be wrong about that. When asked what she thinks of me, my wife Marigold says, 'Difficult.'

At 65 I no longer believe that anything I say or write will have a perceptible influence on what happens, though doubtless I will continue to fulminate. The world is not going to pot, whatever I may say in a rage at the headlines. On the contrary, it will continue to get better and better for most of us, as it has for more than a millennium. I no longer have ambitions of any kind, other than the modest one of seeing a painting of mine hang in the Royal Academy. The things I now most enjoy are going to church to say my morning prayers, listening to my grandchildren and reading in bed at night. My thoughts tend to centre increasingly on the next world rather than this one. Marigold says that such an attitude is not good enough, and that I must form a positive habit of planning and executing a good deed every single day. I agree entirely. But she has spent a lifetime at the service of individuals and to help them comes as naturally to her as to breathe. I have wasted my days battling for or against trends, historical forces, classes, nations, spirits of the age, a foot-soldier in the war of ideas. I hate worthy committees, meetings, discussions. I am not even sure I like people, unless I know them. My instinct, with forward strangers, is like Harold Pinter's: to bristle and ask, 'Were we at school together?'

Marigold, asked for further guidance, says resignedly, 'Just try being nice, then.' But when, how and to whom? The last time I offered my seat to a lady in the Tube, I got an earful of feminist theory. Tubes are rather edgy places these days and all the rules have changed. One *grande dame* I know says that, when she sees a black man sitting by himself in a bus, she sometimes takes the seat next to him to show goodwill. 'But,' she adds sweetly, 'one's gesture is liable to be misunderstood.' I know what she means. When I was an undergraduate I recall a visiting potentate – I think it was Sir Stafford Cripps – observing, 'It is the sign of a gentleman always to pay a courtesy to the plainest woman in the room.' I have followed this counsel intermittently. Recently, at a gathering of Lord Weidenfeld's, I spotted a likely candidate whom I vaguely knew: a woman with a heavily lived-in face poised unceremoniously on top of a torso like a dressmaker's dummy. So I sat next to her and was polite. Alas, she turned out to be a gossip columnist and, short of something to fill her space, wrote that I had designs upon her virtue. Ye gods! What have we here – the latest politically correct phantasmagoria: dinner party rape? A new case of Bardell v. Pickwick?

Good deeds, then, are more easily said than done. Malcolm Muggeridge once remarked to Graham Greene, 'I am a sinner trying to be a saint and you are a saint trying to be a sinner.' But what of the uninteresting majority like myself who desire neither notoriety nor a halo, just to slip into Elysium unnoticed with a pass degree or even an *aegrotat*? It occurs to me that the kind of benefaction which works best is one which gives as much satisfaction to the doer as the recipient. It is a quarter of a century since I ceased to be an editor and the only thing I miss is the thrill of discovering new talent and, still more, the chance to help young authors to write better. It is a melancholy fact that, in the harsh world of journalism and letters, few possess the knowledge or the time or the desire to instruct their juniors. I come from a family of teachers and it is in my blood. So, nowadays, I take a pupil or two, to coach them through their first book. I find this among the most delightful work I have ever undertaken and a form of philanthropy entirely lacking in condescension, patronage or moral uplift. Moreover, in an age of sloppy syntax, gruesome grammar and polluted prose, there must be some merit in helping the young to honour words. Enough to give a lift to the spirit of a superannuated man, anyway.

6 November 1993

CINEMA

THE REMAINS OF THE BOOK

Mark Steyn

THE REMAINS OF THE DAY

I don't suppose it was difficult, but the best decision P.G. Wodehouse ever made was to write in Bertie Wooster's voice – breezy, slangy, peppered with misfired shots at elegant erudition. Jeeves is fine in small doses, as quoted by Bertie, but left to run at length his discreet circumlocutions would rapidly transform him, in the eyes of his readers, into one of the all-time crashers.

That was presumably the challenge Kazuo Ishiguro set himself in *The Remains of the Day*: write a story told by a dull, fastidious pedant and try not to wind up with a dull, fastidious, pedantic book. Such distinction as the novel possessed derived from the voice – that of Stevens the butler, struggling in 1958 to make sense of a life devoted to the service of one of history's fall guys, a Nazi-appeasing peer. Motoring round the West Country, Stevens gradually realises how unsuited he is to a less formal world: he is no good at, as he puts it, 'banter'.

This is a novelist's device – a man who has learnt to employ language as a means of avoiding feelings finds he has no language with which to express feelings. No doubt someone somewhere could find a cinematic equivalent for this, but James Ivory and his screenwriter Ruth Prawer Jhabvala don't even try: as with their previous collaborations, this film is content to look like an adaptation rather than attempt to be anything in its own right.

In the book, we squeeze between Stevens's lines to glimpse what's really going on: Lord Darlington's a dupe, the butler's in love with the housekeeper. On screen, it's laid out like a dinner service, underlined by heavy symbolism (bird trapped in drawing-room is released through window and *spreads its wings*), double-underlined by the dialogue which substitutes for the novel's self-examination: 'Why do you always have to hide what you feel?' Miss Kenton asks him. Golly, so that's what it's about. Only in the final moments, when the audience supplies the romance the characters can't admit to, does the movie pull off the book's trick: it's what's *not* happening that drives the plot.

". . . so I'm like, 'Wow, you know, communications is where it's at, right?' . . ."

In New York the other night, I caught a television commercial for the film. 'A world of devoted service,' growls the dark-brown American voiceover, as we see Anthony Hopkins (Stevens) with James Fox (Darlington). 'A life of unspoken longing' – Hopkins with Emma Thompson (Miss Kenton). Immediately afterwards, Joss Ackland turned up as a pussy-stroking Nehru-jacketed Bond villain to extol the virtues of Energizer batteries. From 'You rang, m'lord?' to 'Not so fast, Mr Bond' isn't so very far. But fussy, soft-spoken civility is more interesting from a megalomaniac psychopath than from a docile servant. The Hopkins act works in *Elephant Man* or *Silence of the Lambs* in counterpoint to what's going on around him. Here, he's too perfectly cast.

The rest of the film, meanwhile, is perfectly wrong, losing not only the voice but also the point of view: pre-war as seen from post-Suez, a time when it wasn't only butlers who were experiencing twinges of doubt about the old certainties. On screen, it's mostly just the Thirties with the odd flash-forward to the Fifties and, as it's Merchant-Ivory, everything looks swell anyway. Drab Fifties austerity? Don't you believe it. Ivory takes no chances: improving on the novel, he upgrades Stevens's car to a Daimler, the seaside resort, the Palm Court, the boarding-house, everything is blissfully untouched by post-war decline.

Well, you retort, the US Fifties didn't look much like *Happy Days* or *American Graffiti*. But it's not a lack of historical accuracy so much as dramatic tension. Ishiguro's Stevens is engaging because the world is clearly not as he sees it. But, viewed through Ivory's lens, Britain is as reserved, deferential and impeccable as Stevens himself. Poor people, peeling paint, scratched cars, factory furniture, all know their place – off-camera. Indeed, in Stevens the butler, Ivory seems to have discovered his on-screen alter-ego. When the new Earl proves unable or unwilling to maintain Darlington Hall, Stevens finds himself in service to a rich American. Similarly, with this film, Ivory has an American co-producer, Mike Nichols (!), and a Hollywood studio, Columbia. Merchant-Ivory have stumbled upon their true niche, as cinematic butlers to anglophile Americans: everything buffed and polished, exquisite manners – and they never give offence.

13 November 1993

A CLEAN BREAK WITH FAIRNESS

Alasdair Palmer

Humbug is the stock-in-trade of democratic politics. Still, there is something spectacular about the humbug that has surrounded the Child Support Act and Child Support Agency, even by the prodigious standards being set by the present government. 'Children Come First' was the title of the White Paper which was enacted in 1991, and the Child Support Agency's (CSA) literature is littered with pictures of happy, skipping children. But the Child Support Act is not about promoting the interests of children. It is about saving the Government money – a laudable aim in itself, and one which it is entirely appropriate for a Conservative administration to pursue. The point of the Child Support Act is to replace income support, which comes from taxes, with maintenance payments from fathers, which do not – thus saving the Exchequer around £500 million. The new legislation does not aim to provide large sums of extra money for the raising of children, nor to ensure that fathers spend more time with them. *Children* don't come first. Taxpayers do. The Government would have saved itself a lot of trouble if it had admitted it.

'The Child Support Agency will trace absent parents and assess, collect, and, where necessary, enforce payment,' wrote Peter Lilley, Secretary of State for Social Security, in the CSA Framework Document. The CSA was sold to Parliament and public as the mechanism which would track down feckless fathers who had abandoned their wives and children, making them pay for their upkeep. Is that actually the CSA's priority? One internal CSA memo stresses that the agency should not bother with cases 'which will need a lot of effort to extract money. The name of the game is maximising the maintenance yield – don't waste a lot of time on the non-profitable stuff!'; another says that 'higher savings can be achieved if we prioritise as follows: absent parents in work with higher than average earnings; absent parents in regular contact with the parent-with-care; absent parents without a second family. . . ' None of those categories sound like feckless, disappearing fathers. But they are men with money. When asked, 'Why do you rob banks?' a notorious thief replied: 'That's where the money is.' The same principle explains why the CSA is targeting men already paying maintenance.

The suspicion that the CSA is not too concerned about disappearing dads is confirmed by looking at how the agency allocated its resources. There are six major regional Child Support Agency Centres. In the Hastings Centre, which handles the South-East, of the 500 people employed in finding ways to increase maintenance payments, how many work on tracing fathers who have abandoned their children? Just four. 'They will trace maybe five fathers a month,' says one man who works at the Hastings Centre. The other 495 people are dedicated to increasing payments from fathers already paying some form of maintenance. Those within the CSA tell me this pattern is replicated throughout the other five centres across the UK.

The CSA's publicity stresses that it aims to end the situation where (as Peter Lilley has written) 'less than one in three absent parents pays any regular maintenance to support their children'. The clear implication is that the other two in three are feckless, disappearing dads whom the agency will bring to justice. But the truth is that the majority of those men are not feckless fathers refusing to face their responsibilities, and both the CSA and the social services department must know it. For the decade prior to the CSA, the Government had been busily encouraging 'clean break' divorce settlements – settlements where one parent, usually the father, would pay a large lump sum, or cede the family home, in return for being released from an obligation to contribute maintenance payments. The idea was that a single, one-off payment was fairer, more reliable and less liable to generate interminable wrangles. It would cut out the courts – beyond specifying the amount of the lump sum to be paid, they would not be involved – and everyone would be better off as a result.

'Clean break' agreements were particularly prevalent in the north of England, where wages were so low that securing the family's assets looked much more attractive than receiving a meagre monthly maintenance payment. As a result, up to 90 per cent of divorces were settled with a single one-off payment from husband to wife. Are the large numbers of fathers not paying regular maintenance the result of increasing fecklessness and irresponsibility? No. They're the consequence of previous government policy.

Now government policy has changed. 'Clean breaks' have not proved to be the hoped-for panacea. More and more women who received one-off payments instead of maintenance have ended up dependent on income support and family credit. Last year, £3.4 billion was paid out. The Government, perfectly reasonably, wants to cut that figure. The men who made 'clean break' settlements are an obvious source of money. The CSA has targeted them. It has overturned the previous court-agreed settlements, and demanded that fathers now start paying regular maintenance to their ex-wives.

Not surprisingly, a lot of the fathers feel extremely aggrieved about this. They have married again and had new families. When a demand to pay £200 a month to an ex-wife arrives, it can be devastating. Fathers devoted to the children from their first marriage find they can no longer afford to see them. Barry Seagrove had his maintenance tripled to £360 a month. It will leave him with just over £3 a week spending money after he has paid his mortgage. The CSA has advised him to sell his house.

The injustice of seeing a 'full and final' divorce agreement broken by the Government can hurt as much as the financial hardship. 'The whole point of the divorce settlement I agreed was that it was final. I would never have given up my house if I had known I was going to face maintenance bills,' says Gary Crozier, a carpenter in his thirties from Gretna, with a strong Geordie accent and a stronger sense of unfairness. 'I'm not against the principles of the CSA. But a deal is a deal. You can't just abandon it. If you sell your house, you don't expect the buyer to come back five years later and say, "Hey! I paid you too much. Give me ten thousand quid." But that's the kind of thing the Government is doing by coming back to me for more money.'

It also seems to be breaking with a fundamental principle of English law. You can imagine how most people, including MPs, would react if the tax laws were altered along the same lines. The letter in the brown envelope from the Inland Revenue would read: 'You made a capital gain five years ago and paid 40 per cent tax. The rate has been retrospectively increased to 60 per cent. You now have a month to pay us the extra money.'

That parallel is not accepted by the CSA. Alistair Burt, the minister responsible for it, has a simple answer to men who made 'clean break' settlements, went on to have second families, and who now find themselves in financial trouble because the CSA requires them to make new maintenance payments to their ex-wives. He says they should have thought of that before getting married again. Mr Burt here introduces an interestingly novel principle into British life. He seems to believe that citizens have an obligation to anticipate government policies, and plan their lives around them *before* those policies have even been thought up by anyone in government.

The difficulty of pulling off that trick has led a number of fathers to share Mr Crozier's conclusion that the legislation is unfair and unjust. 'It would be OK to introduce a policy which ruled out 'clean break' settlements from now on, and stipulated high maintenance payments. Then people could make their plans. But it's just wrong to retrospectively change agreed settlements which people have built their lives around,' he mourns. His ex-wife was perfectly happy with the original arrangement, and did not want it changed. But the CSA contacted her, and told her that unless she authorised the agency to pursue her former husband for maintenance payments, she would forfeit the income support she was claiming. Under the circumstances, the ex-Mrs Crozier agreed. 'It's not her fault. I just want a bit of fair play from the Government. At the moment, I'm not getting it.'

Susan Deas, his solicitor, may succeed in getting it for him. She has taken Mr Crozier's case to court, arguing that the CSA's demand for maintenance annuls the original deal under which he gave the family house to his wife, who has since sold it. Gary Crozier's lawyers argue that if he has to pay maintenance, then he is entitled to at least half the proceeds of the sale. 'We're not arguing that the Child Support Act should be overturned. What we are saying is that since it violates the terms of the original 'clean break' settlement, that settlement, and the distribution it established, is void. Everything has to be renegotiated.'

Should Mrs Justice Booth agree, it will open the way to thousands of similar cases. And that may defeat the whole purpose of the Child Support Act. Instead of saving public money, re-opening 'clean break' settlements will involve spending enormous amounts of it. Not just on court fees – most of the men and women going to court will be legally aided – but on women who will have to pay back large sums of money to their ex-husbands, or sell their homes. They will then be more dependent than ever on state hand-outs. That may hurt their children. But, more importantly to Government, it will cost taxpayers a bundle.

No one at the CSA seems to have anticipated this challenge, though clearly, on Mr Burt's principle, they should have done. But then the Child Support Act was pushed through with immense speed: it took just one year to go from announcement to enactment. That is a very short time to frame legislation dealing with problems as fraught and complex as those thrown up by divorce. Most of the detail specifying who was to pay how much was not in the bill itself. It was enacted through statutory instruments – which of course do not come in for the same degree of scrutiny.

Partly as a result of a failure to think through the consequences of the legislation, and partly because of the intemperate haste to make the CSA save money immediately, the whole enterprise is in danger of being discredited. Those who work in the agency have told me that there is no hope of reaching the target of £500 million savings. Some of the centres failed to open on time. Plymouth, for instance, was unable to handle its workload for six months. Other centres were supposed to process it, but they hadn't the manpower. The result is an enormous backlog of cases, plus a large number of straightforward blunders. Women who live with their husbands – to take one example – have been sent angry letters demanding they name the absent father of their children. Some have found that replying, 'He's living with me and our children!' does not stop the flow of threatening letters from the CSA. To take another example, fathers who had successfully defended paternity suits in the courts have found the CSA demanding they pay maintenance for the upkeep of children belonging to someone else.

All of this would, in normal circumstances, lead to a reappraisal of the initial goals set for the agency. But Ros Hepplewhite, the chief executive, is on performance-related pay. If she fails to meet the targets, she forfeits those lucrative bonuses. So instead of trying to adapt the agency to what is manageable in the first year, the reaction has been a greater drive to achieve those impossible goals – do it now!

faster! That has not been good either for the accuracy of the agency's work or for the perception that it is acting fairly.

The CSA is supposed to be being managed like a private company. The senior managers, however, have not exactly been drawn from the shock troops of capitalism.

13 November 1993

DIARY

Stephen Fry

The experience of reading newspapers for a week has reminded me of our great national genius for headline writing. I spotted a screaming banner in a tabloid last week which ran 'Nude Etonian Murdered By A Hooker's Junkie Lover'. This I thought deserved some kind of palm for containing six words each of which is a sub-editor's dream. Only 'By' and 'A' are redundant. It managed to be free of wordplay too. Some years ago I was invited to lunch by the late Mark Boxer, who was editing the *Tatler* at the time. He wanted to offer me a job, but was being rather coy about describing it. 'I need you to take a look at each month's edition and *smell* it,' he said. 'Find some way of linking everything together. Think about how various features and articles can be reflected on the cover.' At last, after much puzzlement, I suddenly grasped what he was driving at. 'You want me to write the *puns!*' 'Yes!' he cried, thumping the table with joy. For a few months I did as I was asked. If the front cover contained a girl in a scarlet frock, then the 'spine line' would say 'Red Dress The Balance'. Even date puns were obligatory: 'Feb. & Groovy', 'June Know Where You Are Going?' and 'Nov. Under You're Feeling Blue'. If there was a major feature about Catholic families inside, the cover would promise 'The Smart Sect: Roman Britain revealed' or some such tummy-rubbish. Fashionable film and book titles would dictate headlines too. An article decrying the influence of Britain's leading design guru would, as a matter of course be headlined 'Conran the Barbarian', just as profiles of the Chancellor today are invariably subbed 'Beyond Our Ken' or 'Kenneth Clarke Ha Ha Ha'. I lasted no more than three months in this atmosphere. My friends just couldn't take it. 'Ah, the Articulate Laurie,' I would say, 'Hugh are you?' There is no sign of the epidemic being halted. Last week's *Spectator* could not resist headlining Simon Courtauld's article on fish 'Absolutely brill'. It may be time for legislation.

On the subject of legislation, the nation is now ready, it seems to me, for action to be taken on the political correctness front. Am I alone in noticing this alarming new development? It has become impossible now to utter a sentence without the barons of the new trendiness insisting on the inclusion of the words 'standards', 'individual', 'values', 'responsibility' and 'family'. It doesn't matter in what order they occur or what meaningless nonsense they denote, the words must dominate what statesmen like to call our 'agenda'. Eight years ago I wrote an article in the *Listener* wondering at the half-cocked stupidity of politicians displaying such impertinence. The trendy belief in family values had already been going for a good seven years by then and there seems even now to be no end in sight. Nobody minds that the Conservative governments of the last 15 years have contained at least six adulterers and two homosexuals at cabinet level and dozens more on the back-benches. If these men want mistresses, love-children and boyfriends, then good luck to them. The British are a decent, tolerant and friendly people and like to see their fellow citizens enjoying themselves in a kindly, responsible and adult way. What really gets our goat is when these same men and their colleagues stand on podia in seaside towns at Party Conference time and tell us how to behave in private; what causes us pain and indignation is to hear them lecture the nation about the virtues of the family and deride those of us who prefer not to have our moral horizons dictated by the *Daily Mail*. The Family: that noble institution responsible for 70 per cent of all murders, over 80 per cent of incidents of child abuse and a full 100 per cent of all cases of incest.

13 November 1993

LOW LIFE

THE UNKINDEST CUT OF ALL

Jeffrey Bernard

I have been brooding about the man whose wife cut off his penis and I have been doing my brooding with my legs crossed. Thank God I don't live in America. The cheering of American females came across the Atlantic after the deed was done and it is still ringing in my ears. Even the few harridans who have visited me these past few days have had a spring in their step.

But there are aspects of this penisectomy which puzzle and intrigue me. The husband has been found not guilty of rape. If he had been guilty then he should have been punished severely, but I think that parting him from his member was a little over the top. The man must be a fool as well. If a woman climbed into my bed with an eight-inch kitchen knife I think I would get the hint. It would be a clue of sorts, anyway.

Then, why did she drive off with the severed organ? She could have flushed it away or given it to the dog, but she drove off with it and threw it in some long grass, wasting valuable police time in the search for it. Apparently a severed penis will last for 18 hours if it is kept cold. Don't I know. You could add a few weeks to that. But while he waited in the hospital for the wretched thing to be returned it seems that he bumped into an old chum and they fell into conversation. He should have been bleeding to death but luckily for him a clot formed which saved him. But to stop for a chat in that condition does, you must admit, take some balls.

A couple of surgeons who must be quite brilliant managed to sew it back on and it is to be hoped that they sewed it back the right way round. My man at the Middlesex Hospital would have put a titanium plate in it as he did my hip to make sure it couldn't happen again. But what with the nerves having been severed the idiot will get no joy when he next pulls it out for a trial run and it serves him right. Mind you his wife should have left him and gone back to Ecuador. Her drastic measures speak volumes for the Latin temperament.

Women here, though, don't need knives. I know female scribblers who can emasculate a man with one withering glance of contempt. But a major worry and anxiety for me now is that when it is my turn for an old flame to perform a penisectomy on me it will not be sewn back because I am a smoker and we know how doctors feel about helping smokers. Oddly enough, Central Television telephoned yesterday to ask me if I would consider going on a show in which they are to discuss teenage smoking. I said I would but mulling it over in my mind last night I have decided that I would have little contribution to make to the show. I do think that smoking is silly and bad, but I also think that telling people what they can and cannot do is worse in some ways. The Government's aim to keep everyone alive for ever while at the same time ruining the National Health Service is a mad contradiction.

Edwina Currie was bad enough, but she has nothing on the awful Virginia Bottomley, who would have made an excellent health minister in the Third Reich, although storm troopers were notoriously heavy smokers. She would willingly throw a bucketful of penises into the long grass like the Ecuadorian wife and we would all end up grovelling in that long grass arguing about which one belonged to whom. In that event there would be some whopping lies told, with Norman probably foolishly laying claim to a large black job. Yes, I fear the lady from Ecuador might have started a new fashion which will become all the rage.

20 November 1993

TIME TO RESTORE PRIVATE LIVES

Clive James

A hidden camera is far enough. Intercepted telephone calls were already far enough, but we were too fascinated with the results to be sufficiently disgusted by how they were obtained. The results obtained by the hidden camera are nothing remarkable, if you discount the good looks of the subject, which we knew about anyway. The manner by which those good looks were on this occasion recorded, however, was so repellent that even the tabloid editors – including, apparently, the editor of the *Sunday Mirror*, after his fellow editors rounded on him – finally realised that a line had been crossed, although none of them seemed to grasp that they had all crossed the same line years before.

Thugs who had been making a good living beating up helpless victims suddenly discovered that one of their number had supplemented his bare hands with brass knuckles. 'You fool,' they cried, 'don't you realise it's supposed to be *fists*?'

One of the characteristics of the totalitarian mentality is to erect opportunism to the status of a principle. To describe the behaviour of a pack of not very bright journalists in totalitarian terms might sound extreme. But it is another kind of wishful thinking, and a dangerously misleading one, to suppose that totalitarian impulses don't exist in a democracy. They are repressed, but they are there. One totalitarian impulse is to create a subhuman class which may be persecuted without compunction because it is beneath compassion. The moral squalor of French journalism under Nazi occupation was no sudden putrefaction. The rot set in with the Dreyfus case. Anti-Semitism polluted French journalism – even the higher, literary journalism – in a long process which had established the Jews as a special case well before the Nazis arrived to round them up.

Mass murder was only the sudden physical translation of a long spiritual contempt which had been propagated in French journals. Some of the journalists were not without talent. But they were without pity, and what had given their callousness free play was the principle of free speech. It was a cruel paradox.

In Britain the same paradox now ensares the famous. It takes a less cruel form, and is scarcely likely to have such a vile outcome; but while being careful not to diminish a great tragedy by equating it with something inherently more trivial, one can still suggest that there is an instructive comparison to be drawn. In recent years there has been a steadily growing tendency to treat the famous as if they were without the right to a private life – always an important step in depriving a group of human dignity, even if, as in this case, there is no further wish to deprive it of life itself. (Quite the opposite: to ensure a supply equal to the demand, the press is ready to help almost anyone become famous, if only to provide fodder for the style-file supplements that we all deplore even as we fight over the first look.)

It can be said that with politicians and other public officials the private life and the public role are intertwined, so that everything they want concealed, even if it breaks no laws, should be open for inspection. (It *was* said, often, by Richard Ingrams of *Private Eye*, although when his turn came he was quick enough to decide that he had been a private citizen all along.) But the thin argument grows thinner still when it comes to those public figures who are famous for their achievements. Some of them seek publicity for all they do, and so should be ready to take the flak with the kudos; but clearly most do not, or if they once did, learned better, holding, surely correctly, that the appreciation they attract is for their public performance, and that their private lives are their own business. Since most journalists obviously feel the same way about themselves, they know they are wrong to contend otherwise, but increasingly they have done so anyway, the contention growing more hysterical as its self-serving basis stands revealed. It has been years now since anyone prominent in any field could offer himself to be the subject of a profile without taking his life in his hands. By the time open season was declared on the Prince and Princess of Wales, bad faith among journalists had already whipped itself up into a righteous passion. It is often said in print, in the more august journals, that the royal family made a mistake in letting publicity into the Palace; but this is just a pious way of saying that they asked for it. The idea that they brought it on themselves is basic to the cast of mind which invents a subhuman class as a preparation for giving it the treatment. From the Peloponnesian war onwards, for the guards watching the prisoners starving in the rock quarry there has always been that consoling thought: *It's all their fault for letting us do this to them.*

The more august journals have had good sport in recent days pointing out that the less august ones are steeped in confusion, what with the *Sun* high-hatting the *Mirror* over tactics scarcely less questionable than its own. Posh editors ought to shed their delusions. To anyone on the receiving end of this stuff – which includes the public, who feel far closer to the Princess than to any editor – the press looks like one thing, and that thing is a juggernaut: oppressive, relentless and overwhelmingly nasty. The cheap press stirs up the muck and the expensive press sifts through it, spreading it about so that everyone gets a whiff.

This unfortunate vertical integration of grunge and informed comment is naturally best exemplified by the Murdoch papers, whose upper-echelon editors have long been obliged to pretend that their colleagues down in the yellow depths have nothing to do with them. Wehrmacht commanders who claimed to have got all the way from Berlin to Moscow and back again without noticing what the SS was up to were not believed. Those who did notice but said it wasn't their responsibility deserved a hearing, but couldn't complain if they were heard sceptically. Not that I hold, as some do, that Rupert Murdoch is an evil tyrant. My energetic compatriot is not to be dismissed so easily. He is a man of principle. But the principle is commercial. He has well-reasoned intellectual objections to any institution that can't be quoted on the stock exchange. His broadsheet editors, however strong their illusion of independence, are perforce caught up in his heroic voyage to a future where no tradition, however hallowed, will restrain enterprise.

But other broadsheet editors should be slow to assume that they aren't at least partly in the same boat, even if they are kicking in the opposite direction to its drift. By discussing the mess that the tabloids have created, they can't help but reinforce the impression that the press has turned into a remorseless machine for chewing up the private lives of eminent people and spitting out the pieces.

Editors of responsible broadsheets and magazines, suitably horrified by this latest excess, nevertheless announce that a privacy law would be a cure more virulent than the disease. They are probably right, but could be surprised by the dearth of public outrage if such a law is brought in. Nobody outside the system really believes that voluntary curbs will work for long. Like Mr Murdoch's sudden conversion to a decent reticence, they will be seen as a stratagem, a lull declared by the storm. The best answer would be for the posh papers to leave the pop papers strictly alone in their strange world of soft-core pornography and freeze-frame soap opera. The pops would be less noxious if they were isolated. For that to happen, however, the political parties, and especially the Conservative Party, would have to stop co-operating with them. Hillary Clinton has never written a column for the *National Enquirer*. It is not pleasant for admirers of Virginia Bottomley's sunny face to see it smiling above her byline in some festering rag featuring transsexual mud-wrestlers on the opposite page, and it was always a poser, when Lady Thatcher was in power, to see her keeping company with Woodrow Wyatt, considering the company *he* was keeping in the *News of the World*.

Both in money and in votes it pays to slum, but the poisonous side-effect is to lend the junk papers legitimacy, and so foster the illusion that journalism is a profession, instead of what it is, a trade. Plumbing is a trade because the man who fixes your tap and the man who wrecks your sink are both called plumbers. Medicine is a profession because the man who takes out your diseased kidney is called a doctor and the man who takes out your healthy one and sells it is called a criminal. The solidarity between good and bad journalists is illusory. It would help if they were not all so keen to sit down together at such functions as the annual *What the Papers Say* luncheon, which I myself lost the urge to attend when I realised that I might inadvertently clink glasses with the editor who helped to kill Russell Harty.

Splitting the quality press from the trash press would not be easy, especially within the Murdoch empire as at present constituted, but if it could be done it would at least have the benefit of resolving the permanent identity crisis of Peter McKay, who fills half his column in one kind of paper lamenting the fatigue induced by reading about the Princess of Wales in the other kind of paper, to which he himself regularly contributes on the subject of the Princess of Wales. Ben Jonson would have made him the hero of a play. Kinder spirits would put him out of his misery.

Meanwhile the Princess of Wales is in hers, and the Prince along with her, if I know him. I do know him to speak to, and her too, but in both cases the speaking acquaintance will undoubtedly evaporate when this piece comes out, because both of them must have long ago grown sick of having their relationship talked about in the press, and the press definitely includes *this* part of the press talking about *that* part of the press. But with the damage done, I might as well throw in my two cents' worth, to go with the million dollars' worth of unsolicited advice that the sundered twain are inundated with every day. I think that the Prince and Princess of Wales, much as they both loathe what press intrusiveness has done to them since their separation, have rather underestimated its role in driving them apart in the first place, and that if they could put some of the blame where it belongs, instead of all of it on each other, they might be persuaded to get back together behind the barricades, if only to put up a fight against this monster before it consumes the rest of us.

The monster is not republicanism, but press intrusion into private life. As it happens, I am for the monarchy, but only as a preference. In my own homeland, Australia, the alleged tide of republicanism is already flowing the other way, largely because the people have begun to remember that Prime Minister Keating, who is so certain about Australia's future as a self-assertive nation state, was once equally certain, when he was Treasurer, about its future as an economic miracle. The benefits of retaining an off-shore, cost-free head of state who is out of politics and sets a limit to ambition have begun to sink in, helped by the stridency of the abolitionists, whose personal aspirations are all too apparent.

Even if Australia were to go republican, however, the monarchy here, though it would be badly damaged, would probably survive. It will probably survive even if the Prince and Princess of Wales divorce, although if the explosion propels young William early to a tottering throne he won't thank his parents for giving him a broken home as a prelude. What might or might not happen to the monarchy, however, is not the main reason why these two should renew their alliance. The main reason – and this comes from conviction, not from mere preference – is that they have let the press define for them what a marriage is, and in so doing have made a mistake with potentially ruinous consequences for everybody.

The press is not qualified to keep the conscience of the married. At almost every level, with the occasional exception of a proprietor miraculously immune, its practitioners have done everything except stay married. They know more about divorce and remarriage than they know about marriage. For the Prince and Princess of Wales the journalists promoted an ideal marriage, and then detected a bad marriage, and finally condemned a sham marriage, but in all three cases it was a fantasy, because all they had ever been talking about was a difficult marriage, and all marriages are difficult. Every marriage has something wrong with it. Marriage has something wrong with it. What it has wrong with it is people. The more individual they are, the less they are designed to live together. If two people were meant to live together easily they would have half a personality each. Mr and Mrs Rupert Murdoch might be an ideal couple – he bringing out the *News of the World*, she running the beautiful house in which it is never read – but scarcely any other couple is. A lasting marriage isn't dreamland: it is reality.

As things are now, the Princess, though brave as a lioness, is being dragged down. The Prince should overrule any advice from his camp which suggests that he can survive her fall uninjured. He will be dragged down next. They have already had sufficient experience of living apart. The time has come for them to live apart together, drawing what profit they can from everything they have so harshly found out. With their private life restored, they might each love other people. It would be no great innovation. Most people who love once love again, and have even been known to fall for the person they once married, after realising that the person they let go was in a trap, and the trap was in themselves. We might delude ourselves that what happens to the beleaguered couple in private will still be our concern, but really it will be unknowable, as marriage, in its essence, always is. But there will be an important practical result.

They will be back in business, and for that they both have excellent qualifications, both mutually and as a complement. We have been encouraged to forget, in the hubbub, that the Prince of Wales is a man out of the common run, a fact he would have had less trouble proving had he been born a commoner. (Indeed if you think that the chief role of the royal family is to exemplify an ordinary life, his excess of ability has always threatened to unbalance the whole institution.) What has been less noticed about the Princess, largely because of her startling glamour, is that she has a good mind too. It is not an academic mind (journalists who read three books a year have always been swift to point that out) but it is an original one, and she has learned to speak it with increasing precision, even as the hyenas close in.

On the subject of the children they are more in agreement than they might suppose. One of the first things I heard him say was how determined he was, when some potentate gave him a miniature electric-powered sports car for the boys to ride in, that the boys would never get to see it. When the Princess flies economy class with the boys now, she is pursuing the same idea. They might have different opinions about how to realise it, but the aim is the same. They both want the children to know what reality is, and there she can help him. Neither of his parents was born as heir to the throne: he has had to find too much out for himself. She knows all there is to know about being a child from an unreal background.

In that last dubious advantage lies the key to those qualities she has more of than he does. The reaction she gets in the hospitals and the hospices is no mere contrivance. The wounded and the lonely spot her immediately as one of them. And even if there were an element of the actress, how bad would that be? Female journalists whose every sentence is an imposture are fond of belittling her as histrionic, but where do they suppose the histrionics come from? If she plays a part, she plays it from a deep impulse, and from the same impulse comes an authentic gift for making the weak feel that they have a representative. No wonder the Queen seems desperate at the thought of losing her.

For all I know, the Princess is a hell of a handful close to. But she is a man's woman if I ever saw one. Falling for her is a lot easier than falling off a log. The problem is what to do about her next. Having married her, the Prince was obliged to watch her grow and change, while she had to cope with all the ways in which he was determined not to alter. I imagine his life-lines entangled her like a net. Their life together would have been difficult anyway. But publicity made it impossible. It was just too good a story.

The only way out of the story is to get back to reality. With private life regained their public life might be managed better. It will still be to some extent a PR operation, but at least the publicity will be for something that can thrive in the limelight, as no marriage ever has, or ever can. They will have a battle on their hands, but even if they are living apart, if they are living apart together they are well equipped to fight. All he needs to accept is that he is the Hurricane and she is the Spitfire. In the Battle of Britain, the Hurricane was the worthy gun-platform that could take the punishment and the Spitfire was the bobby-dazzler that could turn inside the German fighters and demoralise their pilots with its sheer speed. The Hurricane broke them up and the Spitfire knocked them down. In the flypast afterwards, the Spitfire flew first and got most of the publicity. But it took both of them to win. There is a hint there about protocol. The Prince might consider letting her walk in front to mop up the photo flash, while he takes the credit for his wisdom. A change in procedure is all it will be.

But the institution will have been preserved. And let us be in no doubt about what institution that is. It isn't just the monarchy, which might very well be coming to the end of its time, although I hope not at the hands of those who see a role for themselves in its replacement. It is private life, the touchstone of civilisation, our only guarantee against the mob – which is us too, but at our worst.

20 November 1993

FOG IN THE CHANNEL, CONTINENT CUT OFF

Anne Applebaum

Brussels

For anyone accustomed to the gentle Euroscepticism of the British Isles, a quick trip to Brussels provides an unexpected jolt. First thing in the morning, a high-ranking envoy of the German government pointed his finger directly at me. 'You people,' he said, 'you people, sitting up there on your island in the fog, you have no idea what goes on over here.' Just after lunch, a long-serving Eurocrat continued, 'Here on the Continent, the mainstream view is that, through ever-closer union, we will create a state-like entity.' By evening, I was better prepared. 'We are holding to the idea of monetary union, and we are holding to the commitment to monetary union as well. We have lost ground but we will still do it, in 1998 if not 1996, in 2001 if not in 1998.'

The feeling one has when staggering back home across the Channel can only be described as culture shock. Over here, there are newspaper stories about 'Europe going our direction', and Foreign Office statements along the lines of 'we have halted the centralising tendencies of the Community for good now', and confident preparations for the European summit on December 10, which is bound to 'go Britain's way'. Over there, meanwhile, diplomats, politicians and Eurocrats alike express a determined dedication to the ideal of united Europe, and a pronounced frustration with British triumphalism. 'You would think things would be different now,' one (British) Eurocrat said to me. 'But at the last European Council meeting a colleague turned to me and said, "Wouldn't you know it, it's 11 to one again, Britain standing out against the rest." What could I say?'

In Brussels, it is as easy to see this cultural difference as it is to hear it. It reveals itself in the mini-Euro-flags painted on the sides of Belgian buses, and the super-Euroflags draped across Belgian war memorials, and in the small shop, not far from the European Commission, which sells not only Euro-flags but Euro-mugs and Euro-pencils (one for each of the 12), Euro-T-shirts and Euro-silverware (guess how many place settings). The public flags can be explained away by the Belgian government's commitment to the Community, but the shop speaks of something deeper. It is a commercial venture, after all. Someone must be buying Euro-paraphernalia, and whoever it is, isn't British.

The difference is one of attitude as well as symbol and rhetoric. 'Look at me,' a British resident of the Belgian capital said to me over lunch. We were sitting in the European Council cafeteria; the food (fishsticks) was appalling, a sure sign of institutional seriousness. Only completely aimless bureaucracies (the United Nations, say, or the European Bank for Reconstruction and Development in the Attali era) have truly good food. 'Look at me. I'm married to a European. I live in Europe. I believe that the European Community is a good thing. But I can't imagine putting a Europe sticker on my car, or pinning the European flag to my lapel. It would be . . . embarrassing.'

It was not supposed to be this way – not at all. Throughout the long process of Maastricht ratification, John Major and Douglas Hurd argued loudly that signing the Treaty would give Britain more influence in Europe, would place Britain in the centre of the European project. Without it, Britain would belong to a 'second-tier' Europe. The train of European integration would leave and Britain would be stranded on the platform.

But now the Treaty has been signed and ratified, Britain still seems, curiously, as out of step as ever. The Belgians fly the European flag, the British do not. The French put the European flag on coffee mugs, the British do not. Everyone in Brussels appears to think that progress towards economic and monetary union has been temporarily slowed, but will continue anyway; that, after all, was part of the European Community's vision from the very beginning. But the British do not. The British seem to believe that progress has been halted, that attempting to continue is folly, that anyone who thinks otherwise is mistaken. This is not to say that the Continentals are right and the British are wrong; but the difference in perceptions is striking.

In fact, it appears that Britain has not only failed to gain influence in Europe, but has rather lost influence of late. However rosy things look from the Foreign Office, in Brussels one is told over and over that the continued acrimony within Britain over Maastricht, together with some of the changes which the Treaty itself will bring, have driven Britain farther away from 'Europe's heart' than ever before. This is not to say that Britain doesn't have a voice in negotiating trade treaties or various economic laws, or that Britain's much-praised diplomats do not enjoy tremendous respect. But on the big issues, those central to what everybody else perceives to be the goals of Europe, Britain's voice is now less important than ever.

It is true that, at first, the British Government's political difficulties with ratification didn't matter. After all, the Danes had a spot of trouble, and the French nearly did; the German process took longer than the British. One British MEP told me that John Major, who is very popular on the Continent, scored Brownie points in Europe for his tenaciousness.

But given the difference in political style between Britain and the Continent, it was impossible for even John Major to stay in European good books for long. In late September, the British Prime Minister published an article in the *Economist*. The piece was wholly predictable – it advocated Gatt, enlargement of the Community, more jobs for unemployed Europeans – and went virtually unnoticed in Britain, where its main tenets are taken for granted. Not so across the Channel. 'Have you seen this?' A Commission bureaucrat waved his issue in front of me last week; his copy was underlined in red ink, with little stars next to the paragraph where the Prime Minister had written: 'I hope my fellow heads of government will resist the temptation to recite the mantra of full economic and monetary union; if they do recite it, it will have all the quaintness of a rain dance and about the same potency.' The famed British sense of humour had missed its mark again. 'A rain dance,' howled the Eurocrat. 'A *rain dance?*'

'It was a very brave article,' I was told at the Foreign Office, but if the comments were intended for the Tory party conference, as they no doubt were, then why the *Economist,* which is read far more assiduously abroad? Or if the remarks were intended for abroad, why use a peculiarly British tone, almost guaranteed to offend? The same tone, also designed for domestic consumption, appeared again in several speeches at the Tory party conference, an event attended by the usual team from the German Christian Democratic Party; all of which has only helped to bring the usual exasperation with the British into the foreground again. It seems almost as if the British, simply because of the way they talk about Europe, were destined to offend everybody, just when acceptance seemed within reach.

Whether one wants to call it forward or backwards, the Community also seems to be heading in directions which the British are not prepared for. For example, the Maastricht Treaty gives more power to the European parliament, and consequently encourages the formation of cross-European political parties. This is the sort of thing that German Christian Democrats love; not only does the CDU send inspection teams to Tory party conferences, but they donate money to help other Christian Democrats win elections, particularly in eastern Europe. Party-to-party contacts are an integral part of German foreign policy. But until recently Britain's Conservative MEPs were not even members of the European People's Party, the conservative party of the European parliament. Now the MEPs are members (to the chagrin of Bill Cash, among others) but the Tories still do not belong to the governing body.

This seems like a minor detail – until one remembers that the leaders of the European People's Party, including six heads of state, hold regular conferences usually before meetings of the European Council. Helmut Kohl is there, Felipe Gonzalez of Spain is there, but John Major is not, and won't be, because too many of his backbenchers would scream treason if he appeared, and too many others just don't care enough to push the idea. I asked a recently elected Tory MP what he thought of the European Peoples' Party. 'Doesn't matter much, does it?' he said, his voice trailing off. 'Just more nonsense from Brussels.' No one else thinks it's nonsense, but there it is. Like other MPs from both parties, he appeared to view the European parliament with suspicion: more power for them, less for us. Perhaps that is one reason why the British still do not send the sort of senior politician to the European parliament that others do: Giscard d'Estaing served in Strasbourg, but not even Edward Heath could be bothered. As for Mrs Thatcher, she could never even bring herself to call the institution anything but the 'European Assembly', as if 'parliament' was simply too offensive.

Over the long term, Britain's inability to take European institutions seriously has resulted in one or two major failures, most notably the placement of the European Monetary Institute, the proto-European Central Bank. It should have been in London (which trades more currency daily than the rest of the Continent put together), but no one could put such an institution in a country so sceptical of monetary union; it could have been in Bonn, which would have been better from London's point of view, because Frankfurt being the German financial capital, a bank in Bonn would be less competition for the City. But Britain lost that argument too, and the bank will be in Frankfurt.

Though it is an old problem, the extent to which the British and other Europeans appear to be living on different planets, even in the post-Maastricht era, is curious. Asked about new British initiatives, one very senior British official referred proudly to British contributions to the European debate on unemployment; asked about his concerns, the same British official said that he was privately shocked by the money which the Community pays out to southern Europe: £7 million daily to Greece and Portugal, £13 million to Spain. I put these two subjects to an equally senior German diplomat, a man representing a country which is meant to be on Britain's wavelength. To the unemployment debate, he merely snorted, 'Oh we know about this, it's just the same old thing, more arguments about deregulation. We've heard it all from Britain before.' Asked about Mediterranean expenditure, he drew himself up: 'These sums are the price of European unity, so these sums must be paid.'

Even British journalists seem, perversely, to have become hate figures of a sort: everyone in Brussels reads the British press and listens to the BBC, and everyone knows that the British press and the BBC are, by Brussels standards, anti-Brussels. Meeting a member of the British press is a chance to get even. My appointment with one of the more senior Germans in Brussels prompted the line, 'You British, you just sit up on your island in the fog.' Another distinguished bureaucrat preceded our conversation with a ten-minute lecture on the iniquities of British foreign policy, ending with more finger-pointing: 'You have a sentimental, backward-looking concept of former glory and eventually you will have to come to terms with that.' Not actually being British myself, I found this educational, if somewhat odd.

None of this is to say that the European Community hasn't changed at all; of course it has, and it has even changed in some of the ways which Britain originally wanted. Certainly the mood is different, certainly the commitment to free markets is stronger, certainly no one talks about monetary union happening with anything like the speed which was once expected. Certainly there are now strong, anti-federalist forces in the rest of Europe, in Bavaria, in France, even in Belgium itself. There will be more national debates, as opposed to supranational bureaucratic decisions, and more tolerance for opposing points of view.

But the tone in which Europe is discussed in Germany, France and

Spain remains very different from the tone in which Europe is discussed in Britain. It is a matter of rhetoric, language and the way things
are put. The British, with their aversion to grandiose words and
symbols, have simply failed to take on board the seriousness of the
European project, which, however often side-tracked, is the same as it
was in the days of Jean Monnet. European parliaments make them
nervous, European flags make them giggle, an article on Europe is a
chance for the Prime Minister to display his sense of humour. On the
Continent, the European parliament is an important place to jockey for
influence, the European flag is a common household decoration and
John Major's article was considered offensive. Similarly, when
Europeans wrestle with the idea of federalism, they are debating something which they believe to be very powerful and real. When the British
do the same thing, the discussion usually takes the form of a rant
against 'fat bureaucrats in Brussels' or 'airy-fairy ideas' or the 'rain
dance' of monetary union. Europe becomes a scapegoat in Britain for
all sorts of things: when a British bus has an accident, the European
Community's failure to legislate safety-belt laws is blamed, and no one
seems to find that extraordinary.

Yet that kind of thing is picked up in Germany and France and
Belgium, where it becomes further justification for the continental
vision of British intransigence. In a speech at the last party conference,
Sir Leon Brittan himself pointed out that people in Britain 'sometimes
talk about Europe as if nobody in Europe ever listened to what we say'.
It is equally true that when people in Europe talk about Europe, it often
seems as if no one in Britain ever listens to what they say.

But rhetoric is rarely just that; usually, it is reflection of something
deeper. The truth is that even after all the fuss of the last year or so the
British still seem, at least to an outsider, to be deeply uncomfortable
within the Community. Living on an island in the fog is different from
living on a landmass; a maritime history is different from a continental history; a tradition of constitutional continuity is different from a
tradition of upheaval and warfare. British-style confrontations are
different from continental compromises, and British forthrightness is
incompatible with continental idealism. None of those things were
altered by signing the Maastricht Treaty, however sincerely John Major
hoped they would be. On the contrary, the conflict in Britain over the
European project comes up again and again. The recent CBI conference,
during which a supposedly pro-European prime minister was criticised
for not being European enough, was only another illustration of the
depth of the internal British struggle.

It seems odd, in fact, that the idea of dropping out of the European

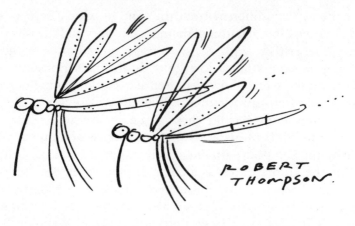

'Fancy a bite? I know this great little Italian!'

project altogether is not more widespread in Britain. Even the most
ardent opponents of the Maastricht Treaty won't bring it up, as if it
were politically incorrect to do so; yet even the most ardent supporters of the European Community know how different Britain's agenda
is from that of others in Europe. Maybe now that the macho thing has
been done – the Treaty was passed, ratification happened, John Major
showed who was prime minister after all – it is time for Britain to drop,
ever so quietly, into the second tier of the two-tier Europe which is
going to emerge anyway, when eastern Europe comes in at the end of
the century.

Perhaps this is not a prospect which Britain should fear. Remaining
within an enlarged free-trade zone, the British could let the rest of
Europe get on with the rest of the Maastricht project. There would still
be remarks about the pound turning into the equivalent of the
Ukrainian coupon – along with the Swiss franc, presumably – but it
might leave everyone better off. For if British influence now is at a low
ebb, it will surely appear even lower in a year or two, when the federalist project starts up again, when the European Monetary Institute
begins turning itself into a bank, when the newly powerful parliament
makes itself heard, when discussions of the new European defence and
foreign policies begin – and when all of the subjects which bother
Britain come up again, as they inevitably will.

27 November 1993

THE MEASURE

Francis Harvey

There's hardly a better way of doing
nothing than sitting on a Lough Eske wall
speckled with green and orange lichens and
overshadowed by foxgloves four feet tall.

Even better is to teach your children
this art of doing nothing at all
by making them sit at the lake beside
you on top of a lichened drystone wall.

And after all that they'll probably leave
you sitting alone on your Lough Eske wall
with nothing except foxgloves to show you
what they were like when they were four feet tall.

4 December 1993

ANOTHER VOICE

FOR EACH PRINCESS KILLS THE THING SHE LOVES

Charles Moore

Having attacked press intrusion into royal privacy, I feel in quite a strong position to defend the press from the latest charge, that it has driven the Princess of Wales from private life. It is her separation from her husband, and that alone, which has changed her role.

The Princess is only royal by association. If that association weakens, so must her status. Princess Margaret divorced Lord Snowdon and he sensibly got on with taking photographs. Princess

Anne divorced Captain Mark Phillips, and now he teaches people in Ireland how to hunt. The Princess of Wales cannot avoid being subject to the same process of relegation. Trying to continue as before was bound, even with the best will in the world, to be competitive. And the best will in the world was not there.

So the speech she made at the Headway luncheon last Friday was in bad taste. It was melodramatic to choose the occasion which she had attended a year before on the day that her separation was announced. It was unnecessary, in fact, to make a speech at all. A statement could have been issued (and should have been issued at the time) saying simply that, in view of her separation, the Princess was withdrawing from public life and intended to devote herself to the upbringing of her children.

Instead of which, the Princess decides that this is an occasion for telling us her feelings. She says that press interest affected 'my personal life, in a manner that has been hard to bear'. Yes, it has been terrible, but who let her friends talk to Andrew Morton? If she were still with her husband, press intrusion, however vile, could not hound her out.

'I hope you can find it in your hearts,' the Princess goes on, 'to understand and to give me the time and space that has been lacking in recent years.' Why should it be a question for our hearts? Why should we, the public, be invited to say, 'Yes, we love you, Diana. And because we love you, we'll let you leave us', the implication being that, loving her still, we shall have her back later? It is irrelevant whether we love her. It is irrelevant whether she needs time and 'space' (what depths of rubbishy psychology are plumbed in that single word). All that is relevant is that she is gradually becoming unroyal and should therefore retire from the scene.

Even in her thanks to 'the public in general', the Princess turns what should be a matter of courtesy into a play on the emotions. We have given her, she says, 'heartfelt support', and our 'kindness and affection have carried me through some of the most difficult periods'. But that's not what our kindness and affection were there for. They weren't there to carry her through anything, though it is nice that they did. They were there in deference to the monarchy, in whose life she played an important part. We thought that she played it extremely well, and were grateful. It is becoming clearer that, despite her real gifts, we thought wrong.

In a pedantry which irritates my colleagues at the *Sunday Telegraph*, I am forever saying, 'There is no such person as "Princess Diana" ' and insisting that she is given her proper title in all copy. I am right technically, but wrong psychologically. She is 'Princess Diana', a person who has come to imagine herself as inherently royal rather than royal only in reference to a relationship with somebody else, a woman with a sense of destiny rather than a sense of duty, a heroine from a school-girl's magazine. 'The Princess of Wales' is a description, a title held by several women in history. 'Princess Diana' is she alone, beautiful and dangerous and unstable.

It is harsh to say all this about someone who came to something very difficult very young and has suffered since, but it needs saying because the Cult of Diana goes on and may even flourish more in her retirement. The Cult of Diana is part of the religion of sentimental egotism which is replacing religion itself. It was no accident that the Princess's last big engagement before her speech was to attend a Concert of Hope for World Aids Day, or that Esther Rantzen attended the luncheon and declared herself 'profoundly moved'. All those egos scrambling for 'personal space' like the great powers used to scramble for Africa. All that display of emotion as a display of self. All that 'fighting back tears' so that people know how interesting and vulnerable you are. 'You do not cry about yourself,' said this paper's thoughtful High Life correspondent on *Desert Island Discs* last week, 'but about things like soldiers marching.' That principle is not understood by the Cult of Diana.

'. . . the curse of sentimentality,' writes I.A. Richards in *Practical Criticism*, '. . . is not that its victims have too much feeling, but that they have too little, that they see life in too specialised a fashion and respond to it too narrowly.' Sentimentality is emotion for its own sake, deliberately willed or deliberately partial, emotion whipped up or played for, self-dramatised, not self-understood. Sentimentality takes a good cause – Aids victims, abused children, the royal family – and exploits the emotions associated with them. It is the guiding principle of the Cult of Diana.

The material for that exploitation is always there, Richards points out, but anyone with proper feeling would treat it with restraint: 'If the mere fact that some girl somewhere is . . . lamenting were an occasion for emotion, into what convulsions might not the evening paper throw us nightly.' The Cult of Diana glories in such convulsions.

They are very destructive and very exhausting, particularly for an institution like the British monarchy. Some newspapers claimed this weekend that the court or 'the Establishment' had been ruthless in harrying the Princess of Wales. Ruthless! They have been restrained almost to the point of insanity. They have not been able to stop her acting as she wishes or saying what she wants; and when her Cult has attacked them, they have had no power to answer. Indeed, they remain bound by a loyalty to her, so long as she is Princess of Wales, which the

character called Princess Diana seems neither to recognise nor recip-
rocate. Imagine them pleading for 'time and space', and you see at once
how much higher standards we impose on them than on her.

But in the end the Princess is right. It is her we should feel sorry for
and find it in our hearts to understand. For the Cult of Diana is killing
the thing it loves.

11 December 1993

MISTLETOE IN MY HAIR-NET

Ian Thomson

'I'm afraid you've had an emergency operation for a fractured skull.' A
blurred but familiar face divided into three, then two and finally into
focus as the English friend who shared my flat in Rome. I protested,
'But why me?' The image dissolved and I was out again.

Some hours later I awoke outside what must have been, to judge by
the sharp ammonia stench, a latrine. A sign at the end of the corridor
announced: 'SAN GIOVANNI, ROME: CRANIAL TRAUMATOLOGY CLINIC'. Five
or six nuns swished past, each bearing what resembled a carafe of white
wine. They were pursued by a man wearing a cotton-wool beard and a
belted red tunic. 'Mind how you go with those pee jugs!' he joshed. The
sisters made a strange noise like startled poultry.

Shivering from the cold, I found I could not sit up; like a bedlamite,
I had been strapped to a low iron trolley out in the corridor. Fairy lights
on a small silver tree nearby fizzed and crackled from a faulty connection as I groaned for assistance. Father Christmas was chivvying
another group of sisters. 'You can't just leave him there like that!' he
seemed to be saying. There was a smell of canteen slops and carbolic
soap.

Nuns were frequently to be seen at the Roman hospital of San
Giovanni; it is affiliated to the ugly basilica of the same name. Soon
enough a couple of Catholic sisters came to untie me, hastily providing
a bowl into which I emptied the previous night's supper. One of them,
a big-thighed, strong-buttocked creature, yanked sharply at a piece of
plastic tubing. A light bulb popped in my head and I blasphemed with
the pain: '*Madonna!*' I had no idea I had been rigged to a catheter.

'*Calma, calmati!*' soothed the nun as she plumped my pillow. 'It will be Christmas soon.' To which she added with surreal irrelevance: 'There's nothing to stop you going to Vigil Mass after surgery.'

Prior to surgery, the last my friend had seen of me was as a group of flustered doctors, white coats flapping, hurtled me out of casualty on a trolley, swing-doors banging on our way to the operating theatre. '*Stai ferma!*' they shouted at the terrified girl. 'Stay right where you are!'

Five hours had elapsed between my collapse in the bedroom of our flat and being discovered there with the telephone dangling – in best Hitchcock tradition – from its hook, fingerprints of blood on the walls and floor.

It was a close brush with mortality. The operation for an impacted fracture with resultant haematoma – a swelling composed of blood effused into the connective tissues of the brain – had lasted three hours. During most of this time my friend was kept in the dark about my chances of survival. After constant pleading, a nurse (or nun) agreed to telephone the operating theatre. '*Coma oppure morto sicuro,*' came the verdict. A coma, if not death. During this ordeal my friend was unkindly ordered to remove her shoes: her restless pacing up and down was disturbing other patients asleep in the corridors.

Surgery had left me with a hole in the back of my skull where the haematoma had been evacuated. It was the size of a healthy tangerine. My head had been swathed in bandages like a mummy's, and a hair-net pulled tightly over the dressing. The quaintly named Dottore Milza (Doctor Spleen), who performed the operation, cautioned me against the hole. 'You are fortunate not to be in a persistent vegetative state,' he remarked in accurate medical English. 'But you are missing some bone and therefore less thick-skulled than before.'

'So what's to be done?'

'May I suggest a silver plate? We can glue it over your cavity. You'll be grateful for the protection.'

I didn't like the sound of this: how could one get through the metal detectors at an airport with a silver plate in one's head? But I trusted Dr Spleen. A stocky man of regimental bearing, he gave an impression of brisk efficiency. Clip-board tucked under his arm like a swagger-stick, he tapped the glass of his watch, saying, 'We'll see you after Christmas for therapy. Cheer up. We can always stick some mistletoe in your hair-net.'

I found it hard to believe that this could be Europe, let alone the capital of Italy, at a time of goodwill. Certainly it made no difference to the urinals of San Giovanni that we were about to celebrate the solemn Nativity of Our Lord: they remained as squalid as those aboard the second-class Naples-Palermo express. The food was usually a stew of fish and rice swimming in oleo-margarine, or else half-boiled lumps of pork gristle, soft and tallowy. Patients would resignedly refer to it as 'grasso di rinoceronte', rhino-fat.

After three days I was moved from the corridor into a ward where the walls were decorated with old Kodachrome photographs of Mount Vesuvius and Sophia Loren. The basilica of San Giovanni itself – or its blackened façade – was dimly visible from a single frosted window. A grim place. At least the food improved as Christmas approached. On a good day one might find a few currants peeping from the custard. We ate this pudding in respectful silence, as though a coffin were in the room. One evening, though, a patient yelled at a startled nun, 'What is it? What's this stuff?'

We all dropped our spoons. Professor Testardo was a newcomer and yet to learn the ropes. 'Next thing you'll be flavouring the rhino-fat with frankincense!' he continued in mellifluous Italian, beaming strangely. A university professor, it was rumoured that Testardo was seeing double after falling downstairs and not quite right in his mind. He wore glasses, with a wad of cotton-wool stuffed behind one lens. It was no surprise when he bumbled into a model of the manger, toppling the shepherds out of Bethlehem. 'Watch where you're going, headcase!' Father Christmas scolded. 'We won't put the three kings in there if you're around.'

For some days now Professor Testardo had been practising his English on me. ('I am so sick of speaking the language of Dante and Fellini.') He was fascinated by the words 'And a partridge in a pear tree', and would mumble them as he eased his legs out of bed in the morning. His routine at this hour was always the same: on with the slippers, off to the urinals (mindful now of the miniature crèche), then over to the window where he'd remove his glasses and cover up each – left hand, right hand – to assess the state of his double vision. '"An-a partr-eee-dge in-a pear-a-tree". Is it so?'

'So I may also say, "Goody gumdrops"?'

The chaotic organisation of San Giovanni at Christmas was not without its compensations. There were rarely any night-nurses on duty in the men's ward where I was recuperating, so visitors were allowed to sleep there and tend to their relatives through the early hours. After midnight my friend would metamorphose into Our Lady of the Bedpans, prevailed upon to run all sorts of errands from procuring pain-killers to raising the alarm whenever an incontinent lost a catheter. 'Signorina, signorina!' the men beseeched. As far as I was concerned, the nuns in their coifs and black habits had been trained in the school of Torquemada (my right arm had gone blue from their injections) and I needed their help like the hole in my head.

Cries for attention often came from the patient they called Luigi 'Sure Thing', a huge and porcine man whose unhappy habit was to break wind after lights out. For such a visual phenomenon, Luigi had a small voice and (apart from those nocturnal eructations) a quiet manner. It was not always so: they say he had been a safe-burglar in the Roman underworld. A rival had coshed him on the head – it must have been a really haymaker of a wallop – and Luigi drifted in and out of a coma now. A great scar like a railway track ran across his forehead, reddish against the waxy patina of his skin. Surgical polythene bags full of urine hung like udders below his bed.

Every afternoon Sure Thing was visited by three black-clad female relatives from Sicily, the oldest of these bearing more than a *soupçon* of a moustache. They came with unusual Christmas presents – wedges of pungent cheese, loaves of unleavened bread, a type of Spanish pepper with such a devilish kick to it that it was known as a *diavolesco*. In a surrealist parody of the Adoration, they would prostrate themselves before Dr Spleen and offer him a gorgonzola sandwich. It was as though they divined a shamanistic power in the surgeon, the power of life or death over their beloved Luigi. But Sure Thing was not long for this world; resignation was in the colour of the clothes and sorrowful eyes of his visiting relatives: a colour like the darkness of earth and death.

The holy terror of San Giovanni was Mustah. Impossible to know what he was like before brain surgery, Mustah – a Tunisian in his late teens – was now quite demented. He would hurl things at the nurses (a pillow, a slipper, even an empty plate) or spend hours gazing at an image of the Christ Child that hung above his bed. On Christmas Eve, Mustah lobbed his pillow at a trolley-load of test-tubes, scattering shards of glass across the ward. 'Mustah!' – a priest came to counsel the problematic patient – 'Do you know what hell is like? It is as hot as Tunis in July and everyone is made to recite a thousand Hail Marys.'

It failed to make an impression. All Mustah would say was, '*Ho paura di nessuno,*' I'm afraid of no one. Not that the nurses helped; they only encouraged Mustah in his antics, teaching him to wolfwhistle, which caused them piquant amusement.

Supper that Christmas Eve was little better than the usual rhino-fat. It consisted of paltry strips of turkey followed by a suety dish served under plastic fly-covers. 'There is one well-known remedy for hunger.' Professor Testardo sucked on a tooth noisily. 'Know what it is? A damn good dinner. Asparagus risotto, baked oysters with parmesan cheese, poached sea bass in orange marinade. And any God's amount of partridges in pear trees.'

'What about brains?' This from Sure Thing.

'Only in Albania,' said Professor Testardo.

'*Ho paura di nessuno.*' Mustah gave an idiot grin.

At midnight I wiped the condensation from my bedside window with a pillowslip. A china-blue half-moon hung in the sky above the basilica of San Giovanni where they were celebrating Vigil Mass. I could clearly see a group of hospital patients, dressed in pyjamas, running as far as they could towards the Egyptian obelisk in the middle of Piazza San Giovanni. I recognised Father Christmas among them. A delirium born in sleep, perhaps; but the hare-brained escapade cheered me greatly.

On Boxing Day I was visited for therapy by Dr Spleen and a group of trainee doctors. 'And how is our Englishman this wintry morning? In fighting trim, I hope.' The tests involved a lolly-stick pressed against the tongue, noting the response of pupil dilation, tapping the knee-caps with a rubber hammer. I also had to walk across the ward in a straight line and lift up both legs simultaneously – not easy when your head is supposed to remain on the pillow. Worse was when Dr Spleen decided to test my multiplication tables in Italian, something which always caused me the greatest of difficulty even in English. With every incorrect answer (in fact there were no correct ones), the doctors cast one another nervous glances and then proceeded to the days of the week. Here I had no problem; my spoken Italian had become quite fluent – unaccountably so – since the day I received a blow to my head.

'Very impressive.' Dr Spleen raised an eyebrow. 'It's hardly the Berlitz method, but a cranial cavity can certainly work wonders.' Then he unexpectedly snatched away the book I was reading, *A Christmas Carol*, to challenge me on the author's name.

Surely we can do better than this, I thought.

By the sixth day of Christmas boredom was beginning to take its toll. Professor Testardo had decided to moan a good deal ('I have a headache that aspirin cannot cure'), while Mustah was reduced to angry silence after failing to set fire to the cattle shed with its figurines of Mary and Joseph, the ox and ass. I had no dressing-gown – only a raincoat; and no slippers – only a pair of sandals. The nurses sniggered at my sartorial elegance as I took a daily shuffle round the hospital with the help of my friend. At least I could walk now, albeit with a weird sense of balance. 'The fall and rise of a Rome patient!' Dr Spleen congratulated me.

The walls of his office were hung with fabulous diagrams from a dissection handbook. *'Gray's Anatomy!'* exclaimed Dr Spleen. 'A far greater work of art than *The Divine Comedy.'* The delicate fibres of the optic nerve resembled the veins in a dead leaf, a diagonal dissection of the brain like a great pink cauliflower. And the names! Fissure of Sylvius, Orbiculus Ciliaris, the Limbic Lode. 'The mistakes made by us surgeons are innumerable, you know.' Dr Spleen hemmed and hawed a bit. 'Quite a few patients have died under me.' I decided then to have the silver plate fitted in London.

On the twelfth day of Christmas, Epiphany, the three Magi were added to the beleaguered manger. 'What does my true love send to me now?' Professor Testardo seemed sad at my departure. I had been informed by the head nurse that another haematoma casualty was on his way, and that it was now time for me to leave. Having said goodbye to my fellow inmates, a porter handed me a black refuse bag with my clothes – the trousers, he said, had been incinerated because they were blood-stained. Now bearded and unrecognisable, I hobbled out.

It was snowing in Rome, the first snowfall in ten years. Soft flakes were falling over the Capitoline Hill and the Colosseum, like down from a pillow fight. Despite the comical horrors of San Giovanni, I had enjoyed my convalescence there. The pervasive goodwill among patients, the regal solitude of the sick-bed, all this had made my illness oddly pleasurable. And I wasn't sent a bill.

18/25 December 1993

THE ETHNIC CLEANSING OF ULSTER

Simon Jenkins

Drive over Ulster's Sperrin hills, descend into the valley of the River Foyle and spread out before you is the ancient city of Derry. The scene is one of unparalleled public spending. Handsome roads and bridges dart between modern estates and community centres. Historic buildings sparkle afresh. Smart factories line the river banks. Derry has been at peace for over two years now. New jobs have arrived, bombings all but ceased (until December following the Anglo-Irish declaration). Only the security towers that dot the horizon recall that this country is still policed without consent. Derry, like many Ulster towns, is a modern San Gimignano.

But Derry is now 'behind the lines' – as exemplified by the official abandonment of the old name of Londonderry. John Hume's nationalist SDLP has won Derry politically and even his rivals for Catholic affection, Sinn Fein/IRA, see no point in bombing and killing their own. The ancient Protestant settlement on the west bank of the River Foyle that was begun by the Stuarts and survived the siege of 1689 has ended. In just a decade of 'ethnic cleansing', the Protestants have been driven from their historic redoubt in the old city across Craigavon Bridge into Waterside, like Croats over the river in Mostar. The Protestant Apprentice Boys no longer jeer down from Derry's walls on the Catholics of the Bogside. The Catholics have scaled those walls and driven them out.

Some Protestants went quietly. Some needed threats and bricks through their windows. They knew they were beaten and no British soldiers could save them, however thick the walls of the Strand Road fortress, however high the turrets of Rosemount police station. The Foyle is the new border. Old Derry is an Irish city. Its bars, newspapers, celtic lettering, heritage centres are a different country from Belfast or Newtownards or Armagh. Protestants are now migrating east even from Waterside, towards Coleraine and Limavady and across the River Bann into Antrim.

Politics is still about territory. Tribes still occupy and vacate that territory in search of security. They may go first at weekends to caravan lets on the north-east coast, then to relatives, finally to resettle. But they go. Since the start of the latest troubles, the number of segregated areas in Northern Ireland has more than doubled. When the British installed direct rule in Ulster in 1974, they inherited what was still largely an integrated province. They have created a segregated one. Over half the population now lives in wards comprising more than 90 per cent people of the same religion. How can this apartheid be ruled as one land?

The answer given by two decades of British government is as a colony. I have visited Stormont Castle regularly over these years. Each time I see a new secretary of state settling elegantly back in his chair, crossing his legs and reciting the same message – be it Jim Prior, Tom King, Peter Brooke or Sir Patrick Mayhew. They say the terrorists are 'tiring of the struggle' and are on the run. They explain how, sadly, the local politicians are a mediocre bunch who cannot be trusted with power. None the less, talks about talks are 'on offer' once they persuade their communities to 'eschew violence' and put down their arms.

At this point the walls of Stormont echo the Punjab and Kenya, Cyprus and Aden. When direct rule began it was described as a 'temporary' measure while local democracy was re-established. The Government's emergency powers were equally temporary. In the 1980s, direct rule was gently redefined as 'temporary pending the cessation of violence'. Occasional secretaries of state, such as Lord Prior, have mooted political reform: talks-about-talks or 'rolling devolution' or a power-sharing assembly. But one or other group of local leaders invariably walks out. Their communities continue to polarise and segregate. The politics of Ulster have atrophied. The province has settled into Whitehall's default mode, rule by decree. Ulster has joined Gibraltar as one of Europe's last colonies.

In the early days of direct rule, ministers camped out in a wing of Stormont Castle and entertained guests to take-away meals. Soldiers lived rough in old barracks and community halls. The vast 1930s Stormont parliament building – 'unmistakable symbol of the Northern Ireland state' says the guidebook – awaited the promised return of democracy. All was in vain. Now the former governor's palace at Hillsborough has been reopened. Pictures of Anglo-Irish beauties have been taken out of store. Guards have been dressed in Georgian gaiters. The local grandees – O'Neills, Abercorns, Hamiltons, Montgomerys – have been consulted and appointed to the committees and quangos by which Ulster is ruled. Diminutive ministries are headed by young British ministers flown out to Belfast on special planes from Northolt to get their knees brown.

The army has changed its role too. It still 'supports the civil power'. The old friction with the Royal Ulster Constabulary has largely ended. But like most colonial armies it has been obliged to build itself ever bigger fortresses and spend ever more time defending itself. Britain has built in Ulster the most awesome and hideous urban citadels to appear in Europe since the Middle Ages. The border is lined with outposts designed with wire mesh and concrete to resist the IRA's Mark 15 mortars. They sit like crusader castles, challenging the enemy to attack. In Dungannon two new bases, one army and one police, tower over each side of the town, grimly declaring Britain's sovereignty over the wild lands of Tyrone.

Military briefings have changed too. They used to relate successes in defending the public and in catching terrorists. Now they talk more about the defence of bases and the capture of weapons that might be used against them. The cost is astronomical: one barracks building in Dungannon base reputedly cost over $10 million. The security forces' work rate is fierce: 750,000 vehicles were searched ten years ago. Over the past year no fewer than 11,601,937 vehicles were reportedly searched. In some operational areas, barely a dozen active terrorists are holding down a thousand troops.

Meanwhile Ulster has been disinfected of democracy. In 1970 a report by the businessman, Sir Patrick Macrory, decided that the best way to reform the six gerrymandered county councils (plus Londonderry and Belfast) was simply to abolish them, leaving 26 subordinate district councils with parish pump functions. Local government was vested in the then Stormont parliament and its cabinet, a micro-Westminster. In 1974, this parliament was usurped by the British Government and since then Ulster has been ruled by a secretary of state under order-in-council. The only democracy left is that this 'governor' answers questions from Ulster MPs at Westminster rather than in any local assembly. (Ulster is closer to the French than the British colonial model.)

I believe Macrory's reform had more to do with Ulster's recent fate than any other measure. Politics lost all power of local self-renewal. The only elections, to Westminster and Strasbourg, were on a sectarian basis: the Westminster parties refused to organise or permit Ulster candidates under their names. With no chain of accountability and no need for party discipline, electioneering was reduced to the rantings of rival extremists. In the latest poll by International Social Attitudes, Northern Ireland was found to be the region least interested in politics in all 21 nations surveyed. Small wonder its MPs have been virtually the same for 20 years.

Ulster's middle class of doctors, lawyers, professors and businessmen has shifted from democratic politics into the greater comfort of patronage. If they win the eye of the secretary of state, they can join the housing executive, the tourist board, the arts council, the many development agencies. Junior ministers are the new district commissioners, dispensing grants and jobs. Those who stay long enough, such as Nicholas Scott and Richard Needham, become established proconsuls. In no other role can a British politician enjoy such power untrammelled by democracy.

Needham's pride and joy was the revival of Derry. He poured tens of millions of taxpayers' pounds into the city, to bolster John Hume's SDLP base against Martin McGuinness's Sinn Fein. 'One call from Hume to Stormont and the cheque was in the post,' was the local reprise. The tactic worked. The 30-strong city council, no longer gerrymandered to give the minority Protestant Unionists control, is now composed of 17 SDLP members and just 5 Sinn Fein. Though it has only district powers, such as rubbish collection, leisure and marketing, such is Hume's status that Derry enjoys *de facto* self-rule.

The SDLP dominance has enabled the council majority to share a modicum of power, including the mayoralty, with both Sinn Fein and the surviving Unionist members from Waterside. A rough-and-ready respect for the territorial space of the minorities has emerged and (until recently) an end to local violence. Business confidence has risen. Only the presence of a Protestant RUC and the ubiquitous British military fortifications hold Derry back from a stable peace.

Derry is the exception that should prove the rule. It is one bud of local self-government which has been permitted to flower in Ulster. The reason is cynical: it suited the British Government to prove that Sinn Fein has little support at the ballot-box. The outcome is to re-partition Ulster at the banks of the Foyle. But the outcome is also peace. If in Derry, why not elsewhere, why not in South Armagh? An overwhelming majority of Ulster's population lives in districts dominated by one or other 'tradition'. Why not draw new county boundaries and give them back the powers they had before 1970, subject to stringent audit of any discrimination? That way power could be shared federally, territorially – as it will never be shared in a unitary state under Stormont.

I believe this holds the key to a 'bottom-up' constitutional settlement. Last summer saw a remarkable report on the politics of Northern Ireland. It was by a commission chaired by the Oslo Professor Torkel Opsahl. Since it was published during a lull in violence it was mostly ignored. Opsahl recorded the views of those of all persuasions who have thought most deeply about Ulster over the years, and attempted to synthesise them. The story was a virtual monotone. By stripping Northern Ireland of democracy and making violence the focus of policy, British governments had committed the oldest colonialist fallacy. They had treated democracy as the reward Ulster would get if it gave up violence. Instead they should treat democracy as the only route whereby violence might be marginalised and diminished. That British ministers in the 1990s should need reminding of this is sad.

One Opsahl witness after another deplored Ulster's democratic deficit and Britain's obsession with 'first defeating the IRA'. Direct rule, said the Unionist politician Kenneth James, 'prevents elected representatives from learning how to govern, and absolves voters from accepting responsibility for their actions. Direct rule is a recipe for political stagnation in which the terrorist thrives.' Nor, many felt, would the answer lie in reviving rule from Stormont, an institution that embodied the hatreds, posturings and tribal warfare of old Ulster.

Sir Kenneth Bloomfield, former head of the Northern Ireland civil service, admitted to Opsahl that power-sharing was never likely to work and that 'the answer may well be to diffuse power to [local councils] and build in the strongest possible safeguards against abuse by elected majorities'.

Sir Charles Carter, former head of the Northern Ireland economic council, advocated bold devolution to councillors, who at present have so little to do they just 'waste time striking political attitudes'. Local majorities should be forced to shoulder responsibility for planning, libraries, local roads, perhaps even for primary schools and clinics, with safeguards for minority civil rights. This was not a matter of size, said Carter. Multipurpose authorities as small even as Ulster's districts exist all over Europe. They are the building blocks to peaceful cohabitation between the communities.

Already power is shared in some degree on 11 of the existing 26 district councils. At this level, people know each other and are the more able to tolerate each other's arguments and needs. As in former Yugoslavia, it is the failure of more distant authority that drags integrated communities apart. But power is most easily shared where one side is dominant and not under threat, as will never be the case at Stormont. The essence of political reform in Ulster is to acknowledge segregation – even the fact of ethnic cleansing – and try to construct tolerant self-governing communities across the divide. The way lies not through artificial, enforced powersharing but through the power that is shared by local compromise, by the give-and-take of citizens who know each other.

I believe Britain cannot 'leave' Northern Ireland. That is plainly against the wish of the majority, and much of the minority. Ulster will, like Scotland, need its secretary of state. But areas led by nationalist/Catholic councils will form their own links with the South, as many districts do now. Ulster is part of the island of Ireland and the existing all-Ireland mechanisms must remain operational for both security and economic development. 'Troops out' is a matter of logistics, not of sovereignty. 'Ministers and civil servants out' is the first priority. Political reform cannot wait on a solution to violence. There will not be one. As the Ulster specialist, Clare Palley, has often said, only chemists have solutions. The (tentative) lesson of modern Derry is that peace comes from a shift in the political culture. It does not precede it. Nor does it arise from a repetitive chant of 'peace declarations' from London and Dublin.

Ulster collapsed into violence in the mid-1970s as a simple consequence of Britain's failure to update the province's political institutions. A corner of Europe had been allowed to rot politically, like Sicily. The symptom was mayhem. The need then, as now, was for political reform. Then, as now, Britain's preferred answer was a power-sharing executive at Stormont with institutional links with the South. Under the Faulkner leadership this was tried and it failed. For 20 years British politicians have been struggling to re-establish it. They have not succeeded and they will not succeed. Meanwhile, Britain has stayed, fortified and entrenched – entrenched physically and mentally.

In private conversation, John Major's commitment to cure Ulster's ills is palpable. Lady Thatcher had consigned Ulster to outer darkness from the moment of Airey Neave's death. She even permitted herself the indulgence of the 1985 Anglo-Irish agreement. This repeated the error of Sunningdale in 1973, that a deal between London and Dublin has some restraining effect on Ulster extremism. What is curious about Mr Major's Downing Street declaration is that it seems to repeat the same error. It is just more of the same.

We all have our own special lens through which to view political conflict. Mine is that central government may be a good judge of how best to govern a country, but is rarely its best governor. Mr Major's reforms in England and Wales of education, the police, the courts and local government suggest that centralism is now his prevailing ideology. Centralism prevails too in Ulster. But centralism is vulnerable to its own distortions. In Northern Ireland it places a premium on violence because bombings and murders are what hit the London headlines. Whenever there is an atrocity in Northern Ireland, the secretary of state promises the same ritual, a 'review of security'. He never promises a review of democracy. It is like responding to small-pox with a box of patches.

The Downing Street declaration cons firms that violence is still top of the Ulster political agenda. Indeed it goes further. It offers the paramilitaries a *de facto* veto on political reform, implying that reform cannot proceed without their presence at the negotiating table. Far from marginalising them, it puts them firmly at centre stage. Never has the IRA received so much attention. Never has it deserved so much neglect. This is crass. It is no way to proceed. And there is another way.

1 January 1994

BLACK MISCHIEF

Amity Shlaes

Brooklyn Heights, New York

Winter is a merry time in Brooklyn Heights and this one has been particularly festive. The children of the Wall Street lawyers who live here spend afternoons building snowmen in each others' gardens. The wives of the Wall Street lawyers come home from work around six o'clock and chat about property values with their neighbours as they hang elaborate wreaths on the bevelled glass of their brownstone doors. The Wall Street lawyers themselves arrive only around midnight, but bear in their pockets magnificent bonuses – golden shards of the merger bonanza and a runaway stock market. At last, the whole snowy neighbourhood seems to sigh, the bleak recession-time is over. Maybe, goes the thinking – perhaps in this New Year – things might get back to normal.

Might get back, that is, except for one little problem. The problem is one that says to all tame urban inhabitants of 1990s America, and in particular to white inhabitants: you will soon be in the minority, and the official city – employees, courts, juries, laws – cannot protect you. Brooklyn Heights residents pride themselves on being bold city leaders, though, so they don't talk about 'fear'. They refer to their problem in code, and they call it 'the subway'.

For Brooklyners, the subway is an unlovely and unavoidable necessity. Brooklyn Heights grew great because it is close to Wall Street, and some of the cupolar rooms of the nicest mansions of the biggest lawyers' houses peer right out on to the Staten Island Ferry. Between Brooklyn and Wall Street, though, lies the soggy East River. There is a bridge over the river – the rickety Brooklyn Bridge – and there is a car tunnel, the clogged Brooklyn Battery. But, to cross that river, someone in the lawyers' families – the husband, say, when he is in a hurry, the daughter, who has to get to her East Side girls' school – has to descend into the Court Street entrance, face humanity and smell the urine, and ride the train.

The subway, of course, has always been an adventure. First came the vandalism and graffiti, back in the 1970s, but that threat was quickly tamed by the view that converted it to art: make pictures on the wall, and you will become famous like Keith Haring. Then came crack and necklace-snatching, so that riders took to turtle-necks, turning their engagement rings around and storing their Rolexes at home (this did a lot for the fashion among Wall Streeters of cheaper timepieces like the Swatch). Then came token-sucking, the disgusting sight of a man or woman bent down, lips pursed, to suck tokens out of the token deposit machine in order to buy themselves a token for a free ride.

Several recent events, though, have made it clear to Brooklynites that they are now facing a more threatening change. The splashiest example was Colin Ferguson's murderous ride on the Long Island commuter line, not because he killed six people – all countries have occasional wild gunmen – but because his manic hostility to whites is shared by many of the city's non-madmen. It is hostility shared by the black teenagers who push white teenagers out of cars when they are trying to board a crowded train. It is shared by the (black) city employee behind the bullet-proof glass at the token booth, who looks at two simultaneous arrivals – one white, one black – and says to the black one with a pointed and gratified smile, 'You go first.'

The latest fright – at least before Colin Ferguson's personal ethnic cleansing – came last month from Washington, when the Supreme Court declined to hear, let alone revoke, something known around here as 'the McCummings case'. In early 1984, a 71-year-old named Jerome Sandusky was waiting for a train at Manhattan's 96th street stop. He was accosted by a mugger – Bernard McCummings – who held him in a choke-hold and tore at his pockets. Police arrived and stopped the crime, and Mr McCummings did a bit of time.

That story, though, is not the 'McCummings case'. The McCummings case is the mugger's own crusade for 'social justice' in the modern sense of the term. It happened that, in trying to stop the criminal, the police shot at him, and in trying to stop him, made him a paraplegic. So Mr McCummings turned around and sued the city for 'excessive force'. An urban jury awarded him $4.3 million. Not excessive, Mr McCummings and his lawyer thought, for the loss of the use of his legs and a sex life. But a lot more than Mr Sandusky got and a lot in the eyes of the urban taxpayer.

The basis for the jury's decision – and the judge's advice to the jury – was item one in new-era law: a 1984 New York rule that said policemen may use guns solely as defensive weapons. In other words (McCummings' lawyer's), his award was 'an affirmation that Bernard was wronged when they turned him into a paraplegic'. In other words, the Brooklyn riders whisper, the police down there at the neighbourhood's subway stop can't help you, because they can't be like Clint Eastwood and yell, 'Stop or I'll shoot.'

'I do hope her first marriage is more successful than mine was'

Another case in another of Brooklyn's Heights neighbourhoods, in this instance the less smart Crown Heights, had an equally troubling resolution. Heights is a neighbourhood of three communities: Orthodox Jews, Caribbean blacks and American blacks live in unfriendly peace there. (To get there its locals ride the '4' and '5' trains, which make stops in Brooklyn Heights.) One day two years ago, an Orthodox Jew had a car accident and – must we spell it out? – unintentionally ran over and killed a black child. The black community rose up and within hours black youths had jumped on and knifed to death a visiting rabbinical student from Australia. The city's lawyers found the bloody weapon and extracted an identification of his murderer from the dying man. The murderer, a teenager, also confessed on video-tape. But a black-dominated jury on Brooklyn Heights Court Street, right over the heads of the lawyer commuters, freed the defendant, and afterwards went out for a celebratory dinner with civil rights lawyers and the freed gangster.

What, we say at our cocktail parties, does this mean about white life in Brooklyn Heights? 'I haven't read the paper since the McCummings thing,' said one lady to me flatly. Others adjust their blinkers to take in only a bit more light. Mostly, citizens concentrate on the dos and don'ts of subway and home safety. A list of recent rules for survival, heard and overheard at such parties in the past couple of years, goes something like this:

'You must not wear a sheepskin coat no matter how shabby.' (A man in Rockaway was killed for his sheepskin before the eyes of his pregnant fiancée.)

'Your teenager must never carry a Jansport backpack.' (The gangs that ride the trains favour that particular brand.)

'You must not walk home alone from the train late after work.' (Gangs with guns target middle-aged men on foot; if they're driving they lock them in their own car boot.)

If only you can handle yourself right, the logic goes, you will be safe. Few people, though, mention the truth: if by some misfortune you happen to get mugged, the policeman standing at the Court Street subway stop cannot protect you. If by some misfortune you find yourself on trial at the Court House there, you may face a row of Brooklyn faces that look different from yours, and they may not give you a fair hearing.

Demography plays a role here. In a city that is becoming ever more diverse – ever more Asian, ever more black, ever more Hispanic – it is ever harder to find one's white self before a white jury. The real issue, though, is not race. The statistics bear out the truism that minorities are the greatest victims of minority crimes in cities like New York. But demography has also wrought a turnover in America's officials, lawyers, and judges, and those educated in a post-1968 era with a heavy civil rights focus most often find it more interesting to vote, judge and litigate on the side of the criminal. When out-of-control American tort law, the kind that permits the size of Mr McCummings's award, is backed up by city officials and a judiciary anxious to placate the politicised rage of a succession of minorities, the result is something more dangerous than a city with a simple crime problem. A fortnight ago in the capacious Jacob Javits Center in Manhattan, the black minister Louis Farrakhan drew cheers from his largely black audience when he mentioned the deeds of the subway killer Colin Ferguson. The audience cheered again when the minister suggested that America's new concern about crime was racism in disguise – that being 'tough on criminals' really meant being 'tough on black people'.

New Yorkers, even before the commuter-car massacre, had elected a white, hard-on-crime prosecutor mayor. But Rudolph Giuliani, the new man, cannot himself control a New York establishment that busies itself defending 'social victims', or single-handedly reverse the Supreme Court or bring about legal reform.

Meanwhile, the circle of physical liberty for Brooklyn Heights, or communities like it, gets ever tinier. You will be safe on the subway, the mantra here once went, 'if you don't ride the train at night'. In the rough 1980s that became, 'if you don't ride the train in non-rush-hour times'. 'If you don't ride the '4' or '5' trains' was the new rule after Crown Heights, or look, one could add, obviously Jewish. 'If you don't commute to Long Island' is this month's law, following the Ferguson murders.

'If you walk across the Brooklyn Bridge, you can avoid the subway altogether,' the Wall Street wives advised this winter. Then a girl was raped on the Manhattan-side entrance.

1 January 1994

TRAVEL

NATIONAL SMELL OF URINE

Christopher Howse

Sin is always different abroad. In Mexico there are still seven deadly ones, but the temptations are foreign to an English temperament. Since the peasants of Chiapas decided to rise up when I was there, I shall start with:

Anger. It was a tropical evening. It was either him or me. He lay there on his back against the wall, trying to fend off the blows. All I can remember is my hand rising and falling again and again. The next thing I knew he was dead.

He, of course, was a cockroach, and a particularly fine specimen: about three inches long with delicate yellowish colourings about his thorax and wing-casings. The only problem was that he was in my bathroom and seemed to be making himself at home. I didn't want his six feet going anywhere that either of my bare two went, particularly at the same time; and I don't like things that go scrunch in the night. What finally did for him was some Boots spray anti-perspirant; God knows what it does for me.

Gluttony. Christmas Day was a fiesta that I expected to be accompanied by mariachi bands and excited crowds. It turned out to be much more English in character – in other words, the bars closed up at 7.30 on Christmas Eve and the shops stayed shut for two days. I thought I should have to survive on four water biscuits and two Club World chocolates in a little cardboard box, courtesy of British Airways.

The trouble was that people back in England had given me very good health advice: don't take ice in your drinks, don't eat salads, on no account eat those tempting *tacos* sold by typhoid-infested Indians at the roadside. That doesn't leave much scope.

Now, in Mexico City, unlike London, the Underground runs on Christmas Day, so I went to the great national shrine of Our Lady of Guadalupe, where the basilica, which has room for 20,000, was full of holiday crowds. Outside in the summery sunshine children ran around with balloons and little windmills. I saw a man breaking up a block of ice in a gutter where a dog had pissed, to cool his home-made orangeade. Everywhere there was the national smell of urine, burning charcoal, dust and frying *tacos*.

I don't know if I could have resisted temptation, but I was saved from Montezuma or worse by the discovery of the Café Popular (on the Calle Cinco de Mayo): such black black coffee, such crumbly *polverones*. It is clean and open 24 hours. Even if you're not starving, I recommend it.

Envy. On 27 December 1839, the Scottish-born wife of the first Spanish ambassador to Mexico, Frances Calderon de la Barca, wrote: 'The weather is lovely, the air fresh and clear, the sky one vast expanse of bright blue, without a single cloud.' On 27 December 1993 the sky at the end of the street was brown, the newspapers were proclaiming the worst pollution known and I had developed a hacking cough. It was time to head out of the valley of Mexico City.

I did envy Señora Calderon the pastoral peace of the Mexican suburbs (even though she had to dodge cannonballs in the street during one of the regular *pronunciamientos*). But as the bus climbed over the surrounding mountains, the scene changed from the car-choked 1990s to a pre-war English countryside; stooks of wheat stood in the fields beside oaks in full leaf. Altitude makes all the difference, and as the bus careered down again round hairpin bends the temperature rose and we were among palm trees, tropical flowers and strange long-tailed blackbirds making whooping noises. Within an hour and a half I was sitting with a cooling drink in the garden of Sanborns, the ersatz English drugstore in Cuernavaca, the Harrogate of Mexico. But it does have 16th-century frescoes in the cathedral.

In Cuernavaca I bought some pure alcohol to put on my blisters. It was called El Viejito (The Little Old Man) and the bottle was labelled *potable*. I don't envy the little old man.

Avarice. Where do you put your money if every shadow in the street could be a mugger? Decentralisation is my motto, and so it was that I had the cash in the hip pocket and the credit cards in the inside jacket.

Hence my unorthodox reply *sotto voce* to the priest when he proclaimed the Gospel at Mass in the pretty colonial church of San Francisco. He said, '*Lectio evangelii secundum Lucam*.' I made the sign of the cross, felt my hip pocket and replied, 'Fuck, I've been dipped.'

I knew exactly how it had happened: that cheerful Cantina Rio Plata the night before, with the guitarist and the Dos Equis brown beer and the boot-black doing his round and the little Indian boy selling (or not selling) chewing gum and the Magno brandy all the way from Spain. It would be all too easy to brush past me at the bar and extract the goodies from my pocket.

Halfway through the Gospel next morning I found the cards in the other top pocket, next to the airline ticket. At the end of the Gospel the people answered, '*Laus tibi Christi*.' This time I joined in.

So much for decentralisation.

Pride. Mexicans have a lot to be proud of. I didn't see a single volcano or pyramid, but there are plenty of both around. I did see the most perfectly preserved baroque church in the mountain-side silver-mining city of Taxco. It is called Santa Prisca and has 13 reredoses rising 60 feet around the walls, so thickly encrusted with gilt ornament they look like the giant larvae of caddis-flies touched by King Midas. S. Vital, S. George, S. Isidro, S. Estolano, S. Joachim, S. Emerenslana, S. Pedro Arbues, S. Vicente De Paulo, S. Lorenzo Levita and a hundred more – and two dozen Virgin Marys.

Mexico Cathedral itself is vast and stuffed full of modernist scaffolding to stop it falling down (the earthquake plus water extraction). It was there I saw a thin Indian and his barefoot wife and their very dirty little child attending Mass one morning. They knelt on the marble floor; his hat lay on the altar rails and in it was a roll of bread, their breakfast for the day. That was humbling.

Sloth. The flight to Mexico takes nearly 12 hours (British Airways direct, three times a week). Now, even curling up with a good Trollope, that means quite a few hours of boredom, discomfort, anxiety, dehydration and annoying neighbours. Do you go World Traveller at £633 or Club at £2,126? I went Club because British Airways gave me a ticket, and very nice it was too: *High Noon* on the way out and *It's a Wonderful Life* on the way back. Lots of room too. I slept.

Lust. I wouldn't, if I were you.

29 January 1994

NO PONTIFICATION IN THIS REALM OF ENGLAND

Ferdinand Mount

Is it possible that, after all, we shall come to think that Catholic Emancipation has turned out to be a mistake?

For a century and more, we have applauded the surrender of Sir Robert Peel and the Duke of Wellington and congratulated ourselves on the openness and tolerance of our civil arrangements. British Catholics, for their part, responded with decorum and patriotic enthusiasm. If the same spirit of give-and-take was less evident within the Roman Catholic hierarchy – in its attitude, say, to mixed marriages or attendance at services in other churches – then we trusted to time and the example of the Church of England to erode the edge of prejudice.

The contribution of Nonconformists to the moral and political life of the nation might be more stirring; the contribution of British Jews to science, business and the arts might be infinitely more dazzling. But Catholics had shown not only that they were just as British as the rest of us (which we already knew) but that the Bishop of Rome and his minions were no longer a threat to the public peace. Over the last 20 years, that mutual confidence has grown, as the Catholic hierarchy, even in Ireland, began to relax some of its prohibitions and rather gingerly to take part in inter-church activities.

Yet suddenly the most insensitive Protestant nostril cannot help detecting an intrusive whiff of incense, the dullest Anglican ear cannot fail to catch a note of triumphalism. I could scarcely believe it when the Church of England's decision to ordain women inspired Cardinal Hume to muse out loud on the prospect of 'the conversion of England'. I find it still harder to believe that the conversion of the Duchess of Kent should prompt Mr Piers Paul Read to ask if they could have their churches back and Lord Rees-Mogg to speculate on the possibility of a

Catholic monarch. It may be said that Lord Rees-Mogg is to all intents and purposes an American smart operator disguised as an English gentleman, rather in the style of P.G. Wodehouse's Soapy Molloy, and that Mr Read is a notorious tease. But there is no disguising the note of stifled excitement in the pronouncements of Catholic spokesmen and journalists. 'The Church of England is finished,' cries Mr William Oddie with all the exuberance of a recent convert. 'Is the cause,' asks Mr Paul Johnson, 'for which St Thomas More died on Tower Hill, St Edmund Campion was hanged, drawn and quartered at Tyburn, Cardinal Newman preached, Cardinal Manning fought and schemed, and a host of great writers – Belloc and Chesterton, Maurice Baring and Evelyn Waugh, Christopher Dawson and Ronald Knox – devoted their splendid talents, now at last in sight of victory?'

Victory. Ah, so there was a war on, after all. The ambitions for the conversion of England were never abandoned, never even modified, but only expressed *sotto voce* for tactical reasons. It will be said that they are only talking about peaceful competition. That's what Khrushchev claimed when he said 'We will bury you', and we didn't take very kindly to that. After all, those same publicists have never made any secret of their loathing of the Church of England. In column after column, they have poured forth their contempt for its spirit of accommodation and conciliation, its attentiveness to the hopes and aspirations both of its members and of the millions of non-religious citizens of Britain – in short, for everything which which we now think of as Anglican. (If any of my remarks should happen to give offence to good Catholics, they might care to reflect that the Anglican church and clergy have had to put up with a thousand times worse from Catholic polemicists – Islamic and Jewish commentators occasionally join in the fun too, but it is the Pope's big guns who dominate the media.)

Nowhere was this rooted antipathy more evident than in the attitude of Catholic journalists towards the Church of England's decision to ordain women. All the concentration was on the anguish of the smallish Anglo-Catholic minority who 'no longer recognised the Church they were brought up in'. The fact that the vast majority of Anglicans and non-Anglicans were mystified by the fuss was brushed aside. After all, it is possible to have been a devout churchgoer all one's life and listened to several thousand sermons without ever hearing a single word about the maleness of the priesthood. The theological justification advanced by Bishop Graham Leonard (before he poped) sounded to the average Anglican more like a description of some outlandish fertility rite. Ask the natural Protestant question – Would Our

Lord have opposed the ordination of women? – and the answer seems self-evident, for 'there is neither Jew nor Greek, there is neither bond nor free, there is neither male nor female: for ye are all one in Christ Jesus'.

Nowhere is the desire for *reconquista* more evident than in present-day Catholic historiography. Distinguished historians like J. J. Scarisbrick and Eamon Duffy have made considerable headway in convincing their non-Catholic colleagues that throughout the Reformation the English people clung passionately to the old religion which was being taken from them by a minority of fanatical Protestant radicals. By this means, the intervening centuries of fierce popular anti-Popery are neatly stepped over, and the Roman Church re-established not only as the one genuinely Catholic church but also as the church of true-born Englishmen, which is soon to come into its own again.

Yet our self-understanding of Englishness – the tolerance, the mildness, the irony – is intimately connected to the much later development of the Church of England, after the Civil War, after the Glorious Revolution. This Englishness may be illusory or fleeting, we might be better off without it, but without the Church of England it would not be the same.

Nor am I much impressed to be told how prominent British Catholics are in the patriotic fight against the dreaded Maastricht Treaty and the bureaucrats of Brussels: Mr William Cash, Lord Rees-Mogg again, Mr Johnson, Mr Conrad Black. This seems to me to prove precisely the opposite of what it is supposed to prove. It is exactly because the Maastricht Treaty was never a real threat to the things we hold precious – because, like many another flawed treaty we have signed, it was always likely to be a dead letter before the ink was dry – that the paranoiac literalism of the Catholic campaigners against Maastricht seemed to have a fractionally deranged and, I can't help adding, alien quality to it. If France is anything to go by, Catholicism and nationalism make a prickly, inward-looking combination.

It would be equally deranged to argue, contrariwise, that the real threat to our institutions and our way of life comes today, not from Brussels, but from Rome. The Catholic Church, has, after all, undergone a certain amiable anglicanising over the past few decades: its narrowness, its snobbery, its anti-Semitism, its obsession with authority have lost much of their old bite. All the same, the old reflexes are still there, and make it all too easy for critics to ask what really is the difference between Roman Catholicism and Islamic fundamentalism.

It would be much nicer if we did not have to ask such questions and if some of our best friends could continue to be the affable and self-effacing papists we used to know.

29 January 1994

BOOKS

A MODERN WORK OF GENIUS

Warwick Collins

THEORY OF WAR
by Joan Brady
Abacus

Joan Brady's *Theory of War*, which recently won the Whitbread Book of the Year prize, is one of the most remarkable and accomplished fictions to come from these islands perhaps since William Golding's great seafaring trilogy which began with *Rites of Passage*.

The work is so coherent that it is only in attempting to classify it that one begins to perceive its daunting, complex structure. It is novel, historical excavation, and philosophical treatise, ironic comedy and revenger's tragedy. Its tone is both mordant and serious. The book's length, a mere 209 pages, gives some idea of its economy and compression. Nothing is included which is not necessary to the whole.

The philosophy may be based, loosely and somewhat ironically, on Clausewitz's classic, but its approach to the subject matter is concentrated and merciless. Brady has chosen as her theme the exploration of slavery. But this is not black slavery, it is white slavery – the selling of one white by a second white to a third white – into what was called 'bounden' labour. Fact and fiction merge in the sense that both Brady and her narrator had grandfathers who as children were sold into bounden labour. But perhaps the real theme of Brady's novel is America, or rather the difference between the manufactured image, the American dream, and another America that emerges – meretricious, ugly and somehow extraordinarily compelling – from these pages.

The unblinking nature of Brady's gaze is exemplified in pungent description. Meeting her uncle's new wife, the narrator thinks:

> She had one of those faces that are purely American. Even at whatever ancient age she'd reached (and plainly she'd been around quite a while), there was nothing in the skin, nothing in the eyes, nothing around the mouth to betray a single thought or a single experience; all was as hygienic as an unwrapped roll of toilet paper, no hint whatever that anybody had ever lived there: a safe house rather than a face.

The biography of her grandfather Jonathan, the slave, is told with a passionate detachment – how he is broken for labour; how he is tied down and his teeth are gruesomely extracted to serve as false teeth for rich folk; how he finally runs away and reaches a railway. It is in her descriptions of the railway, its lore and strangely doomed characters, that Brady's prose reaches its great heights of poetry. With the possible exception of Ondaatje, no one writes as she does of the complex relationship between men and the machinery which they serve. No one has described more beautifully the great steam engines, called *Mogul* or *Consolidation*, which sometimes kill their operators as casually as a wild animal. In these passages alone, the novel expresses a vaulting ambition above nearly all other writing of the past several years. Almost the entire middle section of the book is quotable, but a typical passage is the following, when a train carrying redwood logs on a bitterly cold day begins to break in half:

> At dawn, the train began to ease its way downhill. Icicles hung from the redwoods and from the chains that held them. The wind was so sharp it froze eyelashes together. A change in the locomotive's exhaust is the only warning of a brake-in-two a railroadman gets. Hear that? That easing of the sound? That's your reference point. That's what measures you – tells you who you are. If you're quick you can catch the mistake before it's actually made. But nobody was quick enough on those icy redwoods in that icy, whistling wind – not Jonathan, not College, either, not Hecox, the bear of a conductor himself. The train quaked. The redwoods swung in their chains. The back half of the train pulled away from the front, paused, then cannoned forward. Well, what can you expect? You've got to die sometime. Bire sprouted from the wheels: this really happens, fire from metal on metal, and it catches the brush on either side of the track as though the train itself has become molten like lava that ignites whatever it touches along its path.

As part of her extraordinary vision, Brady has chosen, as her dark angel, her villain, a Democratic senator, who has transformed himself seamlessly from huckster salesman peddling faulty goods to politician peddling populist illusions. He has an unfailing eye for other people's weaknesses, not least that of the protagonist, who first encounters him as the son of the man, Alvah Stoke, who has bought him as a slave. Senator George Stoke must rank as one of the more successful grotesques of fiction. Yet it is part of Brady's skill that we find ourselves able to feel a surreptitious sympathy for the old phoney. We first encounter him as elderly senator, inclined to take hold of a piece of litmus paper, and threaten a colleague:

> I'm gonna put this up to your face just like this, right? And by the quivering cunt of the unfucked mother of Christ, it's going to tell me whose ass you had your nose stuck up last night.

Brady's prose is not so self-conscious as Cormac McCarthy's. It is more integrated and less highly wrought than that of Ondaatje. But it rises to the the same powerful heights, sometimes even beyond, because she is obsessed by her subject matter. The moral depravity of slavery is clearly branded deeply into her soul. At the end of the book an author's note reads:

> My grandfather was a slave. This isn't an uncommon claim for an American to make if the American is black. But I'm not black, I'm white. My grandfather was white, too. And he was sold into slavery not in some barbaric third-world country; he was sold in the United States of America. A Midwestern tobacco farmer bought him for $15 dollars when he was four years old. Not many people know about such sales, though they were common just after the Civil War.

In the same brief author's note, Brady calmly records psychological reverberations through the generations of her own family:

> The slave's life my grandfather led until he ran away at 16 so scarred him that no one who came near him afterwards could escape the effects of it; four of his seven children – including my father – ended up suicides.

What Brady's novel demonstrates above all is the height literature may reach when moral force is allied with high technical virtuosity. By comparison, the fictions of our own fashionable leading writers, with their combination of rough-boy stance and nervous, if not slavish, political correctness, appear somewhat anodyne. Which of them (Amis, McEwan, Barnes *et al*) would have the courage to deploy as villain a politician who had both a laudable record in radical reform, and a soul as dark as an unlit basement?

Critics are fond of the notion that they can judge novels. In practice, when a novel reaches a certain stage of excellence, it begins to reverse the process, and to judge its critics. Brady's book has received remarkably little critical attention so far. The same is broadly true of literary prizes. They may be designed to bestow upon a novel the prestige of a venerable committee of judges. But at this level, the novel reacts back and brings prestige to the prize. For, in awarding *Theory of War* the Whitbread Book of the Year prize, the Whitbread selection panel has done itself greater honour than it has done the book.

Brady is one of a small number of Anglophile American novelists who, while residing in England for much of their lives, are nevertheless haunted by their country of origin, and write in a manner which would be inconceivable if they were not Americans. Russell Hoban and Paul Theroux are other examples. Oddly enough, their very obsession with the less salubrious aspects of their original culture also does America a sly honour. *Theory of War* is like a backhanded slap in the face of the American ideal, delivered with all the power of a thwarted lover. It will be interesting whether in the longer term the novel can establish a genuine foothold on its home ground. Perhaps, amongst the American reading public, who seem to take to heart such slush as *Love Story* and *The Bridges of Madison County*, there is room in some corner for this magnificent and excoriating novel.

5 February 1994

CENTENARY OF A DOUBLE-CROSSER

Simon Heffer

'Macmillan was such a double-crosser that when he hadn't got anyone to double-cross he would double-cross himself to keep in practice.' More than 30 years after Enoch Powell served Macmillan as a minister, his opinion of his chief has lost none of its pungency. Talking last week to Mr Powell and his colleague in Macmillan's cabinet, Lord

Deedes, I found views still divided on the legacy left by the first Earl of Stockton, who would have been 100 next week. But it is unsurprising that there is no agreement about Macmillan now; so devious was he that it is hard to gauge the truth about him, or what he stood for.

In July 1962, at the last Cabinet meeting before the Night of the Long Knives, Harold Macmillan pushed back his chair and produced some sheets of paper. He said he had been reflecting over the previous weekend, and wanted to share his thoughts with his colleagues. Superficial thoughts they were, too, but many of those colleagues made a show of agreeing with him as he read them out. 'And,' says Enoch Powell, 'the heads which nodded like cuckoo clocks were the ones that were to roll; and no head nodded more vigorously than the head of Lord Kilmuir.'

Of the seven Cabinet ministers knifed that day, Kilmuir, the Lord Chancellor, was the most shocked by his fate. 'I got the impression that he [Macmillan] was extremely alarmed about his own position, and was determined to eliminate any risk for himself by a massive change of government,' he wrote in his breathtakingly self-serving memoirs. 'The stupidest Lord Chancellor ever' was how Macmillan described Kilmuir, only to trump his judgment by replacing him with Sir Reginald Manningham-Buller. So angry was Kilmuir's three-quarters-of-an-hour interview with Macmillan that the Prime Minister forgot to tell him he was to be advanced to an earldom; he and his wife, still stunned, discovered it while listening to the wireless when they reached their house in Sussex that evening.

That legendary episode of selfish panic, which showed Macmillan's 'unflappability' for the pose it was, was the beginning of the end of his premiership. Kilmuir was shocked because he had made the mistake of taking Macmillan at face value; which prompts one to wonder what exactly he thought Macmillan was. To the historically minded, the answer should be obvious. Macmillan was a Whig, and he always behaved whiggishly. Not of the aristocracy, he acquired the trappings of so being. His mother, an American and fiercely ambitious for her son to be part of the establishment, drove him on through Eton, Balliol and the Guards. She built a *nouveau* neo-Georgian house for the family, which he inherited. Most significantly, Macmillan pleased his mother by marrying a daughter of the Duke of Devonshire. At the beginning of his marriage his wife's family despised him, and Lady Dorothy herself devoted much of the prime of her life to committing adultery with Bob Boothby.

Many of those who remember Macmillan, like Mr Powell and Lord Deedes, both of whom served in the Cabinet after the Night of the Long

Knives, see Lady Dorothy's adultery as a great spur to Macmillan. He had something to prove after his rejection, and threw himself into politics: notably, championing the poor in his constituency of Stockton-on-Tees. This social conscience was no pose; he felt so strongly about the Baldwin government's treatment of the unemployed that he resigned the Tory whip. However, the 'Lady Bountiful' aspect to it did help contribute to the wider illusion about him. Thanks to his mother's energy and his wife's rank, Macmillan was able to identify himself with landed society. Once within their stockade, he was prepared to sacrifice almost anything else to stay there. Enoch Powell dubbed him the actor-manager, and says now that 'he actor-managed himself into the upper classes. Part of the pose was the grouse moor, the duke's daughter.'

He also affected an ignorance of the middle classes from which he had sprung (claiming to have heard a lot about them after he became prime minister, he asked an adviser to find out 'what do they want?'). For the working classes, though, he professed great and lasting affection, as the man from the big house should. His unforgettable finale in the House of Lords, when roasting Mrs Thatcher's government, saw him brooding sadly on how the miners (who, on a number of occasions, had threatened to bring the country to a standstill in the depths of the Second World War) were 'the best men in the world'.

'Don't underestimate,' says a friend of Macmillan's family, 'the shock that people like him felt in coming back from the war in 1919. Their class was under threat. His whole career was dedicated to keeping the lower orders sweet so that they would not do what they had done in Russia and Germany.' As such, Macmillan, the Whig pragmatist, was immune to ideology or economic sense; his perceived duty to defend the social order by participating in the safe management of inevitable decline was clear to him from the moment he returned from the trenches. Moreover, this attitude infected a generation of politicians who served under him. It has still, indeed, not been expunged from the soul of the Conservative Party, even after the Thatcher revolution.

That is not his only dubious legacy. His showmanship, manifested as the blending of serious governance with vulgar stunts encouraged later politicians into a habit of patronising and conning the public that lingers to this day. Worse, the panic of July 1962 scarred the Tory party for years. 'The continuing effect of Macmillan,' says Mr Powell, 'is the loss of a generation.' Mr Powell says it was unnatural to bring in so many inexperienced ministers at once. Men who might have succeeded if brought on more slowly and gradually were thrown in at the deep end. Some failed, others burned out before their time; what survived was not always attractive. A climate was created in which Mr Heath, just three years later, could become leader of the Conservative Party. Macmillan's priority was always his own survival; and when even he realised he could no longer survive, he was determined for the party to continue in his own image.

In October 1963 Macmillan thought he had terminal cancer; either he panicked again, or, for actor-managerial reasons, the idea was allowed to get about that he was much more ill than he was. He was certainly furious to have resigned over a mere prostate problem, only to find subsequently that de Gaulle, afflicted with the same condition, was carrying blithely on. Macmillan's bizarre, but typically manipulative, decision to tell the Queen he would be resigning a few days hence, and to proceed to give her advice on whom she should pick, was unconstitutional.

The Queen was taken in by it, however, not realising that Macmillan had arranged the circumstances in which he could cling on to power long enough to try (successfully, as it turned out) to hijack her prerogative. He told her, in a secret memorandum published by his official biographer, Alistair Horne, that he favoured Lord Home not because he had 'been thought of as a last-minute method of keeping out Mr Butler', but because he was obviously the best man for the job. The real reason seems to be that Home was the only senior minister who had never crossed Macmillan. Horne says that in the diaries Home is 'the only member of the administration never to attract any opprobrium . . . there is nothing but respect, and liking'. Home also, according to that memorandum, was 'the best of the old governing class'. This is exactly what Macmillan thought he was himself – or at least, what he had spent his life trying to pose as – so Home, the genuine article, was the ideal choice, if only from that point of view.

In January 1957, when the Queen had asked Macmillan to conduct her government, he had taken Heath, his chief whip, off to the Turf Club to celebrate with oysters and champagne. The premiership began with an excess of style over substance that accurately presaged what was to follow. Alistair Horne reports that while Macmillan and Heath tucked in, the premier speculated about how Rab Butler, his rival for the leadership, would have celebrated had he been favoured. 'Plain living and high thinking,' he concluded waspishly. That was the difference between the two men. Though both had substantial private wealth, Macmillan was happy with ostentation, perhaps as a substitute for deeper contentment and as a mask for his insecurity. Bill Deedes is in no doubt why Macmillan disliked Butler: 'Butler saw through him.'

Mr Powell is not so sure. After Butler became Master of Trinity, he was dining with Powell at the college, and said to him, in the tone of one who has just made a great discovery: 'Mollie and I have been talking. We don't think Harold's a nice man.' Though both men were highly educated, Butler was the one to think about politics fundamentally. Macmillan was destined to use his talents mostly to manipulate colleagues ('He was a great psychologist,' says Mr Powell). That, certainly, was what made him the more successful politician. Macmillan was, says Lord Deedes, 'quite ruthless in his manipulation of people. He understood the Machiavellian theory of politics: stay in the saddle at all costs, then you can control events.' Though no ideologue, he was a brilliant controller, if not always of events, certainly of men; especially when he thought his survival depended upon it. 'Greater love hath no man than this,' said Jeremy Thorpe after the Night of the Long Knives, ' that a man lay down his friends for his life.'

Lord Deedes gives a less well-known example of Macmillan's ruthlessness. Having decided that a junior colonies minister, Cub Alport, should not have a future, Macmillan offered him the job of High Commissioner to the doomed Federation of Rhodesia and Nyasaland. In a typically venal use of patronage, Macmillan sweetened the pill by offering Alport 'a little something to wear under your tie'; in this instance, a life peerage. When Alport returned after just two years he no longer had his seat in the Commons, nor a place in the government, nor even the consolation of a KCMG for a job well done.

Everyone – well, almost everyone – who met Macmillan testifies to his charm and courtesy. He was, eventually, a class act, but then he had had years of training, many of them on the back benches, to perfect his role. Yet he was a cynic who professed to have no cynicism. As well as referring to his charm and his courtesy, many who knew him seem also inevitably to refer to him as a 'fraud'; for some, though, that appeared to be part of his charm. Lord Deedes thinks Macmillan took A.J. Balfour as his model, pretending not to care very much about anything and determined not to be 'flapped'. 'The act,' says Lord Deedes, 'was to conceal his ambition.' 'Putting on a show,' says Mr Powell, 'was part of his personality. A screen and a protection between himself and the outside world suggests some internal debility.' Macmillan dubbed Mr Powell 'Aristides' after the Greek who was ostracised for his pursuit of what was just. ('A mistranslation,' says Mr Powell. 'It should be "righteous".') Mr Powell stops short of describing Macmillan as a conman, preferring a milder term. 'To call a politician a confidence trickster is to accuse him of excelling at his profession,' he says.

Macmillan's economic legacy was dire. He didn't, or wouldn't, understand economics. He showed no willingness to tackle the trade unions (his unpublished diaries, quoted by Horne, are spattered with references to how beastly their wage demands are, reflecting his impotence to do anything about them). He was unbothered by the size of the state, with its plentiful nationalised industries and its manpower expansions that imposed a burden on the taxpayer and on prosperity. He had 'a manic fear of the recurrence of the 1930s', says Mr Powell. 'He was not interested in the causes of inflation.' Roy Harrod, John Maynard Keynes's vicar-on-earth, was his principal economic adviser. It was what Enoch Powell calls Macmillan's 'saturation with Stockton' that prompted him along with almost every other politician of the time to embrace Keynesianism so wholeheartedly.

Whenever one of his Chancellors tried to tackle the country's economic problems by cutting public spending, that Chancellor – notably Thorneycroft and Selwyn Lloyd – was fired or forced to resign. Heath, as Leader of the Opposition and as Prime Minister, did not deviate from Macmillan's orthodoxy, maintaining the obsession with foreign affairs and belief in interventionist consensus. This creed has had its echoes in Conservative politics of this decade too.

Although Lord Deedes praises Macmillan's international vision, Mr Powell dismisses it. 'He wasn't a statesman. He wasn't working with a concept of Britain. He had an American mother, didn't he?' Macmillan's finest achievement was his part in the brokering of the Test Ban Treaty between Kennedy and Khrushchev, which was also a sign that he had succeeded in his desperate attempt to salvage the special relationship with America after the Suez débâcle. 'He was not over-confident about the strength of Britain,' says Mr Powell. 'It was an early premonition of the enslavement to America that has since taken great strides forward.'

After Suez, Macmillan told the Commons, 'We are a great world power, and intend to remain so.' It was a fantastic display of his cynicism. He was to seek friendship with America and, as an insurance policy, entry to the Common Market, precisely because he knew Britain was not a great power. His performance over Suez was the first public manifestation of his ruthlessness, or, alternatively, of his ability to panic. Harold Wilson said of him 'first in, first out'. Macmillan led the hawks until the going became rough, and then became a dove overnight. He was not above double-crossing the Cabinet in order to achieve that end. Diane Kunz points out in *The Economic Diplomacy of the Suez Crisis*, (Yale, 1991) Macmillan as Chancellor of the Exchequer terrified his colleagues into retreat by informing them that British gold reserves had fallen by £100 million in one week. The next day he was told by officials that the loss was only £30 million, but this interesting news he kept from his colleagues. When he did not panic into retreat, the effort of confronting a problem had a wretched effect on him. He would often be physically sick before making an important speech, and after the Night of the Long Knives was sick for days.

This Whig Prime Minister was a proper Tory in some respects; he understood that Britain was a class-bound society, even if that understanding intimidated him. He believed in the Queen's right to choose her prime minister without any help from the parliamentary Conservative Party, though with help in 1963 from Harold Macmillan. He believed in patronage. He believed in the hereditary principle. These grand historic trappings, however, became more and more incongruous as the country in which they were rooted declined in power and influence under Macmillan's stewardship, and under the stewardship of most of his successors.

Lord Deedes defends his old boss. 'You have to relate politicians to the circumstances in which they find themselves. Macmillan was highly sensitive to all strands of opinion. He had a genuine rapport with the working class.' Nor does he blame Macmillan for his neglect of domestic politics, particularly the economy, during a premiership that concentrated on international issues such as the Cold War and Britain's attempts at entry into the Common Market. 'Never blame a head man in politics who goes for the big one.'

Lord Deedes does, though, blame Macmillan for other mistakes. The decolonisation of Africa, he says, 'happened much too soon. It all fell into the hands of dictators. That had some very unfortunate consequences. But it was a case of domestic politics being played off against the welfare of the Third World.' Anxious to pre-empt trouble from liberal opinion at home, Macmillan displayed a typical trait: be prepared to compromise anything and anyone in order to survive.

At the actor-manager's centenary, many will recall a monumental old grandee the like of which we do not see these days, however hard Sir Edward Heath tries. Others will recall a monumental old fraud. The perceptive will see Macmillan's sad legacy all around. In the censure debate after the Night of the Long Knives, Hugh Gaitskell said of Macmillan that 'his government will be remembered not for the leadership they gave the nation, but as a conspiracy to retain power'. That resonates today. Macmillan may be dead, but his influence, unfortunately, survives him.

5 February 1994

THE LESSER OF TWO EVILS?

Anne Applebaum

This week and last week, and the week before that as well, the columns of British newspapers and magazines have been filled with news of a tragedy which occurred more than 50 years ago. There have been interviews with survivors, photographs of the perpetrators, fresh evidence and memories, almost all sparked by the release of a brand-new, high-quality Hollywood film about the subject – a film which has already been hailed as an 'event', and will eventually be called the greatest achievement of America's most talented director.

The film is *Schindler's List,* the director is Steven Spielberg, and the subject is the Holocaust: Hitler's attempt to destroy the European Jews. But although justified by the ambitions of the film, the extended fanfare for *Schindler's List* – the articles on Auschwitz and the Krakow ghetto, the photographs of Oskar Schindler and the interviews with his wife – is not unusual. Whenever there are films about the Holocaust, a new set of interviews and photographs appears. This happens with a certain regularity.

About this time last year, for example, cinemas were showing *Europa, Europa,* the story of a Jewish boy who survived the war by passing for a German; in recent memory we have also been able to watch *Korczak,* Andrzej Wajda's film about the Warsaw ghetto, *Shoah,* nine hours of interviews with Holocaust witnesses, and *Sophie's Choice,* the story of a woman forced by the Nazis to choose between her son and her daughter, not to mention *Holocaust,* the television series.

The quality and abundance of such films, not to mention the documentaries, the journalism and the novels (even Martin Amis has now written about the Holocaust), together with the extent of the attention they receive, prove that the subject continues to inspire even those who are now too young to remember the events themselves. Nobody finds this either peculiar or obsessive. On the contrary, those who make movies or write about the Holocaust often feel that there is a moral imperative to return to the subject, again and again. Spielberg himself told an interviewer that he made the film because 'I was afraid of the world my children were being raised in, that something like the Holocaust could happen to them'. Because nobody wants something like that to happen to their children, the popular memory of the Holocaust actually strengthens with the passage of time.

And because the popular memory is strong, the Holocaust continues to colour our Anglo-American view of current events, affecting the behaviour of politicians and journalists. When an Asian is murdered in London, no one notices; if a Turk is murdered in Berlin, the world is shocked. The reunification of Germany was greeted with more anxiety than joy: 'I do believe in national character,' wrote Mrs Thatcher in her memoirs, before giving an account of how she tried to stop it from happening. No one seriously questions that 'national character' should be an issue in dealing with Germany; even some Germans argue in favour of a more united Europe on the grounds that only tight restrictions can save them from themselves. But if the memory of the past – as perpetuated in popular culture – can affect the perception of the present, can the absence of memory do the same?

Recently, the writer Robert Harris tried to imagine a world where the Holocaust had happened, but had been successfully concealed. In his novel *Fatherland* – now being filmed in Prague – Harris depicted a fictional Europe. The Nazis have won the war, and thereby succeeded in covering up the murder of the Jews. Germany is run by a new generation of 'reformed' Nazis, who have discovered the more 'difficult' parts of Nazi ideology and are now on the verge of détente with America. The papers which document the order to carry out the final solution are locked away; the concentration camps have been destroyed; the only Jewish survivors are weird old men, whom no one knows whether or not to believe.

Yet the real horror of Harris's vision is that it is true – except that what he depicts is not what might have happened in a successful Nazi Germany, but what actually happened in a successful Stalinist Russia. We now live in a real Europe, in which Stalin won the war, and thereby succeeded in covering up the murder of up to 20 million Russians, Ukrainians, Poles, Balts and others, not including those who died in the war; Russia is now run by a new generation of 'reformed' communists, who have been accepted as legitimate by the world. The papers which document various Stalinist crimes – like the order to kill 15,000 Polish officers at Katyn and elsewhere – were until recently locked away; the concentration camps have been destroyed; the only survivors are now weird old men, whom no one knows whether or not to believe.

Intellectually, most West Europeans and most Americans know that terrible things happened in the Soviet Union over the past century. Many even know that Stalin killed, by means of mass murder and concentration camps, at least twice as many people as Hitler – not because he was a 'worse' or 'more unique' dictator (that is a pointless debate if there ever was one), but because he was in power much longer. Whereas Hitler had time only for one attempted genocide, Stalin managed to stage not only the Katyn massacres, but also the purges in Russia and the artificial famine in Ukraine, the murder of one in ten Balts, the execution of most intellectuals living in the Soviet Union, and the near-liquidation of the Crimean Tartars.

Stalin's crimes did not happen in either a remote place (as did the genocide in Cambodia) or a distant time: they occurred within a decade of the Holocaust sometimes in precisely the same Polish and Ukrainian towns and villages. And yet – Cold War propaganda notwithstanding – almost no one in the West feels these crimes to have been evil in the same visceral way that they feel Hitler's crimes to have been evil.

Tourists in central Europe, for example, who would be shocked by the idea of buying Nazi memorabilia find it amusing to purchase Soviet army-issue belt buckles and hats. Respected magazines like the *Nation* in America, which would be horrified by anyone who argued that the Holocaust never happened, have actually printed articles arguing that the Stalinist Terror was nothing more than American government propaganda. When President Bill Clinton went to Belorussia last month, former communist leaders asked him not to visit the scene of a Stalinist massacre, and he quietly agreed; imagine the outcry if he had been prevented from visiting the site of a Nazi massacre by former Nazis.

Western fellow travellers, who argued that the Soviet occupation of Eastern Europe was progressive and spoke glowingly of communist health-care systems, are not treated with anything like the opprobrium granted to those who trumpeted Nazi propaganda; look, for example, at the different fates of Unity Mitford and Diana (Mitford) Mosley – both fascist sympathisers, both now popularly thought to have been traitors – compared with their sister Jessica Mitford, who became a communist in the 1930s and is now fêted on talk shows when she comes to Britain. Even the word 'collaborator', which is applied to the leaders of Vichy France and other Nazi parties in Europe, is almost never attached to East European communists like General Jaruzelski or Janos Kadar, let alone to pro-Soviet journalists in Britain.

As for Hollywood films and popular novels – there aren't any, at least not on a large scale. The Cold War produced James Bond and spy novels, and cartoon Russians of the sort who appear in Rambo films, but nothing even approaching the quality of *Schindler's List*.

Curiously, Steven Spielberg has made films about Japanese concentration camps (*Empire of the Sun*) and Nazi concentration camps, but not about Soviet concentration camps: they just don't catch the imagination in the same way.

The lack of interest is academic as well as popular. Until five or six years ago, the historian Robert Conquest, without whose investigations of the purges and the Ukrainian famine we would know nothing at all, was often considered a paranoid alarmist for claiming that Stalin had murdered millions of people; after all, most British history books spoke of hundreds. Count Nikolai Tolstoy is still thought to be a crank for daring to point out that British soldiers, under British government orders, used force to send thousands of Russians and Yugoslavs home to concentration camps after the war. Richard Pipes, the Harvard professor who maintains that the Russian 'national character' is an inherently dangerous one (much in the same way that Mrs Thatcher worries about the German 'national character'), is still widely considered too 'right-wing' to be taken seriously.

Officially, attempts to commemorate Stalinist crimes have often been treated with scorn, particularly in Britain. In the 1970s, British Poles attempted to erect a small memorial to the victims of the Katyn massacre in a Chelsea churchyard, and encountered a curious series of obstacles, legal and otherwise. One Anglican official opined that to fix the date of the massacre as '1940' on a plaque would be inappropriate, since that would be tantamount to accusing the Soviet Union of the crime (the Russians always blamed the Nazis, who occupied Katyn in 1941). This, he said would be unfair since the Russians could not defend themselves; besides, the Church of England did not want to 'perpetuate bitter feelings'.

The monument was finally put up, but in Gunnersbury, not Chelsea, with the word 'perished' substituted for 'murdered'. We are, church officials reminded the Poles, 'enjoined to forgive our enemies', which is not something that anyone said to the builders of the new Holocaust museum in Washington, or to the founders of libraries and memorials dedicated to the Holocaust in Britain. Moreover, documents released in Moscow now show that the Anglican officials and Chelsea bureaucrats were under pressure from the British Government, which was in turn under pressure from Soviet officials who called the Katyn monument an example of 'Goebbelsian propaganda'. It is impossible to imagine the British Government responding to German pressure in the same way.

Until recently, many argued that there was no way to commemorate Stalin's victims, because there was no proof of their identity or their numbers. This was always a somewhat disingenuous argument – eye-witnesses and written memoirs abound – but it is true that there were no bodies and no documents, at least not on the scale of the records we have of the Holocaust, and nothing like the film of the German concentration camps brought back by Allied soldiers. But now there is evidence. The order to murder the Poles at Katyn has now been published, complete with Stalin's signature; lists of purge victims exist. Not all the evidence comes from suspect official sources either. Three years ago, I visited by chance a small town in south-west Ukraine. It was a sunny day; I came upon a brigade of men who happened to be digging up skeletons in the square, the remains of a Soviet mass murder. There were no journalists, no television cameras, no publicity, just the townspeople, uncovering bones which they had always known were there.

Now that we do have the evidence, it would seem that this is the time to begin prosecuting at least those East European war criminals who live in Britain. It is not as if it is too late: cases against Nazis living in Britain are still open, and the Simon Wiesenthal Institute in Vienna continues its search for Nazi war criminals internationally, on the grounds that to forgive is to forget. Yet not only is there no thirst for the blood of Stalinist criminals, there is something like an antipathy to the idea of finding them at all. In 1990, when the Home Office set up a commission to write a law enabling the British Government to prosecute war criminals, many people, including at least one prominent Oxford historian, appealed to Mrs Thatcher to get the commission to define 'war crimes' broadly enough to include Stalinist war crimes. But, as published, the War Crimes Act of 1991 defines a 'war crime' as an offence 'committed in the period beginning with 1 September 1939 and ending with 5 June 1945 in a place which at the time was part of Germany or under German occupation'. War crimes committed elsewhere do not count.

To explain why this is so – why, at heart, we are so much less interested in Soviet crimes than in their Nazi equivalent – is not easy. The passage of time is part of it; the fate of the survivors is responsible as well. Whereas the state of Israel has been able to build monuments and museums to Hitler's victims, the Poles and Balts and Ukrainians remained under Soviet rule for another 50 years, unable to speak out, unable to move to America or Britain, unable to write books and make films. Communist regimes also grew less reprehensible with time, as the Nazi regimes would have done: nobody who visited Budapest in the 1980s found anything resembling the terror of the 1950s.

George Orwell thought that an inherent British sympathy for

Russia, born of 150 years' worth of on-and-off alliance, explained why greater attention was paid to Nazi crimes than to Soviet ones. George Urban, a former director of Radio Free Europe, thinks that the absence of war crime trials in Eastern Europe (itself a phenomenon which requires many explanations) has led, in the West, to the 'suspicion that Soviet crimes could not have been so terrible'. Urban says that John Strachey (himself a communist sympathiser) once told him that the explanation lay in the fact that the Germans were always looked upon as civilised Europeans, a part of the human race, which made their crimes seem more shocking. The Russians, on the other hand, are not really seen to be Europeans at all, so what they do is nothing new, nothing surprising, and hardly reflects on us. It is also true that while Hitler attacked the French, the Poles and others, Stalin was perceived (incorrectly) as inflicting terror only on his own people, which somehow made him seem less bad.

Of course there is, and always will be, something peculiarly horrifying about the nature of the Nazi crimes. The random brutality of vodka-soaked Russians, whose victims froze or starved, or sometimes survived quite by accident, seems almost acceptable beside the gas chambers, the careful book-keeping, the extraction of gold teeth and the manufacture of soap. It is also true that the goal of the Nazis was historically unique: the liquidation of the European Jews – as a people, as a race – was a mass murder carried out for its own sake. The murders of the *kulaks* (wealthy peasants) in Ukraine, or of political leaders in the Baltic states, on the other hand, were undertaken in the name of the revolution and of the proletariat, and were clearly part of the regime's consolidation of power.

Yet without shedding any doubt upon the uniqueness of the Nazi crime, one can both question whether the difference mattered much to the victims, and ask whether this explanation hasn't been too easily accepted by Western intellectuals. Visiting Ukraine at the time, Beatrice and Sidney Webb excused the mass murder of the *kulaks* on the grounds that 'it must be recognised that the liquidation of the individual capitalist in agriculture had necessarily to be faced if the required increase of output was to be obtained'. Crimes carried out in the name of the common man have always been more acceptable to the Webbs, George Bernard Shaw, the Red Dean of Canterbury and their successors. Quite recently, a British journalist told me that Soviet crimes could be excused because they had been committed 'in the name of a cause'.

Most of all, the feeling that the Nazis were worse than the Soviet communists is a by-product of the wartime alliance. 'During the

German war,' Evelyn Waugh once wrote, 'it was thought convenient to attribute heroic virtues to any who shared our quarrel and to suppress all mention of their crimes . . .' In effect, it is unacceptable to say that we defeated one genocidal criminal with the help of another; that undermines the moral legitimacy of the entire war effort. Equally, to admit that we went to war to save Poland from brutal Nazi occupation, and that we ended the war knowingly (and Churchill knew very well what Stalin was up to at Yalta), leaving Poland under brutal Stalinist occupation, is to admit that the Allies failed in at least some of their goals.

Instead of remembering Stalin as a terrible dictator, it is rather the warm afterglow of wartime propaganda, the stories of friendly Uncle Joe, which remain with us. After all, our greatest leaders sat around dinner tables with him; after all, Lord Beaverbrook called Stalin 'a kindly man' who 'practically never shows any impatience at all', and Averell Harriman, President Roosevelt's adviser, once said that 'the contradiction between his personal courtesy and his wholesale liquidations always puzzled me'. Yet Hitler too was said to be a charming man; records of his tabletalk show his sense of humour to have been quite keen – particularly for a German.

Whatever the reason, whatever the explanation, it is now a fact: we simply don't feel the same kind of horror about Russian communists or their collaborators in Eastern Europe that we feel about the German

Nazis. We never will. Popular memory will never absorb Stalin the way it absorbed Hitler; popular culture will never perpetuate the story in the same way. So just as our memories colour our perceptions of modern Germany, so too will our absence of memory continue to colour our perceptions of modern Russia.

There is no feeling in the West, for example, that Russia's former colonies have a right to be frightened – even a right to be unnecessarily frightened – about Russian aggression in the post-Soviet era. After German unification, when Helmut Kohl took his time about recognising the inviolability of Poland's borders, a great fuss was raised. When Russia makes claims on Ukrainian territory – the Russian parliament has specifically claimed ownership of Crimea, for example – the silence is stunning. In fact, Russia's territorial ambitions in its former Soviet colonies have been positively encouraged by some in the West, including Douglas Hurd, who believe that the reimposition of Russian rule is the best way to 'keep the peace' in the region. If we remembered – emotionally, viscerally – that a whole generation of Ukrainian intellectuals died in the purges, that up to six million Ukrainians died in an artificial famine induced by Soviet Russians, and that thousands more Ukrainians died fighting for independence after the Second World War, we would feel much queasier about advocating Russian peace-keeping in Ukraine, just as we would feel queasy about German peace-keeping in Sudetenland, however benign.

If we don't care much about Russian behaviour in former colonies, we seem even less concerned with the need to construct a new European security system, one which binds Russia into the international community in the same way that West Germany was bound into Europe at the end of the Second World War. True, this is a complicated project, made more complicated by the fact that we did not conquer Russia at the end of the Cold War, and so have less influence there than in Germany. But nobody is even talking about the problem. Not long ago, I sat in a room with a prominent Nato official and watched as a dozen angry East Europeans threw him question after question about Nato, defence, Russia and so on. After a while, he became annoyed. 'Look,' he said, 'I'm willing to discuss these issues. Nato is willing to discuss these issues. But the governments of the countries which belong to Nato are simply not interested: they would prefer to leave things the way they are until forced to change.'

Most importantly, if Russia begins to go wrong again, how will we know? Because we remember what happened in Germany, we watch carefully for early warnings of a repeat performance. Yet because we do not remember what happened in Russia, we are surprised when

Russians vote for a nationalist with openly imperialist ambitions, and do not know whether to take this as an early warning signal or not.

Such talk – of warning signals, of Russian revanchism, of historic inevitability – does contain an element of paranoia. But if paranoia has its uses in our dealings with a safe, domesticated Germany, surely it has its uses in our dealings with an unsettled, ungovernable Russia. The Cold War is over, we want to move on. But we cannot forget too much, if we are to ensure that, in the words of Steven Spielberg, 'something like the Holocaust' never happens to anyone's children, ever again.

12 February 1994

BOOKS

CRIES AND WHISPERS

David Caute

IMAGES: MY LIFE IN FILM
by Ingmar Bergman
Bloomsbury

The first Bergman film I saw was *Virgin Spring*. I emerged with knotted stomach and have never dared to view it again. Bergman retired from film-making ten years ago but during his prolific heyday one ran slowly to the next feast, uncertain whether it was to be the playful elegance of *Smiles of a Summer Night* (where the Russian-roulette pistol is loaded with soot), the joyous idyll of *The Magic Flute*, the full coffin-load of Fate in *The Seventh Seal*, or the rivetting boredom of *The Silence*. One crept into the cinema braced to fend off the corpses, ghosts, Dr Deaths and demonic chess players which have hissed at Bergman (he insists) throughout his life. Would bride and groom commit suicide at the wedding? Would a dead woman rise from her coffin to give birth to her own mother? Violent slashes of Nordic seascape and dark Protestant soulscape would unfailingly turn angelic faces into gargoyles, and all the while there was that mournful, melodious Swedish soundtrack fluting into the ear, those little circles over the o's and dots over the a's – as if even when foolishly happy Swedes are morally compelled to sound close to death's door.

Now for the cast. The lights go down. Enter Max von Sydow on a donkey.

– It's that tall chap again, the one with the ash-white hair, the cavernous cheeks and the accusing gaze. What mediaeval miseries has he got in store for us this time? You finally get to feel that he's not so much playing a role, a part, as being invaded by it.

Close-up of a woman. She doesn't look too happy.

– Wasn't she in the last one? And the one before that? Is she Harriet Andersson or Bibi Andersson?

Bibi. You can tell by her nose. And she's blonde.

Which came first?

Harriet. Then Bibi. Then Harriet kept coming back.

So which is Liv Ullmann? The one with the lips?

Yes. Bibi introduced Liv to Ingmar. They're all very fond of each other, they love to perform together in Ingmar's films. It's a perfect understanding they have. Swedish women are very grown-up, very Scandinavian Social Democrat, about art and love.

Did he marry them all?

His five wives and eight children are another story – except for Liv's daughter by him. Five of the children were born before he was 30. When he got to 60, in 1978, all eight gathered for his birthday, although he'd heard that some of the older ones were being unsympathetic and leftist about his famous income tax difficulties. He owned a Swiss film company and a Swedish one by that time and he'd been signing documents he never looked at and couldn't conceivably have understood if he had.

Bergman is one of those artists whose golden bricks are baked out of semen and shit, and he's never more vivid than when describing his lifelong bowel problems or how he fouled a Paris taxi after suffering an attack at the top of the Eiffel Tower on a day when the lifts had broken down. The magician of the magic lantern is a highly gifted prose writer who can never quite explain how he became an image-maker of extraordinary power, one of the foremost practitioners of the century's primary art-form, film. He can explain the psychic provenance of his films, he can talk about techniques, editing, photography, light, furious rows with technicians, all the usual stuff, but the genius who emerges after the lights go down has to be seen on the screen.

Beware Bergman on Bergman on Bergman. In recent years he has been conducting his own autopsy non-stop and with the publication of *Images* there are disturbing confirmations of the recycling. Extensive passages from his recent memoir, *The Magic Lantern*, are reprinted and many biographical episodes are repeated. In *Images* Bergman sets out to re-explore his films. The text is based on vast interviews with Lasse Bergstrom, who self-effacingly purged his own questions, boiled it all down, then submitted it to the master for revision. By contrast to the disciplined and evocative time-cutting technique of *The Magic Lantern*, this book leaves the reader constantly groping for the filmography to get his chronology straight. There is no index. However, the numerous photographs are gorgeous and beautifully chosen – a reminder of the cunning, provocative sensuality of the films.

Bergman begins *Images* somewhat portentously – his natural, nasty, self-mutilating wit is slow to make its entrance:

> Watching 40 years of my work over the span of one year turned out to be unexpectedly upsetting, at times unbearable. I suddenly realised that my movies had been conceived in the depths of my soul, in my heart, my brain, my nerves, my sex, and not the least, my guts. A nameless desire gave them birth.

With the help of old notes and workbooks, he sought out 'the blurred X-rays of my soul.' 'My soul' twice in eight lines is an ill omen. Even so, he settles in to the X-raying of each film, often in terms of that now-familiar nightmare, childhood:

> Most of our upbringing was based on such concepts as sin, confession, punishment, forgiveness, and grace ... punishment was something self-evident ... My brother got the worst of it. Mother used to sit by his bed, bathing his back where Father's carpet beater had loosened his skin and streaked his back with bloody weals.

Then you had to kiss Father's hand. Far into his adult life Bergman's relationship with each of his parents remained unhappy, tortured: they haunt his films.

> The driving force in *Wild Strawberries* is, therefore, a desperate attempt to justify myself to mythologically oversized parents who have turned away . . .

Bergman reports that as a boy he was an exhibitionist, fantasist and liar (promising qualities in a future artist). He was also a daydreamer but, he notes, 'a daydreamer is not an artist except in his dreams. It was obvious that cinematography would have to become my means of

expression.' In a tireless frenzy Bergman fed his camera with 'dreams
. . . fantasies, insane outbursts, neuroses, cramped faith and pure
unadulterated lies.' His macabre youthful experiences were made-to-
measure; few of us experienced the privilege of being shut in a mortu-
ary at the age of ten, and left to examine the naked corpse of a pretty
young woman. The boy was plucking up courage to touch her pudenda:
'Then I saw that she was watching me from under her half-lowered
eyelids.'

Bergman's ability to pour out films like a painter at his easel, whenever he felt like it, which was most of the time, has awed and baffled
British and American directors hobbled by the demands of the money
men. His early patron was a man he now mocks, Carl Anders Dymling,
head of Svensk Filmindustri (where Ingmar first worked as 'the lowli-
est manuscript slave'). Dymling abandoned his arrogant, manic,
abusive protégé from time to time – who wouldn't? – but fought to persuade the Svensk Board to sanction *Summer with Monika*, despite its
eroticism and nude bathing scene. As Peter Cowie has written in his
Ingmar Bergman:

> He trusted Bergman when the chips were down and at a time when
> Bergman was by no means accepted as a national institution.

Dymling later described Bergman as

> very short-tempered, sometimes quite ruthless in pursuit of his own
> goals, suspicious, stubborn, capricious, most unpredictable.

Bergman would agree. But in *Images* he strikes back:

> It had become a standing ritual for the head accountant, Juberg, at the
> start of every one of my films, to step into the executive office with his
> accounting ledgers and show what serious losses my latest movies had
> inflicted upon the company.

But then came *Smiles of a Summer Night* (1955), a prize-winner at
Cannes and 'an unexpected colossal success both in Sweden and in
other countries.' The studio began to behave 'not unlike an old maid
who suddenly finds herself being courted by the most exotic suitors'.
The 'old maid' was Dymling, whom Bergman found at Cannes, 'over-
excited and out of control,' selling the film 'dirt cheap to any horse
trader who happened to show up.' Bergman immediately presented
him with the screenplay of *The Seventh Seal* (which he'd already

rejected) and gave him a now-or-never ultimatum. This film clinched Bergman's international reputation but he cannot forgive Dymling for having been the principal 'yes' or 'no' figure in his early career. Normally Bergman is generous about friends and collaborators – punishing judgments are softened or balanced with a beguiling *mea culpa*.

Whom does Bergman admire among the major directors? Tarkovsky certainly, 'one of the greatest of all time? Likewise he professes a 'limitless' admiration for Fellini. Now comes the sting:

> But I also feel that Tarkovsky began to make Tarkovsky films and Fellini began to make Fellini films. Yet Kurosawa has never made a Kurosawa film.

As for Buñuel, he 'always made Buñuel films.' Bergman then asks himself whether Bergman had begun to make Bergman films. The answer is hesitant: 'I find that *Autumn Sonata* is an annoying example.' Most of us could find a few others.

19 February 1994

ANOTHER VOICE

LET US RAISE OUR GLASSES, PLEASE, TO A VERY HAPPY MEMORY

Auberon Waugh

About 890 people die on average every day in the United Kingdom. Nearly all these deaths are sad for someone; a few may cause relief, happiness, laughter. Nevertheless, there is a general feeling that you don't laugh when people die. Death is too grim a subject for laughter, and in any case friends and relations must be considered.

There are three further reasons why we should not laugh at the manner of Stephen Milligan's death, according to John Sweeney in the *Observer*. In the first place he had a terrible squint; in the second place his mother, Ruth, died of a haemorrhage when he was just 15; in the third place he was not homosexual. These considerations make it much harder to poke fun at the manner of his death, Sweeney opines.

Well, that is his point of view. Another suggestion made in the course of a tremendous flea in the ear from my dear wife after she caught me allegedly laughing about Milligan's fate is that we should all concentrate on how desperately unhappy he must have been to have put on women's stockings and climbed alone on the kitchen table to seek some heightened pleasure there. I don't see why this should be seen as evidence of great unhappiness. It is just another way of spending a Saturday afternoon. If he had wanted company, he had plenty of friends, or he could have telephoned the 'exclusive' £700-a-year Drawing Down the Moon dating agency of which, we learn, he was a member. Perhaps he was simply concerned to save money.

So much has been written on this new subject of auto-erotic asphyxiation (AEA) that many feel they have read enough, but it is unlikely that anything more interesting will happen – least of all in the world of politics – for a very long time. The only possible restraint on our endless and joyous discussion must be consideration for the sorrow of Milligan's family and friends. One such is Mr Andrew Neil, editor of the Sunday Times and a fellow bachelor. I do not know whether Neil is also a fellow member of the prestigious £700-a-year Drawing Down the Moon dating agency, but he took the manner of Milligan's going very hard: 'We are forced to conclude that there was a private, dark side to Stephen of which even his closest friends were unaware.'

This strikes me as odd. If I were to learn that any male friend of mine was in the habit of climbing naked onto the kitchen table of a Saturday afternoon, with women's stockings, electric flex and any other paraphernalia of AEA, I might be surprised and amused, but I would not be shocked or upset. 'There is no reason to believe that he would not have ended up happily married,' wrote this fellow bachelor in the course of his tribute to a 'trusted colleague and dear friend':

> That he should even know of the techniques that apparently brought about his death, much less practise them, has startled us all.

Neil has a point there. How do those intending to try AEA ever learn about it? Few of us would imagine that there was much fun to be had on a kitchen table alone with some electric flex, a dustbin liner and a satsuma fruit unless someone had told us. I have been around longer than Milligan and nobody ever told me about it. Nobody discussed these things at Oxford in my day. Was it in the House of Commons tea-room that Milligan learned such tricks, or in the alcohol-free canteens of the Sunday Times? Perhaps there are secret networks of AEA practitioners who hold conferences in provincial hotels and read each other papers.

In a way I hope not, because it would subtract from Milligan's contribution. If we ask ourselves whether, by his death, Milligan has contributed more to the gaiety of the nation or to its sorrows, the answer is unmistakable. Sorry as we are for the friends and relations, Stephen Milligan has made a massive contribution to the gaiety and happiness of us all at a rather gloomy time in the country's history. Nor do I believe that he made a socialist victory any more certain than it already was with Major as leader. But having commiserated with his various friends and relations, I must also admit that well-intentioned attempts to be solemn about his death succeed only in making it funnier. Thus Mr Neil, in elegiac mode:

> His tragic death is all the more of a tragedy because he had just reached the first rung of a political career that would undoubtedly have taken him to the highest offices, where he would have served with great distinction. He is a great loss to family and friends, but also to the Tory party and country.

Oh phooey! The Tory party will never be short of young men trying to climb its rungs, and the country will manage without him. In fact, to the extent that he impinged on my awareness before his magnificent exit, Milligan always struck me as exactly the sort of Conservative the country could do without. On the first occasion he came to my notice he was photographed with a pet fox in one of his constituency newspapers, swearing to vote for an end to the ancient British sport of fox-hunting.

'Stephen was modern, progressive, often ahead of his time,' intones Neil, reporting an undergraduate speech, 'arguing there should be more tax on wealth and inheritance, less on income and earnings. That's my kind of Tory, I thought.' Will these chippy little smartiboots never realise that the interests of high earners and wealth owners are indissolubly linked? No, the fewer of Neil's kind of Tory in the House of Commons (or anywhere else) the better. I never met Stephen Milligan and don't suppose I should have liked him if I had. The fact that he was able to hold the affections of two exceptionally attractive women is no recommendation.

But any doubt I might have entertained about his politics would have been largely dispelled if I had known of his secret habits. He must have known there was a risk of being discovered as he was, and he must have laughed at the consequences. Even if nothing became him in his life like the leaving of it, we owe him an enormous debt of gratitude for cheering us up at this dismal time. He will occupy a much warmer place in our memories than he could ever have done as another vulgar, slippery, bungling Tory Chancellor.

19 February 1994

WHO DO THEY THINK THEY ARE?

Martin Vander Weyer

Helmsley, North Yorkshire
As a latecomer to dilettante journalism, I have an unusual three-way view of the media world: from inside and out, and from the perspective of a previous life.

For part of each week, like a nervous gatecrasher at a *Spectator* garden party, I circulate on the edge of self-admiring throngs of writers and broadcasters, politicians and pundits: perhaps I may sit next to Jeremy Paxman at lunch, or speak to David Mellor on the telephone, or be cut dead by someone who would rather meet Barbara Amiel (I have learned to drop names with the best of them). But for the rest of the time, far from the metropolis, I move among real people – the first group's distant audience, the passive consumers of press and television – who are increasingly fascinated, disgusted or confused, or all three, by the media folk's lack of restraint, by their bizarre judgment of news priorities, by their mischief-making, by their sheer arrogance.

Often I find myself interpreting between the two worlds. At *Spectator* editorial meetings I have been heard to say plaintively, 'I really don't think these internecine trivia have much appeal to the general reader . . . ' Barely a weekend goes by without some tweed-clad North Yorkshire worthy launching an attack which begins, 'Well, you can tell young Mr Simon Heffer from me . . .

Media arrogance is the heart of the problem, and it has two faces, neither altogether acceptable. The one which enrages the burghers of North Yorkshire has to do with upmarket journalists who 'think they're running the country' and their downmarket colleagues who report Back to Basics not as what Mr Major repeatedly says it is but as a bonanza of circulation boosting sleaze, who topple elected politicians for sport.

These practices seem constantly to expand the limits of disrespect and prurience, but they are not new, nor (in their less extreme forms) are they without a coherent defence. The *Times* in its heyday thundered at the government with more *gravitas* than any modern paper; Lord Beaverbrook was more mischievous, and closer to the seat of power, than any modern media magnate.

But today's press has a particular swagger in its gait partly because today's politicians (in their official capacities, if not in their boudoirs) are so subdued. After a generation out of office, the Labour Party is demoralised and ideologically barren; the arguments which really matter are to a large extent encompassed within the spectrum of Conservative opinions. After a generation in office, the Conservative Party has lost the knack of manipulating media coverage to its own advantage and seeks desperately to conceal its divisions and weaknesses. The press, acting in place of the official opposition, seeks quite legitimately to expose them. Less legitimately but in the spirit of the times, it seeks to turn them into entertainment.

The general reader (and some of them are indeed retired generals) accepts this up to a point: he is, after all, thoroughly opposed to hypocrisy and deceit in public life, in whatever form. But when the digging goes on and on, when the same techniques are used to undermine his last illusions about the royal family, when it has such disproportionate commercial rewards for the diggers, he becomes increasingly suspicious.

He may begin to believe the theory, popular with Tory after-dinner speakers in recent months, of a conspiracy among foreign press barons (Conrad Black and Rupert Murdoch that is) to destroy the pillars of the British way of life. Even if the retired military man in his calmer moments can see the absurdity of that claim, he still thinks the press has grown far too big for its boots.

He is perhaps less instantaneously provoked by the second form of media arrogance, but its effect is more insidious and it is beginning to irritate. It is the extent to which the media now regard *themselves* as newsworthy. The changed location on the radio dial of a radio gardening programme or the question of who will host *Question Time* become major stories for the broadsheets, while the tabloids thrive on the sexual gymnastics of television actresses. A car-crash injury to the editor of *The Archers* makes the *One O'Clock News* headlines; Brian Redhead is mourned as if he were more important than the news he interpreted.

It is all so incestuous. Stephen Glover writes at length in the *Evening Standard*'s media section about the *Sunday Times* columnist Lynn

Barber, most of whose column this week is about the importance of newspaper picture-editors. Meanwhile, Joanna Coles (host of *Medium Wave*, part of Radio 4's contribution to the genre of journalism about journalism) fills a page of the *Guardian* with a who's who of all her fellow women columnists, including their salary figures. The *Times* Diary on two successive days invites us to waste three seconds of our precious lives contemplating the fact that the editor of *Vogue* has 'lost her personal assistant to Naim Attallah'.

For crying out loud, who cares? Certainly not the general, although he may be curious to know how much his children's layabout friends in the London media get paid. Although he never really approved of journalists, he was prepared to tolerate them as down-at-heel topers in dim Fleet Street bars; but the sight of Andrew Neil in evening dress has him reaching for his shotgun. Every morning he is presented with more and more verbiage about these people and their organisations. Such ineffable stuff may have its place in the trade press or in media supplements designed to attract job advertisements, but what is so astonishing, to him and to me, is that it fills more and more of the news pages of serious newspapers.

The perfect encapsulation of this trend – and the vanities fuelling it – was to be found in last Friday's *Daily Telegraph*. Just below the report on the Scott Inquiry, we learn that 'TV news broadcasters feel snubbed by Bafta'. Occupying slightly more space than a story about health service job cuts is one about GMTV moving upmarket 'to cater for an increasingly "news-hungry" nation' – sidelining 'Mr Motivator, the resident fitness instructor' as a result. And 'creamy blonde' Diane Sawyer, anchorwoman of ABC television news in the United States, 'doubled her salary to $6 million yesterday', having turned down a bid of 'close to $7 million' from Rupert Murdoch's rival channel. On Wednesday, the paper devoted almost half a page of home 'news' to a report on how 'Mr Blobby, the television personality', reduced a girl to tears at a children's party.

Perhaps these are correct news judgments. It may be argued that the media – most especially television – now play such a dominant part in our lives that news about journalists and television actors deserves to be on the front page, rather than tucked away as pap for the showbiz section. Popular broadcasters are deemed to be sociological icons. But the argument is a circular one – the more you tell people that something is important and the less you tell them about everything else, the more they are likely to agree with you.

Newsprint and broadcasting may be capable of continual expansion, but the time which each reader or viewer can devote to it is strictly finite. Within that finite attention span, real news about the real world is being displaced by febrile media coverage – a cheap way of filling space, an endless opportunity for hacks to scratch each other's backs or to scratch each other's eyes out without bothering to travel further afield than the bar of the Groucho Club. Above all, it is a symptom of increasing narcissism in a world which can't resist congratulating itself on its power and reach.

It is also symptomatic of the blurring of the distinction between news and entertainment. A *Newsweek* editor (so I read in Lynn Barber's column) claims that the Tonya Harding rivals-on-ice story is 'bigger in America than any story since Kennedy's assassination'. 'True crime' programmes jostle each other in the television ratings, and their impact is analysed in a full page of the *Sunday Telegraph*. The Prince of Wales is mercilessly 'fictionalised' in *To Play the King*, and the actors concerned give their personal views on the monarchy to the press. The death of Stephen Milligan prompts Michael Dobbs, the author of *To Play the King*, to write in the *Daily Mail* about how the reality of House of Commons life is more bizarre than fiction. News has become entertainment, entertainment has become news and the commercial value of both is maximised by the confusion.

In this as in other developments in the media industry, Rupert Murdoch was the pioneer. The *Sun*'s coverage of the sex lives of *EastEnders* actors, a hugely successful weapon in its circulation battle against the *Mirror* in the mid-80s, was an early milestone. Asked last year whether his company, News Corporation, which produces more than 60 million newspapers per week, is still, as its name implies, an organisation devoted to the dissemination of news, Murdoch replied, 'We're in the entertainment business to get into people's homes. People will buy a television set or a satellite dish in order to watch entertainment, not news.'

This offers an economic explanation of the media's new-found self-adulation. In business terms, entertainment is bigger than news; but the combination of the two with all their related hardware is a very big thing indeed. The Murdoch empire – newspapers, television and film studios – now touches, in his own estimation, 'more than two-thirds of the planet'. Telecommunications, computing, consumer electronics, publishing and mass entertainment are rapidly converging into one vast industry, linked together by what President Clinton calls the 'digital superhighway' of advanced satellite and fibre-optic communications. By the end of the century it might be equivalent in value to one-sixth of the world economy. Those who are powerful in it will be very powerful indeed. No wonder they are becoming more cocksure, more infatuated with their own reflection.

And they have every possible means of self-advertisement at their disposal. Other industries at other times – oil and steel, for instance – have risen to great economic significance without commanding anything like so much daily attention for themselves. But oil news is just news, whereas media news is self-gratification as well. Consider the vastly disproportionate coverage given to television company takeover bids, or to the matter of who will finally come to own the *Independent*. A quick tap into a computerised cuttings library reveals that the national press has carried no fewer than 1,049 articles, three every day, on the latter subject in the past 12 months. The comparable figure for a genuine industrial icon which also happens to be looking for a new proprietor, Rolls Royce Motors, is 42. (By this measure the future of a seven-year-old newspaper is approximately 25 times more important than that of Britain's most famous engineering company. This from the same press that occasionally wonders why Britain is no longer good at 'making things'.)

This is not to argue that the media must strive for anonymity – like the *Economist* or, in a different sense, like radio continuity announcers – in order to retain authority as a transmitter of information about the rest of the world. But it is one thing to intermediate legitimately in the transmission process in order to add focus, opinion and colour; another thing altogether, a corruption of the power of media technology, to hog the space in order to talk about yourself.

Which brings me around, at last, to the third vantage point of this analysis: my previous life as a member of another profession which came to think itself smarter than everyone else, that of merchant banking. The similarities were suggested to me by Geoffrey Wheatcroft in the *Independent on Sunday*, pointing out that, in the era when newspapers treated politicians with respect journalists were paid much less than ministers. Now the increased economic importance of the media world has allowed its once humble scribes to leap up the salary ladder. 'It is a safe bet,' according to Wheatcroft, 'that no national newspaper editor is paid less than the Prime Minister's £76,000.' Indeed, many of the columnists and television pundits I meet on my weekly forays and defend at weekend sherry parties are (so I read almost everywhere) even more overpaid than I used to be at the zenith of the City's rise.

A banal comparison, my Armani-suited media acquaintances may say, huffing the froth off their cappuccinos. But what happened in the world of money – in the decade of money, the 1980s – offers the sharpest possible parallel to the behaviour of the media in the first part of the decade of information, the 1990s.

In both cases, deregulation and progress in technology created almost limitless possibilities for expansion: the industry was on the threshold of a new era. Proprietors were willing to sink vast amounts of capital into a battle for market share, even if the pay-off was still far over the horizon – even, in newspapers, in a market which is recognised to be in absolute long-term decline.

Meanwhile the talented players earn much more, are given more attention, are allowed more freedom of action, than ever before. Their professional ethics are easily bent to accommodate unmissable opportunities for fame and profit. They believe themselves more important than their customers, and they may well like to think of themselves as running the country (remember Nigel Lawson's jibe at the City's 'teenage scribblers'?).

In the money world, a period of excessive self-confidence led inexorably to a crash in which heads rolled and customer loyalty was destroyed, and the gradual emergence of a chastened industry, much less flamboyant, much more self-disciplined. It may be facile to predict a parallel crisis for the media, but we can certainly observe the similarities of human behaviour: the Greek word is hubris, the arrogance which leads to disaster.

26 February 1994

DIARY

Ruby Wax

God has been cruel to women. Feminists throughout the land will stick a fatwa on my head, but I know from bitter personal experience, having only weeks ago delivered my third child, that these are the hard, cold facts. He has decided that in the last few months of pregnancy, however mighty your education, however many degrees or honours you have, He is going to hack off your IQ points and give you the mind of a fish. Each thought lasts four to five seconds and then fades away into a filing cabinet you'll never find again. I know He in His infinite wisdom would probably say you don't need your intelligence when you're making a baby, so in His infinite wisdom He taketh it away. He tooketh mine away for so long, after the baby was born I couldn't come up with a name. I have been warned that I have 40 days to register my child's name. I am very close to my deadline and live in fear of what happens if I don't come up with something. I thought at first I'd do what the Red Indians do, name it after the first thing you see after it's born, but I don't think 'Forceps' will quite do. I picture my house being surrounded by blazing sirens and some policeman screaming, 'Come out of that house with your hands up and a name!'

But I digress. My brains have gone. Which would explain why I found myself on the front cover of *Hello!* magazine in January holding up my newborn. *Hello!* magazine offers a lot of cash for newborns. If they're still wet you can earn up to five-figure sums. Three years ago *Hello!* magazine called me up and asked if I would pose with my first child. I said 'How dare you' and hung up. Three years later I'm on my third child, my body's crumbled slightly and my brain rather more, so I call *Hello!* magazine and say, 'Remember me? You made me an offer five years ago. Halve it.' So Sven, the photographer in leather jacket, leather pants and leather brain arrived saying things like, 'Yeah, yeah, I love it, give me more, you're looking sexy, spread 'em', to my two-week-old. And I got the cash.

Something I did for a lot of money last week was to rent myself out to Saatchi and Saatchi for one of their 'weekend workshops'. The event took place at a Butlin's Holiday Camp, where the Saatchiites were divided into 30 teams. Each team in turn made a commercial with a home video camera about Saatchi and Saatchi which was to be judged by one of their *grands fromages*. Does it sound like a good way to spend the weekend? My brief was to go around with a cameraman and interview the employees about what their commercials were all about and how they managed to come up with their concepts. I went up to the first team, who had been at work for over six hours. They were scrunched around a white piece of paper with some arrows on it and a few words circled. They said they were still 'brainstorming'. Another group had written in bold felt-tip, 'Saatchi and Saatchi. We've got the energy!' The word 'energy' was crossed out. Then they wrote, 'We've got the ideas.' The 'ideas' was crossed out. And I just said 'You have no idea, do you?' They were all wearing T-shirts which read 'We've got the balls!' with the 'balls' crossed out. Imagine the face of an animal just before you run it over, and you have imagined how happy they looked to see me. I said I was sorry, but Charles Saatchi had acquired me along with some modern art piece of a cow's head being eaten by maggots. He got both of us for the price of one. No one laughed.

I had to do *The Family Show* for the BBC. It is, they said, 'the year of the family'. In fact, it is another gimmick by the BBC to look as though they are conscientious about something other than ratings. They made me go in front of an audience full of angry single mothers, furious old people and bored, joy-riding teenagers, and do stand-up comedy. I would rather have done a musical comedy in a cancer ward. For dessert, Esther Rantzen came on looking sincere and worried to advertise something called Agewatch. Now I love Esther, but the mind boggles at what Agewatch could be. Someone calls in and says, 'I think I might be getting old. Could you come over?' Then an expert comes over with a checklist and says, 'Any sign of a liver spot? Check. Do you wander around aimlessly holding a kettle, but not knowing what you're doing with it? Check. When you sit down does your poop come out of your collar? Check. Yup, you're definitely old.' I think Esther Rantzen will be getting a knighthood out of this one.

For the rest of the time everyone just gabbled on about this awful buzzword of the 1990s, 'relationship'. Is your relationship right or wrong, good or bad? This 'relationship' business is one big waste of time, in this case licence-payers' time. It's just Mother Nature urging you to breed, breed, breed. She doesn't care about star signs. She just wants to make sure there's someone fleshing out the world. Fish just swim upstream to lay those eggs. They don't think about commitment or what kind of car the guy drives, they just lay 'em and hightail it back downriver and float around or whatever they do. You don't need to read *Marie Claire* to learn anything about relationships. Learn from nature. Learn from our friend the spider. Just mate once and then kill him.

26 February 1994

HIGH LIFE

SEND IN THE KENNEDYS

Taki

The Kennedy clan has gathered in force in a Northern Irish courtroom as a back-up to their newest member, Belfast man Paul Hill, one of the Guildford Four. Hill is battling conviction for the IRA shooting death 20 years ago of a former British soldier. He is married to Courtney Kennedy, daughter of Robert Kennedy, the assassinated younger brother of JFK.

The Kennedys' joining in an appeal by a convicted in-law is the stuff of Hollywood. With their two martyred members, a president and a senator, this is strong stuff. Representing the martyrs are Robert's widow, Ethel Kennedy, along with her son, Representative Joe Kennedy (D-Mass), daughters Rory, Kathleen Kennedy Townsend and Kerry Kennedy Cuomo, daughter-in-law of the Governor of New York.

Ethel, Rory and Kathleen I do not know. Congressman Joe Kennedy and his sister Kerry I do, along with other members of the British-hating Kennedys, whose shenanigans I first heard of from a Brit who had married into the clan, actor Peter Lawford. Lawford was waiting for his divorce from Pat Lawford, JFK's sister, when I met him in 1965. The Kennedys then were considered American royalty, and Bobby Kennedy was preparing a return to Camelot and a presidential run in 1968.

So you can imagine my surprise when Lawford – who spoke highly of his wife – let loose on what a sick bunch of people the Kennedys really were. He may have had an axe to grind, but he impressed me as telling the truth. According to him, JFK was the best of the family by far. The father was a tyrant, the mother a cold-hearted Catholic maniac, and Bobby a hater *sans pareil* who passed moral judgment on people while committing adultery non-stop.

Lawford liked Jackie but hinted strongly that Bobby was after her. I only met Bobby Kennedy once, at a party, and his ugly character sure came through. He was aggressive, zealot-like, and kept badgering a Greek shipowner for money. I had met Pat Lawford and Jean Smith, the present American ambassador to Dublin, the year before, 1964, at Porfirio Rubirosa's house outside Paris. Pat was nice but very nervous, and steadied her nerves with booze. Jean was normal but looked unhappy. Her husband Steve Smith was known as the only non-Kennedy who was treated like a member of the family. Steve was loyal and a nice guy, but the pressure of running the family fortune as well as the campaigns of the brothers eventually got to him. He became a very heavy drinker and cocaine abuser, and the cancer that killed him was attributed to his drinking and substance abuse.

In 1974, Ted Kennedy came to Athens with his nephew Joe, back then not yet a congressman. They asked me if I could organise a fun party and I did, introducing Teddy and Joe to two young American friends of my then girlfriend. It turned out a disaster. Teddy got drunk, inhaled what smelled like poppers and then tried to seduce his date, who, incidentally, almost had a nervous breakdown and flew home as a result. (She was an exchange student.) Joe Kennedy lit up a joint while in a taxi with me, and complained like mad when informed by yours truly that the penalty for smoking pot in Greece in 1974 was five years in the pokey.

I also met Bobby Jr throughout the druggy Seventies in places like the back rooms of Xenon, the chic club at the time. Bobby was smarter than his older brother Joe, but mean-spirited, aggressive and conceited. He once asked me whether I had the bottle to keep up with the Kennedys while planning to go down some rapids. Well, at least I had the courage not to take smack, as he did regularly, although he has now beaten the habit.

All the Kennedys I've known have given me the impression that they are unaware that actions have consequences, including a member of their family who once walked into a back room where people were doing something illegal, and sniffed someone else's stuff. He got away with it. As will Paul Hill. Brian Shaw, dead at 21, has no rich American 'royalty' behind him. Hill's 'confession' has been discredited by the film *In the Name of the Father.* Hollywood and the Kennedy clan rule supreme.

5 March 1994

ALDRICH AMES, MY WOULD-BE KILLER

Oleg Gordievsky

I sat opposite Aldrich Ames, the CIA officer who is now under arrest for spying for the Russians, several times. As a senior officer in Soviet counter-espionage, he was there, quietly and patiently listening, at a number of my debriefings in Washington. I liked him more than most of the other CIA officers I encountered. His face radiated gentleness and kindness.

That was a surprise: CIA officers are generally hard and forceful in manner, without illusions about people or politics. I was disappointed to discover they shared many of the characteristics of KGB officers: they can be excessively deferential to authority, and frightened of saying anything they think might upset their boss – behaviour which I haven't noticed (or at least not to the same extent) in the British Secret Service. In America, they work pointlessly long hours: just as in the KGB, so long as the boss's light is on, the subordinates keep working, even if they don't really have anything to do. As soon he quits for the day, the minions leave.

Ames seemed different. In fact, I was so impressed by him that I thought that I had encountered the embodiment of American values: here was the openness, honesty and decency of which I had heard so much. Of course I didn't know at that point that he had been trying to kill me. When I first appeared at the meeting with him in Washington, I must have seemed like a ghost risen from the dead. I believe that I was the first source he betrayed. He received his first payment from the KGB on 18 May 1985, the day after I was recalled to Moscow for inter-rogation.

He wouldn't have known my name at that time, but he would have heard about the kind of information that was coming from me. It would not have been difficult for him to work out that the British had a very important and knowledgeable KGB source with a Scandinavian background working in London. There was only one officer in the London office who fitted the bill: me.

Ames would have known exactly what he was doing in betraying the information: he was sentencing the victim to death. He knew any important source he passed on to the Russians would be shot – and most were. He has the blood of a dozen officers on his hands. He would have had my blood, too, had I not managed to escape before the KGB had any evidence (other than Ames's tip-off) against me.

So when I turned up in Washington, sitting at the table opposite him, he must have been a little surprised. If he was, he didn't show it. Not one breath of nervousness escaped from him. Newspaper reports have portrayed him as a craven wimp ordered about by his wife. I can testify from personal experience that he must have an extraordinary amount of mental toughness. I've been in that situation: you attend meetings, you go for a drink, you chat in the corridor with your colleagues – and you attempt to destroy everything they think you are working for. I had a moral commitment to the work I was doing for the British, but even so the strain was almost intolerable. Ames was after only one thing in co-operating with the Russians: money. But he seems to have coped with the pressure outstandingly well. His main worry doesn't seem to have been getting caught, but getting wet in the rain.

He did one or two outstandingly stupid things, like buying that Jaguar. He must have known the first rule for double agents: don't ever attract attention to yourself. Driving that car to work was like a sign saying 'I'm guilty!' Even so, that wasn't necessarily what led the CIA to suspect him. I don't know what happened, but I believe that information from a source run by the FBI may have been responsible. Or it could have been another KGB defector. The current head of the KGB has just been fired, which may indicate treachery somewhere in his department.

I don't know exactly how Ames originally came to be involved in spying, but his wife might have been the original contact. She is Bolivian, and I understand she moved in circles thoroughly penetrated by Cuban intelligence. It is possible that she was employed to target him, or to persuade him to spy. I should stress that the idea that Mrs Ames was a latter-day Lady Macbeth is pure speculation on my part, but it could easily have happened – the KGB would have taken over from Cuban intelligence when it was apparent how important the case was.

Ames's treachery could have been detected earlier. In fact, one CIA officer called Gus Hathaway had suspected there might be a mole inside the CIA as early as 1986. But no one seems to have followed up his concern. Everything seemed to be going so well: the KGB had been hit by several major defections, including mine, and the Western intelligence community knew that the Soviet system was on the verge of collapse. The last thing on anyone's mind was the possibility of Soviet penetration of the CIA. The Cold War was over, we were friends with Gorbachev, so no one cared.

There was also the problem that some of the CIA officers are not all that brilliant. The level is not as scintillatingly high as one might expect. They make up for it by working hard and being thorough, but there are some things you can't make up for that way. The organisation also has the reputation for not being terribly secure. I remember that when I first started working for the British in London I was very eager that they should pass over my information to the Americans. The MI6 officer who was working with me – a very thorough and protective woman – was adamant: 'No! Absolutely not! The CIA leaks like a sieve!' At the time, that shocked me. In my naive way, I thought it amazing that a minor power like Britain should not trust a major one like America. But when I got to America, I found that Americans didn't necessarily trust the CIA either. One FBI agent said to me, 'The CIA? They spy for the other side. We're here to catch them doing it.'

In the KGB, it was virtually impossible to smuggle out documents of any importance. But it seems to have been relatively easy for Ames to take whole bundles of official papers from the CIA. Perhaps they'll tighten up on that now, although there is a limit to what can be achieved by internal security procedures, as my own career shows. The fundamental problem was Ames's character. He must have been a totally cynical individual. Cynicism is a quality sometimes too highly prized by intelligence agencies, for it easily degenerates into total amorality. And that leads to people like Ames, who don't believe in anything except money.

Does Ames's treachery matter? It certainly mattered to the KGB. This week's tit-for-tat 'discovery' of a British spy – the arrest actually took place over a month ago – shows how angry the KGB is about what it sees as the Americans' hypocritical outrage over the discovery of Ames's spying. The KGB are very proud of him. He neutralised a great deal of my work – everything I told the CIA about KGB penetration and methods would have gone straight back to Moscow. And though he didn't kill me, he killed those other people. Gorbachev would have seen reports prepared on the basis of Ames's information, and the details of what the CIA was up to – in Eastern Europe and in Russia – would have fuelled the paranoia of men like Vladimir Kryuchkov, the old head of the KGB, who organised the coup against Gorbachev partly because he thought Gorbachev was selling out Russia to foreign interests.

The Ames case has continuing implications. When an ally like France is caught spying on America, as it was last year, everyone knows it's not really important. It's like a small child misbehaving. But Russia has been so thoroughly infected by nearly a century of totalitarianism that it cannot be regarded as an ally. The former Soviet Union is enormously dangerous, at least potentially. The Western powers continue to devote resources to monitoring it, and quite rightly. The Ukraine, for instance, has more nuclear weapons than Britain and France put together. And if Zhirinovsky comes to power in Moscow, the regime will be worse than communism, because it'll be far less stable – a gangster state without any pretensions to anything else. So, though the Cold War is over, the intelligence war continues. We have to know as much as we can about them, and they want to know as much as possible about us. The KGB is as full of paranoid suspicions about the West as ever.

5 March 1994

A MOST UNDESERVED REPUTATION

Noel Malcolm

Several times during discussions of the Tory party leadership in recent months I have heard a curious expression: 'The smart money is on Douglas Hurd.' It always turns out to mean rather less than it seems to. If one challenges the person who says this with the question 'Would you put your money on him?', the challenge is declined. If one asks which smart people have placed this particular bet, the answer is evasive. What the speaker meant, it turns out, was not that he had heard better-informed people making this judgment, but that he had been listening to other people who were also just repeating the phrase 'The smart money is on Douglas Hurd.'

Of course it isn't. But the phrase is eminently repeatable, because of all the other things that are conventionally said about Mr Hurd. He is the Tories' ultimate 'safe pair of hands'. He 'never puts a foot wrong'. He is the only real 'statesman' in the Government. He is the personification of 'decency' and 'dignity'. To criticise Mr Hurd is not just to show faulty judgment, but to commit an error of taste like being rude about Anne Frank or the Queen Mother. And to ask, as I occasionally have done in a spirit of pure inquiry, what Mr Hurd has actually achieved or what, if anything, he has ever got right is to be met with incredulity and distaste (though not, in my experience, with an answer).

Some of the reasons for this warm glow of admiration are obvious. The Foreign Secretary certainly looks as if he knows what he is doing. He is cool under fire, he speaks well in Parliament and he always turns in a high-quality performance in the television studio. Journalists like him, with good reason: he takes trouble over them, tries to answer questions directly, sometimes even admits that the Government has problems, seems without 'side' or resentment, and contributes a steady flow of articles, book reviews and short stories to their newspapers. Despite his air of the statesman-politician of yesteryear, he is in fact one of the most media-friendly and media-conscious people in the Government – someone who operates much more like a modern American politician than like an old-fashioned Tory grandee.

The method works. The calm, statesmanlike performances are remembered; the gaffes, misjudgments and spoilt opportunities are brushed aside. Who now would recall all unprompted the extraordinary episode in September of last year when Mr Hurd, speaking on Australian television, casually applied a sledgehammer to Britain's relations with China, by attacking Peking's claims to be considered for the Olympic Games? (Some criticism of China's human rights record was well overdue, but to make it a matter of supporting Manchester's forlorn Olympic bid – or, rather, supporting the Prime Minister's equally forlorn populist campaign on that issue – was a strangely pointless and ineffectual way of going about it.) Or who would remember Mr Hurd's signal failure in New York last month, when his opportunity to respond to Gerry Adams's publicity coup with some hard-hitting counter-arguments about terrorism was fumbled and lost?

The idea that the Foreign Secretary has a 'safe pair of hands' is too firmly established to be dislodged by any evidence to the contrary. Last year, for example, the greatest single parliamentary humiliation suffered by the Government came when it was obliged to admit that it had repeatedly misled the House of Commons. It had said that the Maastricht Treaty could not be ratified if the Maastricht Bill were amended in such a way as to exclude the treaty's Social Protocol; but when it saw that the Commons might pass that amendment, it conveniently discovered that the Social Protocol did not matter after all. When Mr Hurd carried out this embarrassing *volte-face*, he received nothing but praise for the 'dignity' of his performance. Somehow it would have been bad taste to point out that he, as Foreign Secretary, bore direct responsibility for the false advice which had emanated from his own department of state.

In the discussions leading up to the Maastricht conference, Mr Hurd had taken a stand on two issues in particular: the extension of the legislative powers of the Strasbourg Assembly and the proposal that 'Europe' might concern itself with defence. Both of these ideas he opposed. On both of them he was defeated. But no one remembers the Maastricht Treaty as a defeat for Mr Hurd, who is well known to be a master negotiator.

Nor is Douglas Hurd the first name that springs to mind in any discussion of the ruinously expensive fiasco of Britain's membership of the Exchange Rate Mechanism. Anyone with a passing interest in recent political history would probably lay the blame for our entry into the ERM at the feet of Lords Lawson and Howe, who 'ambushed' Mrs Thatcher before the Madrid summit in 1989, forcing her to set out Britain's intention to join the mechanism. When she made that statement, however, she attached a number of conditions for joining which remained visibly unfulfilled. The decision to join was pushed through in the following year by a different Chancellor (John Major) and a different Foreign Secretary: Douglas Hurd. As Lord Ridley later recalled, 'Margaret Thatcher confirmed to me in September that she had decided to give way to the Chancellor and Douglas Hurd, who had put heavy pressure on her once more.' When Britain eventually paid the cost of this blunder in September 1992, however, no one thought of connecting it with Mr Hurd, whose judgment is known to be faultless.

Indeed, the Foreign Secretary has a Macavity-like ability not to be there when the consequences of his policies come to light. As Home Secretary he set in train the drafting of legislation which eventually appeared as the Criminal Justice Bill of 1990. The main purpose of this Bill was to reduce the prison population by such means as changes in sentencing policy (for example, forbidding courts to take into account the previous record of the accused). It was left to a later Home Secretary, Kenneth Clarke, to deal with the confusion and anger which this caused among the judiciary; and the blame by then was fastened not on the originator of the policy but on the man who had steered the Bill through Parliament, Kenneth Baker.

When Mr Hurd arrived at the Home Office he had left behind another example of Macavity politics, the Anglo-Irish Agreement: a scheme which he had helped to devise as Northern Ireland Secretary but which, as it happened, was signed a few months after his departure from that office. There are plenty of people in the Conservative Party who will admit that this Agreement was a failure. But there are few who would think of pinning any direct blame for it on to Mr Douglas Hurd – even though he now seems set on repeating the exercise with another equally doomed 'initiative'. (In the Queen's Speech last

November, it was noteworthy that the Government's Irish policy was treated under the heading of Foreign Office business.)

But there is one area of policy where the errors committed by Mr Hurd are so gross and their potential consequences so far-reaching, that he will be unable to escape the judgment of his contemporaries – let alone of history. It is his policy in Yugoslavia and the Balkans, and the intimately connected matter of his policy towards the former Soviet Union. History will certainly judge Mr Hurd, but now even his former colleagues are beginning to do so too. Only last week the former Defence Secretary Sir John Nott made an outspoken attack on Mr Hurd's Yugoslav policy, published in the *Evening Standard* under the heading 'The Weak Man of Europe'. 'British foreign policy is in disarray,' wrote Sir John. 'The Foreign Secretary has become a liability.' In Hans Christian Andersen's story, it was just a little boy who pointed out the true nature of the Emperor's new clothes. But here was a respected senior courtier remarking, so to speak, on our Emperor's new green loden coat.

Although a popular misconception (much promoted by the British Foreign Office) has it that the destruction of Bosnia was caused by a German policy of 'premature recognition', there is an abundance of evidence which shows that the war in Bosnia was already planned by the Serbs and would have been started anyway. What ensured the destruction of Bosnia was not the West's recognition of Bosnian independence, but the arms embargo it maintained against that country, which prevented the Bosnian government from defending its people from attack. The chief supporter of the embargo was Mr Douglas Hurd. It was Mr Hurd who, when the American and German governments both expressed a desire to lift the embargo in February 1992, rushed off to Bonn and Washington to persuade them to change their minds. During his visit to Bonn he explained to the press that 'a balance had to be struck' between 'the German view that a supply of arms to the Muslims was the only fair way of allowing them to defend themselves, and the danger of escalating the fighting'. He did not explain, unfortunately, why persuading the Germans to conform with the second of those two utterly contradictory views should be described as striking a balance between them.

Other distortions of truth or logic were also required in order to maintain this position. From the outset of the Bosnian conflict it was clear to most observers that this was a war against Bosnia planned, instigated, directed and supplied by a neighbouring state (Serbia), and aimed at the conquest of most of the Bosnian territory and the eventual incorporation of that conquered land into a Greater Serbia. The

Foreign Secretary, however, steadfastly described the conflict as 'a civil war' – a piece of obfuscation aimed at preventing people from drawing any comparisons with the case of Iraq and Kuwait. 'This is a war with no front line,' he said repeatedly, while maps showing the front line of Serbian conquest were being printed almost every day in the newspapers.

At the same time, however, the Foreign Secretary felt obliged to go along with the policy adopted by other western countries, which was to put pressure on Serbia (through economic and other sanctions) to end the war. Blithely, Mr Hurd maintained these two lines of explanation side by side: that it was just an internal Bosnian civil war, and that the way to stop it was to act against the neighbouring state which was causing it. The contradiction was no doubt eased by the trust and affection with which Mr Hurd, like so many Foreign Office men before him, regarded the idea of sanctions. So trustful was he that 14 months ago he assured Mr George Soros that the Serbian President would 'soon' be toppled by the popular discontent which sanctions were causing – a staggering misjudgment. (Similarly, he had advised Mrs Thatcher in September 1990 that sanctions 'might succeed' against Saddam Hussein.)

The assumptions which underlie Mr Hurd's disastrous Yugoslav policy reflect his *déformation professionnelle* as a one-time career diplomat. There is the classic Foreign Office belief in the notion of 'stability', which confuses stability with familiarity, and assumes that a strong regional power (Serbia – or, in another context, Russia) will be a stabilising influence, no matter how that regional strength is acquired or maintained. There is the love of diplomacy *per se,* a diplomacy which never recognises the limits of its own power and always prefers setting up new initiatives and 'processes', believing that the world is full of reasonable men who will agree on reasonable solutions. And above all there is a kind of pseudo-realpolitik which thinks it can interpret every problem not on its own merits but as a move in some more elaborate power-play. Thus Mr Hurd's deepest objection to lifting the arms embargo on Bosnia was that it might lead to a situation in which different western and eastern powers were 'backing' different combatants, disturbing the post-Cold War harmony in Europe and the United Nations.

The disturbance of harmony has come about, however: almost every country is now out of tune with Britain. Mr Hurd's policy has earned us the impatience of the Americans and the open contempt of the French. In January the Dutch foreign minister described Britain's policy, on the record, as 'disgraceful'. And in Germany our position is viewed with resentment bordering on real hostility: many German officials and commentators believe (wrongly, I think, but understandably) that the main aim of British policy in the Balkans has been to thwart Germany's own policy objectives in that region. It takes an effort of will now to remember that in the winter of 1990–1, when Mr Hurd was finally given free rein over British foreign policy after the departure of Mrs Thatcher, the creation of a new epoch of Anglo-German amity was the main aim he adopted in Europe. As for the other parts of the wreckage of our foreign policy, they include the widespread hostility to Britain's Bosnian policy throughout the Muslim world, a hostility of which Dr Mahathir of Malaysia is merely the leading exponent.

But there is one government with which relations have improved. When the Russians moved their troops to Sarajevo, and Mr Hurd praised their action as a 'constructive' move, they had reason to believe that this was no empty compliment. They had strengthened his hand against a western policy which, a few days earlier, he had lacked the strength to block on his own. And for their own part the Russians can feel grateful to Mr Hurd for his previous foot-dragging over Bosnia, which has established a useful precedent for any future actions they may take in outlying parts of the former Soviet empire. Douglas Hurd was always against the break-up of the Soviet Union ('We have no intention or wish to undermine the stability of the Soviet Union,' he said in February 1991, when its 'stability' was already past all possible repair). Three months ago he even co-authored an article with the Russian foreign minister, Andrei Kozyrev, in which he stated that armed conflicts in ex-Soviet republics were 'a source of legitimate concern to the Russians, who are worried by clashes close to their borders'. The fact that many of these conflicts were being actively stirred up by Russia for its own strategic purposes (as *Rossiiskie Vesti* admitted only a few weeks later) was of course conveniently ignored.

It is hard to think of any time since 1956 when Britain's foreign policy was in such a shambles. Even during the Suez crisis we had allies whose support was more valuable than that of the unpredictably crumbling Russian government today. But the main difference is that in 1956 the country knew that its foreign policy was a mess; today it persists in thinking – despite all the evidence to the contrary – that it rests in a safe pair of hands.

5 March 1994

BOOKS

HARDER THAN HARD TIMES

Paul Foot

DICKENS'S JOURNALISM: VOLUME I, SKETCHES BY BOZ
AND OTHER EARLY PAPERS, 1833–1839
edited by Michael Slater
Dent

If journalism is 'reporting the news' as defined by our modern news editors, nothing could be less enticing than a huge volume of regurgitated journalism, especially when the volume is the first in a series of four. Experts on news desks everywhere impatiently explain that news, to be news, must be bizarre, out of the ordinary, sensational, 'sexy'. The more news fits that definition, the less long it lasts. News reporting of that kind is essentially ephemeral, and is collected in volumes only to satisfy the vanity of authors or editors.

Charles Dickens had a different attitude to news. From early on in his unhappy youth, he was fascinated by the lives of the people around him, how they ate and drank, how they got from one place to another, how they worked, and above all how they played. He wanted to report the dramas which arose every day in every street from the clash of everyday characters, their aspirations, greeds, fears and hypocrisies. He himself used the word 'sketches' to describe his early reporting of the lower-middle-class London in which he grew up. The word has come on down over 160 years to denote a special kind of writing, apart from and subordinate to real journalism, with which clever writers amuse clever readers in the sidelines. Charles Dickens was never in the sidelines. He was at the centre of real events. He brought his astonishing powers over language to awaken his readers' appreciation and understanding of themselves, their workmates and their neighbours – and they revelled in it.

All his life Dickens's majestic and intoxicating prose was reinforced by two rare qualities. The first was a sense of humour which was as bitter and angry as it was funny. Most important people, he noticed, are absurd – mainly because they think they are important. The more they preen themselves in their self-importance, the more ridiculous they become. Dickens's work as a parliamentary reporter nourished in him a particular contempt for politicians who in his day belonged to two parties representing the rich and powerful, but pretending to represent everyone. His sharpest satire was reserved for lawyers, among whom he had also worked as a clerk. One of these early sketches takes us to Doctors Commons where we are introduced to a 'bewigged gentleman in red robes . . . straddling before the fire in the Centre of the Court in the attitude of the brazen Colossus'. What follows is Dickens at his bitterest best:

> We shall never be able to claim any credit as a physiognomist again, for, after a careful scrutiny of this gentleman's countenance, we had come to the conclusion that it bespoke nothing but conceit and silliness, when our friend with the silver staff whispered in our ear that he was no other than a doctor of civil law, and heaven knows what besides. So of course we were mistaken, and he must be a very talented man. He conceals it so well, though – perhaps with the merciful view of not astonishing ordinary people too much – that you would suppose him to be one of the stupidest dogs alive.

The second quality was compassion for the dispossessed. What disgusted Dickens most about the law courts, for instance, was 'a great deal of form, but no compassion'. His eye was always open to the desperate wretchedness in which so many Londoners unnecessarily suffered. He could describe the despair of such people as well as anyone – the portrait of the doomed woman in his essay on the pawnbroker's shop is almost too much to bear – but he prefers it when the poor refuse to accept their plight and start to argue back. In the same sketch, the woman's drunken husband is roundly abused by an equally poor woman in a magnificent flood of invective which brings the pawnbroker scurrying to the counter to stop the row in the only way he can: by chucking the bully out.

Fashionable Dickens scholars are inclined to turn up their noses at Dickens's early journalism. It has, they tell us, none of the rounded brilliance of the great novels. In one sense they are right. Of course the novels are pulled along more easily by the engine of the narrative. But there is a lot to be said for the raw young journalist Dickens, unspoiled by fame or fortune or by a rather contrived plot. For a start there is in these early pieces none of the religion which got him later. His attack on the ecclesiastical courts (in which a man sentenced to two weeks' excommunication infuriates the court by begging them to excommunicate him for life, since he never goes to church anyway) would have

been widely applauded even at the time. But in his glorious assault on
the wealthy bigots who wanted to put a stop to all enjoyment on
Sundays, he takes on the church at every level. In the high church,
where the clergyman was 'celebrated at Eton for his hopeless stupidity', there is nothing but boredom and hypocrisy. In the 'small close
chapel' you expect from Dickens something more sympathetic. But in
the scene he describes, the form is different, but the content is very
much the same. The evangelist preacher

> stretches his body half out of the pulpit, thrusts forward his arms with
> frantic gestures and blasphemously calls upon the Deity to visit with
> eternal torments those who turn aside from the word, as interpreted and
> preached by – himself.

Perhaps for the same reason, there is much less in this early writing
of Dickens's worst characteristic, his sentimentality. Again and again
even in the greatest of his novels, his satirical scepticism deserts him
while he wallows in a heroine's perfection or in a victim's honourable
and decent forbearance. As he got older and more respectable his sym-
pathies with the poor, which never left him, seemed to take second
place to his relief and admiration that they did not stir themselves to
change the world which so ill-treated them. Even this early mid-
1830s journalism tells us little of the bubbling pot of revolt which
would boil over at the end of the decade. But it is more trenchant,
tougher than the novels. Its author was closer to the grimness – and
the cheerfulness – of lower London life, and could report both more
directly.

I gobbled up these essays greedily, hardly believing at the end that
they take up 550 pages. Their most extraordinary quality is their
durability. The technology has changed hugely of course but the
people, their relationships and their problems seem very much the
same. Dickens's omnibus was not the sort you will find today in
Clapham, but the average man on it is surely at this moment being
irritated by a bore in very much the same way that Dickens described
160 years ago. For contemporary political commentators there is even
a story about public immunity certificates and their origins in the
always strenuous efforts of the authorities to stop important information or documents reaching the public. In one of the most exciting
pieces in the book, Dickens describes an election for beadle (an election much more genuinely representative than an election for
Parliament). Trouble was first whipped up by Captain Purdey, an old
naval officer:

[He] boldly expressed his total want of confidence in the existing authorities and moved for a 'copy of the recipe by which the paupers' soup was prepared, together with any documents relating thereto'. This the overseer steadily resisted; he fortified himself by precedent, appealed to the established usage, and declined to produce the papers, on the ground of the injury that would be done to the public service, if documents of a strictly private nature, passing between the master of the workhouse and the cook, were to be thus dragged to light on the motion of any individual member of the vestry.

Messrs Rifkind, Clarke, and Lilley could hardly improve on that.

12 March 1994

IF SYMPTOMS PERSIST. . .

Theodore Dalrymple

I happened to be visiting friends in Gloucestershire last weekend when the remains of the fourth and fifth bodies were found at No 25 Cromwell Street, Gloucester. Apart from a certain local pride in the national (and perhaps even international) notoriety which the activities of a multiple murderer had brought this otherwise quiet and prosperous county, I detected a slight undercurrent of unease during the dinner party I attended on Saturday night.

The conservatory of one of the guests had been built by the man already charged with three of the Cromwell Street murders, who had most obligingly offered to carry out the work while his employers were away on holiday. Apparently, there are many other conservatories in Gloucestershire built in similar circumstances upon similar foundations.

No one who has regularly to do with murderers can be completely surprised by human conduct, however; and the most perfunctory of surveys of English murder over the last 100 years ought to be more than sufficient to convince anyone that the peculiarity and wickedness of man are not of recent origin.

To take but a single example at random, that of Ernest Albert Walker, a footman, who in 1922 lured a messenger boy to his employer's home and there beat him to death with an iron bar. The police found a note at the scene of the murder, written in the form of a list on black-edged paper, in the murderer's hand:

1. Ring up Sloane Street messenger office for boy.
2. Wait at front door.
3. Invite him in.
4. Bring him downstairs.
5. Ask him to sit down.
6. Hit him on the head.
7. Put him in the safe.
8. Keep him tied up.
9. At 10.30 torture.
10. Prepare for end.
11. Sit down, turn gas on.
12. Put gas light out.
13. Sit down, shut window.

Nevertheless, murder with an indefinitely large number of victims – who knows how many bodies the Gloucestershire police will find or fail to find? – does seem a modern phenomenon, if not in its origins, then at least in its prevalence. One has even wondered whether the writing of articles such as this provides a stimulus to imitation and emulation.

It is in America, naturally, that serial killing has reached its apogee, both quantitatively and qualitatively. There, one such killer intermittently used his murdered mother's skull as a dartboard; another was thought to have killed between 100 and 500 victims (he was a murderer, remember, not a war criminal). The FBI has estimated that there are perhaps 500 serial killers on the loose in the United States, and that nearly 20 per cent of its unsolved murder cases are committed by such people.

One of the reasons for the rise of the successful serial killer, perhaps, is the comparative ease of finding victims in modern mass society. Last year, for example, there were 30,475 reports of missing persons in London alone (the numbers of individuals involved was smaller, because many of them, such as children in municipal homes, would have been reported more than once in the year, having run away several times). Of these, 'only' 558 remained missing, some of whom will reappear in due course, or even many years later. Still, it is apparent that a substantial number of people go missing every year in Britain (about 4,000) and are not found: grist to the mill of the would-be killer.

Moreover, it seems that many more people 'disappear' without ever featuring among the statistics of reported missing persons. The police were unaware of the disappearance of at least two of the people whose bodies were found underneath No 25 Cromwell Street. Any large city hospital receives a small but steady stream of drifters who seem to have severed all connection with those who once knew them, and are now without family, friends or acquaintances. Their complete disappearance from the face of the earth would be noticed by no one. Only the other day, I had a patient, the son of middle-class parents, who had left home some nine months before and had had no contact with them since. When I telephoned the mother concerning her son, she sounded relieved enough to know of his whereabouts, but she had informed no one of his initial disappearance. He would have been a perfect victim for a serial killer.

According to the police, the number of murder victims whose bodies are found but who remain unidentified is less than 10 per year. But this fact does not allow one to answer the disquieting question: *How many people are murdered each year without the knowledge of anyone except the killer?*

Certainly, the population from whom so many of my patients are drawn seem to be one in which a cunning serial killer might operate with ease. It is a population of many young drifters, who move from one address to another without apparent rhyme or reason, in the hope perhaps that the meaninglessness of their lives will be more supportable elsewhere, and whose relations with others are fleeting or transient, while those with their parents (or more likely, parent) are hostile and antagonistic. It is a world in which anonymity is easily attained and maintained, in which incuriosity about one's neighbours, a defence against the violence in which any contact with them whatsoever often results, reaches pathological degrees. If plenty of evil is spoken (and even shouted), none is seen or heard.

It is worth recalling that the serial killer, Dennis Nilsen, was caught not because anybody had missed his 16 victims (the disappearance of only one of whom had been reported), but because their remains blocked the drains of the house in which he lived. Indeed, Nilsen himself, in an unconscious parody of *Guardian*-style thought, asked why society was so concerned for his victims after they were dead when it had done nothing for them while they were still alive. He even managed to persuade himself that, in killing them, he was acting humanely and in their best interest. How lucky they were, he said, to be out of it, to have travelled beyond this modern vale of tears.

Opportunity does not make the crime, of course: a motive and the means are necessary. But with an ever-increasing percentage of single-person households, with ever larger numbers of young people alienated from their parents and almost everyone else, with the blasé anonymity of much of modern life, opportunity for those with a predilection for serial murder will not be lacking. I do from time to time on my rounds meet strange, isolated people, up till now respectable and law-abiding citizens, who confess to me their wish to kill not one person but many, and whose admiration for those who have done so is great. I note down their addresses and steer a wide berth, lest their fantasy become reality.

12 March 1994

LEAD ARTICLE

BREAKING OF A PRESIDENT

Let us say it clearly: the Clinton presidency is finished. But it is not finished in the sense that Phil Gramm, the American Senator who likened the Whitewater scandal to Watergate – and called for President Clinton to resign – thinks that it is finished; it is not finished in the sense that the American journalists baying for Mr Clinton's blood believe it is finished.

The Clinton presidency is not finished because the President has been found guilty of breaking the law, or because the President's wife has been definitively linked to some shady practices at an Arkansas bank. The Clinton presidency is finished because much of the time and energy which Mr Clinton and his staff should be spending on urgent domestic and foreign problems will from now on be directed towards fighting these allegations. For the next two years, the entire American political machine may well grind to a halt while a gaggle of independent prosecutors, Congressional investigators, and prize-seeking reporters do their work: running up large hotel bills in Little Rock, Arkansas, reading through thousands of legal documents, chasing rumours and counter-rumours until they are satisfied (and some never will be) that they know the truth.

The best illustration so far of the coming White House paralysis came this week, during a joint press conference held to mark the visit of Eduard Shevardnadze, the Georgian leader. Mr Shevardnadze, whose country is at the centre of Russian attempts to re-establish an empire in the former Soviet Union, was largely ignored, while President Clinton (close to tears) said that his wife had a stronger sense of right and wrong than anyone else he had ever known. Now, one may agree or disagree with this assessment of Mrs Clinton's character, but surely the leader of America – and, therefore, the most important man in the civilised world – should devote his time and political energy to clarifying more important issues.

The facts of the original Whitewater affair are complicated, to say the least. What we know is that a property development company, founded in 1969 and owned partly by Mr and Mrs Bill Clinton, lost money in the 1980s, along with many similar companies in America. We also know that this company, the Whitewater Development Corporation, was financed by Madison Guaranty Savings and Loan, a building society that went bankrupt in 1989, like many similar savings and loan banks in America, and had to be rescued with government money. Those pursuing this story have alleged, in addition, that Madison Guaranty and Whitewater money was used to finance Governor Clinton's election campaigns; that Mrs Clinton used the company's alleged loss as a tax dodge; that government loans were obtained, at Governor Clinton's request, for Whitewater and Madison Guaranty. Mrs Clinton, Governor Clinton, a host of Arkansas lawyers and bankers all appear to have been working together in ways that bent the law, even if they did not exactly break it.

To anyone who knows anything about provincial American politics, none of this is surprising. Indeed, it is almost inconceivable that anyone who spent his career in Arkansas local politics – or in Chicago local politics, or Texas local politics – could emerge 20 years later without a single stain or conflict of interest on his record. When Mr Clinton was elected, Americans knew that he came from this kind of culture, just as they knew – it came out very clearly during the election campaign – that he was an incurable philanderer. None of the facts of Whitewater, or the further revelations of his sexual exploits, is especially relevant to Mr Clinton's current job, which is President of the United States.

Because of the lengths to which the Clinton White House has gone to cover up the details of the Whitewater story, it is inappropriate to dismiss the whole affair as trivial. But because of the damage which a politically disabled, preoccupied American President could do to the rest of the world, it is absolutely necessary that the story is placed in its proper context. No one doubts that much of the attention being focused on these stories is politically motivated: indeed, Republican politicians have good reason to want revenge for the damage which hysterical Congressional Democrats did to men like John Tower, Clarence Thomas and, during the Irangate affair, Ronald Reagan and George Bush. But however justified, Republican revenge – and Republican interest in recapturing the White House in 1996 – should not be allowed to bring the entire American political machine to a halt.

What America needs is a fast, neutral investigation of the Whitewater affair, as well as a thorough investigation of the more sinister aspects of the cover-up: the journalists who claim to have been beaten up, the papers that were shredded, the unauthorised meetings between investigators and White House staff. What America – and the world – does not need is a campaign of allegations made by leading Republicans, and press hysteria of the sort that has brought down so many able American politicians in recent years.

12 March 1994

THE DESK CAME UP TO MEET ME

Alan Judd

Anyone can get blown up, and sadly it is nowadays not so very unusual. The trouble with telling a story about it is that its dramatic appeal lends to the luck of survival the appearance almost of virtue. It was not, after all, as if I had any choice or endured the event with fortitude. It was not an event to be endured. It happened, in the way things do just happen.

In this respect it is like a road accident, which it also resembles in terms of shock and injury, although people aren't often asked to describe their accidents. Perhaps the fact that it was deliberate makes a difference, that it was both achieved and attempted murder. Even so, having survived with scratches when others lose lives, limbs, eyes, brains makes one disinclined to boast.

It happened when I was serving with the army in Belfast. The murderer carried a suitcase of explosive into the ground-floor reception area of the police station in which we were based. I was working in the room above which had an allegedly blast-proof floor of about eight inches of reinforced concrete. It wasn't blast-proof – I saw the blast rip through it – but it was strong enough to save me.

I was sitting at a desk, writing. Moments before I had been balancing my chair on its hind legs, staring at the ceiling. If the bomb had gone off then it might have broken my neck or back. As I returned to the sitting position, I heard an indistinct shout from downstairs, but took no notice; shouting is not unknown in the army. I was using a fountain-pen to plan on a filing card the novel I was later to write. No doubt I was supposed to be doing something else. I leaned forward, my elbows on the desk and feet and knees almost together; a good position, as it turned out.

A jagged jet of flame shot up through the floor in front of me and I felt a hot stinging shock through the soles of my boots, the seat of my chair and my calves and thighs. I ascended vertically with desk and chair, each in the same relative position, enveloped in a roar like a great wave. It felt exactly as you would imagine. On film it would have been Chaplinesque.

I don't think I hit the ceiling, but I believe the desk did and the inkwell certainly did; its remains were later found embedded. At some point I toppled back and to the right and must have brought my hands up to my head, because that was how I found I'd landed, curled in a foetal position. I don't know how long it was before I reacted; it seemed like no time at all but that could not have been right, judging by how much had happened before I rejoined the world. It really was time lost. I've been knocked out a couple of times, but it wasn't like that because this time there was no sense of coming round.

I was breathing, my eyes were open, I could see. My hands were over my face but I didn't move. I lay still, waiting to feel. My legs felt weighted down and I feared paralysis. Above all, I feared that. I wriggled my toes in my boots. That was bliss. There was no pain anywhere, but liquid spread slowly over my head and face. I carefully moved my hands and stared: red and blue. The red was obvious but the ink took a while to fathom.

The weight was the upturned desk. When I eventually got up it was hard to balance because the concrete floor was ridged like frozen sea and its surface was slippery with books, paper, glass and rubble. Where there had been windows, with heavy bullet-proof steel shutters, were now ragged holes in the wall. The inner wall was pitted with glass. I couldn't see the other end of the room or the door because of a dense, revolving cloud of brown dust. On the ceiling was a large blue stain of ink, dripping.

Outside the street was covered in debris and upturned cars. The

houses opposite looked as if they had been shelled, with gaps in their roofs and walls. One of the steel shutters had gone through the front of a house and into the kitchen behind. The sheer shocking violence of high explosive cannot adequately be conveyed; you have to have been there.

A man was running across the road towards us. They are following up with an attack, I thought – unrealistically, in the context of Northern Ireland. I loaded my Browning, cocked it and took aim. I felt anger and wounded pride. That they had got us was bad enough, but it was unthinkable that they should be allowed to humiliate us by over-running our position. I didn't know whether anyone else had survived or whether I was alone but that didn't matter. It was an immediate, atavistic, unquestioned reaction: fight for your territory.

From somewhere very far back in my mind, but fortunately before I took up the trigger pressure, it was borne in upon me that the man had stopped, was in uniform, wore the red cap of the military police, was one of us. I lowered the pistol down through his body, and unloaded. The telephone was at my feet and, surprisingly, still worked. I dialled 999 and said there had been an explosion. A kindly Northern Irish voice said yes, she knew, love, and thanked me.

The bomb killed a sergeant who was in the room with a Republican family who were complaining about us. He tried to get them out, shielding them with his body and was awarded a posthumous medal, I was told. The baby had some of its brain outside its skull but lived, probably as a vegetable. There were a number of lesser injuries. The murderer, eventually caught and sentenced, may well be out now.

The army is at its best dealing with disaster. Expectation of death is woven into the collective subconscious. It is part of the contract. The system and the book – when in doubt, go by the book – are often clumsy but they come into their own then, provided enough survives. Dead men's kit is stacked and labelled, money counted and recorded, body tags recovered, next of kin informed and death rites – whether hurried battlefield burial or full-dress military funeral – punctiliously observed. The formality and ritual of military funerals make them more bearable; the passing is properly marked, the dead are honoured, the structure sustains.

In this case we did more than necessary. The body was to be buried in England, but our colonel, in an inspired departure from the book, had the coffin routed to the airport not discreetly or ignominiously – an admission of defeat – but publicly and flagrantly, through the very hardline areas, where bombers lived. The IRA made much of their funerals, so we did the same. The battalion simply took over part of the city; all traffic was halted, silence enforced and people in the street made to stand still as the Union-flagged coffin was paraded slowly past. I imagine the gesture was understood, if not appreciated.

I never found my pen but I still have the filing-card. It looks as if the pen exploded onto it, and there is a hole in the middle where the nib must have split as the desk came up to meet me. There is one small, confirmatory drop of blood.

I was later involved, though less intimately, in a much larger and messier explosion. After the first, I had been assured with normal army good cheer that these things always come in threes. I still think of that, balancing on my chair.

19 March 1994

DONNEZ-MOI UN BREAK

Boris Johnson

There used to be an iron law of economics, I think, that when the cro-
cuses were out, or possibly the daffodils, then, first in ones and twos
and then in joyous, colourful clumps, the 'For Sale' signs would sprout
in the streets of London. Clearly, this has not been true these last few
years. As one in search of a house, who has pushed buzzers and admired
rockeries across the nation's capital for two months, my guess is that
this year the choice and availability will be little better.

'It'll pick up,' say the estate agents, the hounds of spring, snuffling
and chivvying. At this stage, surely, any such optimism will make
matters worse. It sows hope, the hope that, if owners will just wait, it
is only a matter of time before prices once again take off. For the
English owner-occupier, the hope is more dangerous than the despair.
My guess is that he or she could have further shocks in store.

Let me at once say that these are merely the observations of a provincial oaf, a bumpkin, stuck away in Brussels for five years, without
the benefit of countless dinner-party symposia on the housing market,
the immense learning on the subject shared by most *Spectator* readers.

But I can say with authority that the mind-set of the London vendor
is to be found nowhere else in western Europe. Speaking as a would-be
buyer (buyor, I almost said), the assumptions seem as demented as
ever.

Despite the punishment of the last four years, the middle classes
cling to the superstition that the natural trajectory of their houses'
value is vertiginously upwards. So strong is this belief that, as far as I
can see, instead of dropping their sights, they would rather sit in a dim,
cold property, progressively selling off the furniture and eating Kit-e-
Kat, waiting, waiting for the market to turn and for the mass mania to
begin again.

In consequence, very little habitable property seems to be for sale,
and almost nothing central and affordable. I know that some of the
potential sellers, in fact, 2 million across the country, are in the negative equity trap, the mortgage being worth more than the value of the
property.

One feels the pathos of these debt desperadoes, the DIY fiends who
have spent tens of thousands wrecking a perfectly good house with

peach-coloured fitted wardrobes and walk-in mirrored bathrooms, all half-built because they ran out of money.

Then there are the other, equally frantic reasons why some want to sell: the young couple in an intensifying hell of noise and perfumed nappy bags; the wife of the musician suddenly stricken by a disabling illness. Take your time, they say, as one tears one's eyes away from the fascinating self-analytical jottings on the bedside table; as one speculates, how unfairly, about their lives; the pitiful testimony of the built-in chopping board, scored with 20 years of devotion to Mrs Beeton, now to be abandoned; the cats, that sure index of unsatisfied human cravings – the flaps, the scratching-posts, the multi-storey cat-baskets.

One almost flinches at how obviously the owner, usually the wife, has made an effort with her appearance, doubtless on the advice of some hectoring property supplement – lipstick, haircut, necklace – and how she has laid out photographs of the minuscule yorkstone patio in the summer when the creepers are in full leaf.

And then, after they have been anxiously watching from the corner of their eye, one hears the painful gush, almost of relief, when they detect that one is not likely to be a taker for the place where they have occasionally been so happy. 'Oh, I think it will be far too small for you, with your baby' etc. One feels so intrusive, so callous.

And yet, however much the heart bleeds for them, these people are fundamentally deluded. The asking prices are still crazy.

I had always thought Notting Hill was meant to be a vaguely bohemian area. Marina and I would be very happy in this house here near Ladbroke Grove, for example, amid the ulcerated stucco of what appears to be a disused international ganja exchange. But Mr Faron Sutaria is asking us to pay £395,000 for the privilege.

Laugh, if you like, at my naivety; but is it not frightening that my generation is expected to go into debt to the tune of hundreds of thousands of pounds to live within a long cricket ball's throw of the west end of the Portobello Road? Am I alone in finding it strange that one's parents, not, *mutatis mutandis*, appreciably better off than ourselves at comparable moments in their lives, were able to buy great schlosses in central London?

As for the present meagre market, some of the more reasonably priced items are acquiring landmark status. Almost every estate agent in London seems to be offering 'this rare opportunity to purchase' a house in Sebastian Street, EC1, which appears to be freshly mortar-bombed. Just pour in another couple of hundred thousand grand, the implication is, just add a roof and, hey presto, a bargain!

We did make an offer on what seemed to be a pricy but just manageable terraced house off Highbury Fields, and the vendors said snap at once. It was only later that a rival agent told us that the Channel Tunnel's underground rail link to St Pancras would require a ventilation shaft and escape hatch somewhere near the kitchen.

The rest of the offerings are dominated by people pitching the price at what they fondly imagine their home should 'achieve' in two years' time. If anybody is interested I could show him a small house in Brook Green, darkest Hammersmith. All right, so it has polished stripped-pine floors and a sunken bath; but it costs £350,000! *Donnez-moi un break,* as we say in Brussels. On the day we saw it, Michael Frayn, the prognathous farceur, was in the kitchen. Maybe that's it. Maybe it's an extra £30,000, just for being the kind of house in which Michael Frayn might have his hands wrapped around a mug of tea, polishing his epigrams on a Saturday afternoon.

And if, in the next couple of years, people did come to think nothing of paying that kind of money, the price rise would be treated as the most tremendous piece of good news, front-page in all the papers, pure Martyn Lewis; whereas, as the Bundesbank president, Herr Hans Tietmeyer, once pointed out, in Germany and elsewhere it would be a bad sign. It has suddenly struck me, coming from Brussels, why the British middle classes will never wear a single European currency, whatever Sir Leon Brittan may say in his new book. It would be like the ERM, only worse. It would be the end of house-price inflation.

26 March 1994

DIARY

John Mortimer

I was fascinated by reports that women's struggle, too long delayed, for equality has resulted in them taking over the pastimes, and some of the potential humiliations, of men. Apparently there has been a startling rise in the employment of male prostitutes which must offer one of the few growing job opportunities to school-leavers. The pay is £60 a time and around £150 for the night, and a young black chef from Guildford apparently does a roaring trade. One client, a 46-year-old doctor's receptionist, told the *Guardian:* 'I am deeply ashamed of doing it, but it makes me feel more alive. After all you only get one life, don't you?' These are words which might have been spoken by generations of men from Profumo to Mellor. I won't say my illusions about women have suffered, but I used to like having them on juries because I thought they were realistic and, unlike men, didn't live in a world of fantasy. Now, however, they have their own porn magazines and are reaching for the top shelf in the newsagents like so many dreaming males. I suppose true sexual equality will come when a general called Anthea is found having an unwise lunch with a young, unreliable male model from Spain.

Another strange moment in the sex war was described to us by an extremely popular novelist. His mother and father, well into their seventies, still lived in his old home in the East End of London. The mother decided to take an English course at the Open University and passed out triumphantly. She then looked about her and wondered what on earth an educated woman like her was doing with an ignoramus like her husband. She promptly divorced him but, being a lady with a generous heart, she still cooks his dinner every day and sends it down to him between two plates and wrapped in a tea-towel on the bus. One woman, hearing this story, told us that it was a well-known fact that many Open University courses lead to divorce.

26 March 1994

LONG LIFE

SOME PARENTS

Nigel Nicolson

An academic called David Cannadine who was once attached to Cambridge but now prefers to teach at a safer distance in Columbia University, New York, has specialised in the abuse of the British aristocracy. For this purpose he manipulates the aristocratic press very adroitly. First his latest book *Aspects of Aristocracy* is plugged in *The Times* and *Evening Standard* diaries. Next he trails the essence of it in the *Observer Magazine*. Then *The Times*, finally sensing a delectable controversy, commissions from him a major article derived from one section of the book, an attack on my parents, Harold Nicolson and Vita Sackville-West. It appeared on Easter Saturday headlined 'The Snobbery that created Sissinghurst'. This is my reply.

Cannadine's main thesis is that Harold and Vita were snobs and failures, and they were failures because they were snobs. They deserved to fail. His evidence lies in the books, diaries, letters and biographies written by and about them, and while he has researched all this conscientiously, his use of it is remarkably selective. For over 30 years my father wrote a diary which I edited, omitting nothing that might be turned to his discredit, for it chronicles the ebb and flow of self-confidence that characterises the life and diary of any honest person. Thus he could write in a moment of humiliation and despair: 'There is a mouse in the lily-pool. I feel like that mouse – static, obese and decaying.' Such confessions are honey to Mr Cannadine. 'Nicolson', he writes, 'gradually recognised his own insignificance.' All his gifts and successes are belittled.

We are asked to believe that as a diplomat he was a failure, when he was regarded as the brightest FO man of his generation and became Curzon's most valued subordinate. As a politician he was a total failure, when in the 1930s he was the most articulate backbench opponent of appeasement. As a writer he was also a failure, Cannadine allowing only his diaries to have any posthumous value, and making no mention of the wit, originality and self-mockery of his writing, best exemplified in *Some People*, nor of the insight of *George V*, acknowledged the best royal biography by everyone, except Cannadine.

Then Vita. What does he make of her? Very little. She was a rotten novelist, poorer poet and a hoity-toity gardener. That she won both major literary prizes of her day and the intimate friendship of Virginia Woolf makes no difference. Like her husband she despised anyone who did not belong to her exclusive society. Even the garden was infected by their class-consciousness. 'In horticulture', Cannadine writes, 'as in everything else, they were consummate snobs.' There must be no 'bedint' suburban flowers in it. Hybrid-tea roses were out, azaleas out. When someone – unknown to me – wrote to *The Times* that in fact there is a bank of azaleas at Sissinghurst 100 yards long, rhododendrons were substituted in the next recycling of the article as symbols of the Nicolsons' exclusivity, when the reason for their absence is that their colours are garish and they take up too much room. Like every other gardener, Vita was inventive in what she planted. She avoided parallel rows of lobelias and geraniums for the same reason that writers try to avoid clichés. Their familiarity breeds tedium.

The whole burden of Cannadine's attack is wrong. My mother and father certainly inherited some unattractive prejudices from their upbringing, just as he has from his, but they do not deserve such a torrent of abuse. He overlooks that they reacted against their background (Vita, Knole: Harold, his father's embassies) as strongly as they were influenced by it. Vita broke with the philistine tradition of her parents to love and practise literature from her earliest age. Offered Belvoir or Harewood as her future home, she chose to marry a penniless third secretary. Her happy but highly unorthodox marriage broke all the rules of contemporary society, which she ridiculed in *The Edwardians* and *All Passion Spent* as angrily as Harold did in *Some People* and *Public Faces.*

Even Vita's chosen isolation from the smart world in her later life appears to Mr Cannadine a form of snobbishness, while Harold's gregariousness is another. They cannot win. To enjoy the company of people who share your tastes and interests does not mean that you despise all others. Vita and Harold were not the absurd creatures of Mr Cannadine's obsession. My father was a man of unusual human sympathy and intelligence, my mother a creative woman of considerable depth and range. But I would say that, wouldn't I?

9 April 1994

MURDER MOST BANAL

John Simpson

Johannesburg

The streets were dark and crowded. I parked at an angle on the steep camber and handed a coin to the ragged black man whose only source of income came from waving white drivers unnecessarily into parking places. In the evening warmth, with the smell of *boerewors* on the air, it felt good to be back in Hillbrow again. Music blared out from a record shop, but it wasn't the one I was looking for; that seemed to have closed down. So had my favourite bookshop, which had stocked good literature and interesting anti-apartheid material during the difficult years.

'What happened to Exclusive Books?' I asked in the nearby chemist's. The elderly white man behind the counter peered at me with curiosity. Exclusive Books had, it seemed, moved out to the safety of the rich English-speaking suburbs. Be careful he warned. There had been a stabbing here only 20 minutes before; Hillbrow was dangerous now. I looked around with new eyes. At 10 p.m. I was the only white person on the street. This had once been my favourite part of Johannesburg, mixed and raffish. The authorities gave up trying to impose apartheid on it as early as the mid-1970s. Nowadays crime and the white exodus to the northern suburbs are imposing a segregation as rigorous as the old one.

The next morning, in the warm, clear weather no one from England ever tires of, I drove round to the place where my family and I had lived when we were based here, 18 years ago. The delightful, sprawling colonial bungalow had been knocked down. Now there was an imitation Tex-Mex estate there called Rancho something. I couldn't even work out where our house had stood, nor the studio from which I had broadcast reports about uprisings in Soweto, the death of Steve Biko at the hands of the security police and the creation of phoney apartheid statelets like Bophutatswana. As for the incomparable garden where the *piet-my-vrouw* birds called in the jacaranda trees and the bougainvillea and the Yesterday, Today and Tomorrow bushes flowered, that had vanished under the concrete abode: gone like apartheid, gone like Bophutatswana.

The area seems grander and more prosperous than ever, like white South Africa as a whole. More frightened than ever, too. 'Immediate Armed Response,' says the sign on almost every house. This means that if you press the alarm button which has been fitted in each room (two in the larger rooms) a truckload of men will screech to a halt outside your gates in less than four minutes. They will be equipped with sawn-off shotguns and a computer print-out with the names of everyone entitled to be on the premises. Anyone else can be shot without problems from the law or the insurance.

There used to be a sign outside one house that said, 'Is There Life After Death? Trespass Here and Find Out.' Now people no longer joke about such things – not when you can emerge slowly from your driveway and be killed by a couple of thugs who have been lying in wait to steal your car. As a result, every householder can have a gun for protection; and the newspapers carry reports with depressing frequency about children who have blown their heads off by accident, women who have dropped their handbags and shot someone in the legs, men who have come home in a bad mood and wiped out the entire family plus the dog. And meanwhile crime continues to rise.

As I drove around, every tree by the roadside was marked with an election promise: 'Vote ANC For More Jobs', 'Only The National Party

Can Stop The ANC', 'The Democrats: No Murderers, No Corrupt Politicians'. Under the promises were the newspaper placards: 'Anxiety Grows In Durban'; 'Massacre Investigation Latest'. Massacres, riots, murders are the stock-in-trade of the news reporters here now. And yet I found it strangely difficult to be gloomy. It wasn't merely the weather, or being back in a country I had come to love: it was the extraordinary change that had taken place.

When I lived here the National Party existed for three reasons: to further the interests of the Afrikaners, to force the British population out of political life, and to keep the black, 'coloured' and Indian populations as helots. The Afrikaners I mostly met were not the intellectuals of apartheid, those kindly, crackbrained souls who believed – though were never quite able to prove – that the Bible ordered different races to live separately; nor were they the quiet, hospitable Boers who farmed the Karoo or the Low Veld. Instead, they were the resentful working-class Afrikaners who disliked everything they believed the British stood for, and who had been empowered by decades of unbroken National Party rule to do whatever they wanted to anyone. 'It's not what you can do for me,' said an enormous, brutal security policeman when he arrested me in 1977 in Soweto (I had made a nervous attempt to be chirpy), 'it's what I can do to you.' He could indeed have done anything to anyone, and the Minister of Justice and the entire state hierarchy would have covered up for him.

I left the pleasant, wooded suburbs with their reassuringly English names (Westcliff Drive, Oxford Road, Jellicoe Street), where everything is intended to make you forget you are in Africa, and drove into Johannesburg proper. There the dirty, littered streets and the sprawling markets show how Africa is taking over. Here there were different National Party posters, this time directed to the new voters: the blacks. 'Once We Imprisoned You Without Trial,' they say, 'Now We've Made The Change'. A few years ago it would have been inconceivable: apologising for apartheid, attracting black voters, allowing blacks to vote at all. Most National Party supporters would have assumed that their power would last indefinitely, and most liberals would have assumed that it would end in bloody revolution. Blood is indeed being shed, but this is neither revolution nor civil war: merely a frightening degree of crime.

The National Party is still run by the very people who voted for apartheid and banned other political parties under a law called, humourlessly, the Prevention of Political Interference Act. Yet we should not assume that those who have been so maltreated for 46 years by the National Party will necessarily vote against it now. One recent poll suggested that although the ANC would sweep home in Natal and the Johannesburg area, the Western and Northern Cape might both be won by the NP. Not all conservative, rural blacks like the ANC, and the forelock-tugging tendency is still strong. And although 'Coloured' people and Indians – and whites – are strongly represented in the ANC's hierarchy, it is generally perceived as a party of and for Africans; and the National Party will be the only real protection against the ANC in the new political system.

It takes time for someone who left South Africa when apartheid was at its height to become used to seeing blacks driving expensive cars and sitting in expensive restaurants being waited on by whites. But it is harder still to grasp that the National Party can now successfully woo people whose interests it once deliberately injured. 'This whole country is changing so much, so much,' said the gloomy old man in the Hillbrow pharmacy, when I went to find out what had happened to Exclusive Books. I agreed; yet to me it seemed a reason for hope. If South Africa can change this much, this fast, then anything can happen. For the first time I began to think that the election might pass off, if not peacefully, then at least without anarchy and disaster.

9 April 1994

'WINSTON REPLIED THAT HE DIDN'T LIKE BLACKAMOORS'

Andrew Roberts

Just before he left office in April 1955, Winston Churchill invited Ian Gilmour, the new owner-proprietor of *The Spectator*, to Downing Street to discuss the magazine's strong stance in favour of restricting New Commonwealth immigration. 'I think it is the most important issue facing this country,' he said, 'but I cannot get any of my ministers to take any notice.'

This month sees the 40th anniversary of the last serious attempt to prevent the creation of a multiracial Britain, what Winston Churchill called 'the magpie society'. It was during his premiership that ever-increasing numbers of immigrants began to arrive here, largely from the West Indies, but later also from India, Pakistan and Ceylon.

It has famously been argued that the Empire was acquired 'in a fit of absence of mind'. Equally, the post-imperial implosion took place without any concerted plan to promote it. Certainly there was no pre-meditated political programme, and no one argued that large-scale New Commonwealth immigration should be encouraged in order to make Britain a better place.

The Labour Government's British Nationality Act of 1948 – the first attempt to define British citizenship – was drawn up at the height of enthusiasm for the concept of Commonwealth. As the Labour Home Secretary, Merlyn Rees, stated on BBC2's *Timewatch* programme on Wednesday, 'That's where the trouble started.' After Burma declared itself an independent republic in January 1948 and Canada took steps to define its citizenship, a structure was considered necessary in the Cold War period which would both bind the ex-dominions to Britain for security and trade reasons as well as act as a fig-leaf to cover the nakedness of post-imperial weakness.

All political parties embraced 'the Commonwealth ideal' with a fervour and naïvety which may seem absurd today. The 1948 Nationality Act supplanted common allegiance to the Crown – which India was also to abandon in 1951 – with the amorphous concept of separate citizenships for the Commonwealth states, plus the status of 'Commonwealth citizen' which gave rights equivalent to those of any British subject. This effectively gave over 800 million Commonwealth citizens the legal right to enter and reside in the United Kingdom.

Cabinet papers show it was the Labour Government which first considered closing this legislative loophole. Two days after the *Empire Windrush* docked at Tilbury in June 1948, bringing 492 West Indian immigrants and marking the start of post-imperial implosion, 11 Labour MPs wrote to Attlee protesting that 'an influx of coloured people domiciled here is likely to impair the harmony, strength and cohesion of our public and social life'. A Cabinet committee under the Labour Home Secretary, James Chuter Ede, was set up in June 1950 to investigate 'ways which might be adopted to check the immigration into this country of coloured people from British colonial territories'.

Throughout Churchill's 'Indian summer' Government of 1951-55, liberal Tory cabinet ministers blocked all movement on the issue. It was during this period that the rate of entry into the United Kingdom achieved its 'take-off' point, rising from 6,000 a year in 1953 to over 40,000 in 1955. In 1961, the year the Government finally curbed immigration, 130,000 entered the United Kingdom.

Employing bureaucratic inertia, electoral scaremongering and dubious political manoeuvrings, the liberal Conservative and

Commonwealth enthusiasts ensured that, despite the Prime Minister's growing agitation over the issue, no change in the legislation took place. By early 1954 Churchill had lost patience, and, as the rate of entry increased exponentially, he warned the Cabinet that 'the rapid improvement of communications was likely to lead to the continuing increase in the number of coloured people coming to this country, and their presence here would sooner or later come to be resented by a large section of the British people'.

In April 1954, after intense struggles in Cabinet committees and ad hoc meetings, conducted by Lord Salisbury and Oliver Lyttleton on one side and Alan Lennox Boyd, Iain Macleod, Lord Kilmuir and Lord Home on the other, the draft Bill to restrict immigration was shelved. It was nevertheless to form the basis of the legislation which was eventually introduced seven years later. But in 1954 the ailing and inattentive Churchill, by then in his 80th year, was unable significantly to alter the course of the internal debate. It took the Notting Hill race riots of August 1958 for the Conservative Government to take notice and begin the drawn-out and politically expensive process of changing a law which could have been amended with relative ease seven years before.

Churchill's views on race did not spring up fully formed when he regained office in 1951, but were held consistently throughout his long political career. By the standards of today – and possibly even of his own time – Winston Churchill was a convinced racist. For all his public pronouncements on the 'Brotherhood of Man' he was an unrepentant white – not to say Anglo-Saxon – supremacist. For such a zealous child of the Empire anything else would have been astonishing. Part of the British Empire's *raison d'être* was its assumption of racial superiority, even if, as with so much of that 'boyish tyranny', this was usually expressed passively.

Neither were Churchill's assumptions about human worth confined to ethnicity. He dabbled in eugenics, and as Home Secretary in 1906 warned: 'The unnatural and increasingly rapid growth of the feeble-minded and insane classes, coupled as it is with steady restriction among all the thrifty, energetic and superior stocks, constitutes a national and race danger which it is impossible to exaggerate. I feel that the source from which the stream of madness is fed should be cut off and sealed before another year has passed.' He therefore instructed his officials to look into the possibility of enforced sterilisation, promising that after 'a simple surgical operation they could be permitted to live freely in the world without causing much inconvenience to others'. Eugenics was taken for granted by many of Churchill's contemporaries across the political spectrum, and it was not too large a step from assuming a hierarchy in human worth to a belief in the superiority of certain racial groupings over others.

In *My African Journey*, the account of his 1907 visit to East Africa whilst Under-Secretary at the Colonial Office, Churchill stated that the British officer class was, 'in all that constitutes fitness to direct, as superior to the Buganda as Mr Wells' Martians would have been to us'. The Buganda tribe were themselves, according to Churchill, the superior one in the region. They benefited from his general policy to 'encourage, as far as may be in our power, a careful patient discrimination between different classes of coloured men'. On that trip Churchill thought the Kenyan Kikuyu 'light-hearted, tractable if brutish children . . . capable of being instructed'. Africans in general were 'less crudely animals' when they wore clothes. After declaring, 'No man has a right to be idle,' he charitably added, 'And I do not exempt the African.'

As Colonial Secretary 14 years later, Churchill averred that 'the Indians of East Africa are mainly of a very low class of coolies, and the idea that they should be put on equality with the Europeans is revolting to every white man throughout British East Africa'. A Cabinet colleague, Edwin Montagu, said that he expected to hear such views from a 'fanatical' white settler, but not from a Minister of the Crown. For Churchill, Negroes were 'niggers' or 'blackamoors', Arabs were 'worthless', Chinese were 'chinks' or 'pigtails', and other black races were 'baboons' or 'Hottentots'. Italians were 'mere organ-grinders', and when an Egyptian crowd attempted to burn down Shepherd's Hotel in 1952 he described them in a memorandum to Eden as 'lower than the most degraded savages now known'.

Not all Churchill's racial characterisations were negative. He believed the Jews to be 'the most formidable and the most remarkable race which has ever appeared in the world'. He felt an instinctive affinity for their genius as well as a historian's respect for their trials, and he supported Jewish aspirations whenever they did not clash with those of the Empire. He may have inherited this philo-semitism from his father, but he certainly gave it a new lustre in his own life.

Indians, on the other hand, he found 'the beastliest people in the world, next to the Germans'. During the 1943 Bengal famine he reassured the Secretary of State for India, Leo Amery, that the Indians would nevertheless continue to breed 'like rabbits'. After one such outburst in August 1944, Amery was prompted to remark of the Prime Minister that he 'didn't see much difference between his outlook and Hitler's'. Churchill's doctor, Lord Moran, believed his master 'thinks only of the colour of their skins: it is when he talks of India or China that you remember that he is a Victorian'. In his conversations it was clear that it was 'the civilising mission of the British race' that drove his imperialism rather than any economic benefits which the Empire might bring. 'If the British people will have a great Empire, if any ray of true glory is to fall upon it,' he had told the National Liberal Club in January 1908, 'they will need an imperial race to support the burden.'

As the great tribal leader of 1940, his speeches were peppered with references to the British race. During the Second World War he unerringly put the interests of the white man over those of the black or yellow one. Sometimes his racial prejudices, which a recent Cambridge conference on Churchill termed his 'cultural assumptions', could work against British interests. He accepted Rear-Admiral Tom Phillips's argument that as the Japanese were shortsighted as a race, they could not make good bomber pilots. It was an opinion he had swiftly to revise after the sinking of the *Prince of Wales* and *Repulse*.

In 1942 the Labour MP, Tom Driberg, questioned the Prime Minister about the 'introduction in some parts of Britain of discrimination against negro troops'. Churchill did nothing to discourage racial segregation, which was both widespread and officially recognised in the American armed forces based in the United Kingdom. When he was told that a black official at the Colonial Office had always lunched at a certain restaurant from which now, because it was being patronised by white American officers, he had been barred, the Prime Minister replied, 'That's all right, if he takes a banjo with him they'll think he's one of the band!'

Neither did this attitude abate with time; Sir David Hunt, one of his Private Secretaries during his 1951–55 period of office, recalls 'Churchill was on the whole rather anti-black. I remember him sending a telegram to [the South African President] Dr Malan and asking me whether he should say "My dear Mr President, *Alles sal rect horn* [all is well]. Keep on skelping the kaffirs!", and then adding, "Better not put that last bit in." ' When the Korean war began he said to a friend dismissively when told of the vast size of the Chinese Red Army, 'Four million pigtails don't make an army.'

The very week he left office in April 1955 Churchill was asked whether he had seen the film *Carmen Jones*. According to Lord Moran's diaries, 'Winston replied that he didn't like "blackamoors" and had walked out early in the proceedings. He asked, a little irrelevantly, what happened when blacks got measles. Could the rash be spotted? When he was told that there was a very high mortality among Negroes from measles he growled, "Well, there are plenty left, they've a high rate of production." '

When 'Young' Winston Churchill, the present MP for Davy Hulme, inveighed a year ago against 'the relentless flow of immigrants to this country, especially from the Indian subcontinent', and called for it to be stopped 'if the British way of life is to be preserved', he was widely condemned. But his grandfather would have been proud of him.

9 April 1994

BOOKS

MY OLD CHINA

Charles Powell

EXPERIENCES OF CHINA
by Sir Percy Cradock
John Murray

I declare an interest. Having long worked with Percy Cradock in the Foreign Office and 10 Downing Street, I believe his was the best mind applied to British foreign policy in the past 30 years: powerful, incisive, independent. It is no surprise, given Britain's post-war history, that his most celebrated diplomatic victory was achieved in retreat, from Hong Kong. But it speaks volumes for Mrs Thatcher's instinctive recognition of true quality that she kept him on to advise her long after the Foreign Office would have let him retire.

Percy Cradock's quality shines through this book, above all a clarity of thought and expression unrivalled in my 30 years' experience of the public service. It is a strange tum of fortune's wheel that someone who devoted his life to producing fastidious intellectual harmony out of the world's natural chaos should finish his career as a source of dissonance; and that years of reticence, indeed Trappist silence, should now be superseded by a peevish public attack on government policy towards Hong Kong and China.

My own contributions to China policy were a sad disappointment to Percy Cradock when we worked together at No. 10. His disillusion dated from a chill December night in 1984, when Mrs Thatcher arrived in Beijing to sign the Joint Declaration on Hong Kong. It was decreed that she should ride in from the airport with the Chinese Foreign Minister. Alarmed at what might pass unobserved and uncontrolled on this journey, Percy beseeched me to force my way into the car and take careful note of anything said. The first part of this mission was accomplished (I came from a more muscular school of diplomacy than the scholarly Percy). But the journey from London had been long and the heat in the car was excessive, with the result that I went instantly to sleep, to awaken only on arrival at the State Guest House, having heard nothing of what had been said. Percy and our Ambassador hurried up expectant, to grill me on what had transpired. Had concessions been demanded or offered? I toyed for a moment with telling them that the conversation was too secret to be revealed – my usual excuse when I went to sleep in important meetings – but Percy's gimlet gaze told me there was no escape that way. I confessed the truth and was ever thereafter regarded as deeply unreliable on the subject of China. In that I clearly joined most of the human race and an even higher proportion of the Foreign Office and Her Majesty's Ministers. China was for the chosen few and not for amateurs.

And exceptional people the Sinologists are, as the book shows. The clinical description of the storming of the British Embassy in Beijing at the height of the Cultural Revolution is on a par with the laconic accounts which mountaineers traditionally give of their most perilous ascents. Beaten, bruised and flung into the gate-house of the Albanian Embassy, Sir Percy quotes Virgil to his colleagues ('Perhaps even these things it will one day be a joy to recall'). Remarkable men indeed, and the women no less, as Birthe Cradock made brave forays by bicycle at the height of the Cultural Revolution to gather intelligence on wall posters, one of the few guides to what was really going on.

Percy's insistence that China policy should be kept to the priesthood did make it possible to have an occasional bit of fun at his expense. I recall in particular a meeting between Mrs Thatcher and Lydia Dunn, the most artful and most decorative exponent of Hong Kong's views. Percy Cradock was alarmed at what two such forceful ladies might contrive if left alone and lobbied mercilessly to be admitted to the meeting. When informed that the great man was outside the door awaiting their call, they conspired to shock him. From the moment he was admitted, their talk became steadily more outrageous, envisaging – would you believe it? – the extension of democracy in Hong Kong and more directly elected seats in LEGCO. Fingers steepled, eyes glinting alarmingly behind his professorial specs, Percy slipped ever deeper into his chair, enveloped in gloom. The uncontrolled discussion of policy was his darkest nightmare.

That may explain the impression from the book that the problems of negotiating with the Chinese were relatively trivial compared with those of dealing with our own side. The Chinese were after all consistent, organised, disciplined and predictable. Mrs Thatcher was none of those things, and Percy Cradock's description of her unique debating style is deliciously accurate, particularly her ability to pop up in the least expected places on the battlefield. His look of exquisite pain at some of the Leaderene's wilder assertions is a joyous memory. Capable of days of trench warfare in negotiation with the Chinese, an hour of all-in wrestling in the Cabinet Room did grievous bodily harm to his preference for an orderly world.

But enough of reminiscence. This is a remarkable book: elegant, perceptive, broad in its sweep yet sparing in its narrative (indeed the bloody Tiananmen Square merits only six dead-pan lines). Those privileged to read his classified monographs will feel instantly at home. It is beautifully written and makes one hope that we shall be treated to more of his recollections.

Yet I am left unsure – both from this book and from an admiring friendship of more than 20 years – whether or not Percy actually liked the Chinese. He had little reason to do so, given his experiences in the Cultural Revolution and the years of tortuous negotiation in the often Kafkaesque world of Chinese diplomacy. His private judgements of their conduct were often scalding. Those of us who knew them less well seemed to like them more. Yet his admiration for China's civilisation and for the traditional mandarin qualities is unmistakable. He describes a Chinese negotiating partner as 'courtly, austere, intelligent and professional'; and the true mandarins would surely regard him as 'one of us'. One is nagged only by the feeling that he has been dragged almost too far into the topsy-turvy world of Chinese logic, where to be a friend of China means being an enemy of one's own government.

The clinical, almost bloodless, approach is most evident in his treatment of Hong Kong: it seems more a problem for the Higher Diplomacy course than a flesh-and-blood issue. The model solution was found in the Joint Declaration, a diplomatic triumph of which Percy Cradock is justifiably proud and protective. But when Hong Kong's people inconveniently changed their minds after Tiananmen Square and wanted a little more democracy, what was the British Government to do? Allow the hallowed text to take precedence over the people? Or seek a little more elbow room within the agreed text to accommodate the Hong Kong people's hopes and fears.

Much foolish criticism has been voiced of the Sinologists and Percy Cradock is rightly indignant about it. For one who stood valiant and unbending in the frontline against the howling mob to be accused of kow-towing is the ultimate insult. He is right that a secure future for Hong Kong depends on agreement with China. But diplomatic agreements are not monuments on the battlefield, to be tended and revered, they are living instruments for realising human ambitions and aspirations. His successors may be less versed in Chinese practices but they should not be condemned simply for trying to cater equally honourably for the changes in both China and Hong Kong since 1984.

16 April 1994

A MESSAGE FROM THE AAAA'S PRESIDENT

Keith Waterhouse

Once or at the most twice a year, when my column in the *Daily Mail* has nothing better to do with itself, I amuse myself by recording the latest proceedings of a spoof organisation called the Association for the Annihilation of the Aberrant Apostrophe (AAAA), of which I am supposed to be the life president.

The response to these occasional reports is extraordinary. There are always a few correspondents who think the AAAA, with its annual rally in Hyde Park and its apostrophe exhibitions in the Albert Hall, really exists and want to join it. For the rest, a single column on the subject is sufficient to trigger off a year's steady flow of enough examples of apostrophic confusion to fill a laundry hamper.

Daily they trickle in: newspaper clippings, handbills, greetings cards, labels, packets, carrier bags, Polaroids of shop fronts, public notices, hoardings, even traffic signs painted on the road ('Bus's only').

They come broadly in four categories. First we have the its/it's and your/you're class, as in 'Its you're birthday!' Then there is the absentee apostrophe – 'Childrens bookshop' is very common, together with other examples so numerous that I once thought of changing my Association's name to the AAAAAA, for the Annihilation of the Aberrant And Apostrophised Apostrophe.

Next comes the anything-with-an-s-in-it apostrophe – Glady's, Ladie's, Brent Cros's. This is a specialist sub-division of the largest category of all, the superfluous apostrophe beloved of greengrocers –

tom's, cauli's, apple's, orange's (I have always maintained that these aberrant apostrophes arrive in bunche's of banana's like tarantulas).

Over the years, my apostrophe crusade has maintained a high degree of interest among readers, who behind a tongue-in-cheek approach are genuinely concerned about slipping English standards. If the AAAA really did exist it would have a membership of thousands.

Now, however, it appears that we have all been wasting our time for, under the heading 'Professor sees no place for apostrophe', the *Guardian* reports that Richard Hogg, Professor of English at Manchester University and general editor of the *Cambridge History of the English Language*, has revealed that he 'would not go to the stake' to maintain the distinction between its and it's, and that he suspects the apostrophe 'may well just decline of its own accord – do you know anyone who still puts an apostrophe in front of bus?'

No; and, indeed, none of us knows anyone who still puts two apostrophes in sha'n't, as the Victorians did; and a latterday Tennyson would no longer write 'Their's not to reason why.' Language moves on, and punctuation is part of the caravan. But should moving on mean the same as moving out?

Hogg is of course not the first distinguished apostrophe abolitionist. GBS, with his shants and donts and wonts, was a famous enemy of the apostrophe to indicate elision, although he didn't object to its possessive use, as in *Widowers' Houses* and *The Doctor's Dilemma*, even allowing the elevated comma to appear in lights. But this is the first time I have come across so utterly passive a case for allowing the apostrophe to die out.

Hogg concedes, according to the *Guardian*, that the mark can be useful to indicate possession in a plural noun, but says it has no use in the singular. So we would have *Widowers' Houses*, but *The Doctors Dilemma*. And that's simplification? As for its and it's, the distinction is 'confusing' – 'Few, except pedants who wear their erudition like a badge, can remember which is which.' Really? It's – it is. Its – belonging to it. Some people are easily confused.

'The apostrophe has only been around for 300 years; we managed very well without it before that,' the Professor (with the aid of a semicolon, whose CV is even shorter) is reported as saying. Yes? Then why was it introduced at all? Because if it hadn't been, the reader would be constantly doing double-takes over such eccentricities as D'Oyly Carte, Well meet again, and Ill see you tomorrow.

As for the apostrophe being in decline, it is not, far from it – that's the trouble. It is increasingly used, in our greengrocer English, where it shouldn't be used, from uncertainty fostered by bad teaching. There may be a case for streamlining the apostrophe, as Hogg mildly suggests, although that would mean more rules of thumb rather than fewer. There is no case for allowing it to go into disrepute without protest simply because that is the way it is heading. That would be to argue that, because an increasing number of people (or amount of people, as Professor Hogg, by his own yardstick, shouldn't mind us saying) do not know the difference between you and I and you and me, the distinction should be allowed to fall by the wayside. Come to think of it, though . . .

16 April 1994

JOHN MAJOR, JUST AN UNDERTAKER ON OVERTIME

David Cannadine

John Major is an extremely lucky man. In the present climate, this may seem a perverse opinion. But consider the facts – and the precedents. During the past 100 years, British history has been littered with the remains of mediocre men who took over as prime minister after a dominant figure left (or was forced off) the stage, and who went down to defeat very soon after: Rosebery after Gladstone, Balfour after Salisbury, Douglas-Home after Macmillan, and Callaghan after Wilson. In each case, the new man took over an administration that was visibly running out of steam and support, and spent his brief months in office combining the jobs of caretaker and undertaker.

If history had repeated itself, John Major's name should have been added to this long list of losers at the general election of April 1992. His qualifications to join this gallery of fag-end failures were exceptionally good. He was replacing a premier who had once been formidable and feared, but who had become out of date and out of touch. He inherited a govermnent that was exceptionally – many thought terminally – unpopular. And he showed little indication of being tough enough, assertive enough or individualist enough to establish a personal ascendancy in the Cabinet, the Commons and the country, which might have enabled him to face the electorate with hopes of success.

But, as we all know, history did not repeat itself in April 1992:

'Go ahead dear, Make all the noise you want'

against all the precedents and most of the polls, John Major won the general election. And he won it because, whereas he was not Thatcher, Neil Kinnock was still Neil Kinnock. This is why it seems appropriate to describe him as a lucky man. Nor is this – nor should it be – the full extent of the Prime Minister's good fortune. For this is a trick of self-renewal which will surely not be repeatable. The temptation to suppose that Michael Heseltine could win them the next election because he is not John Major is one to which the Conservatives may yet succumb. But they would probably be ill-advised to do so.

For their present difficulties are much more deep-rooted than that. John Major – his luck still holding – is the symptom, not the cause, of the Tory party's present unease and unpopularity. But why are the Conservatives in such a mess? Many answers have been offered: too long a spell in power, the lacklustre Cabinet, the declining calibre of MPs, the difficulties over 'Europe', the embarrassment of the Scott inquiry, the 'Back to Basics' fiasco, the succession of sexual scandals, the increasingly hostile press. All true. But not the whole truth.

For underlying these developments is something much more funda-mental – and much more damaging. That is the collapse of public respect for the nation's established institutions. Thus stated, this is hardly an insight of breathtaking originality. These days, it is scarcely possible to open a newspaper without stumbling upon another article lamenting – or, occasionally, applauding – the fall from grace of yet another once-proud British institution: the monarchy, the Church of England, the aristocracy, the City, the Brigade of Guards, the BBC, the NHS, the National Trust, the universities, the Civil Service, the law, the police, the family. Once upon a time, so we are regularly told, these institutions were admired as the bastions of Britishness. But not any more.

It was, presumably, just this concern which underlay Michael Portillo's paranoid pronouncements about 'the new British disease: the self-destructive sickness of national cynicism', which he believes is 'one of the greatest threats that has ever confronted the British nation'. And, on the other wing of the party, Douglas Hurd may be found saying very much the same thing, though in rather less alarmist language. British 'soul-searching', he observed in a lecture at Oxford Brookes University last year, is in danger of becoming 'weakening and ridiculous'. A 'fierce wind' has been blowing 'through the institutions of Britain, uprooting some and damaging others'.

There are many ironies in these remarks, two of which are worth exploring at some length. The first is that it is the Conservative governments which have been in office since 1979 that are largely to blame for the decline in deference and the destabilisation of institutions which Messrs Hurd and Portillo, among many others in the Tory party, now so unhappily lament. They, of course, prefer to blame 'academics, churchmen, authors, commentators and journalists': in short, their much-needed enemies, the 'chattering classes'. But they seem to have forgotten that it has been the Conservatives, not their critics, who have been governing this country for the last 15 years.

Nor should they need reminding that it was Margaret Thatcher who unleashed not just the rhetoric but also the policies, which were confrontational, acerbic, destabilising. As her memoirs remind us, she hated most of the nation's established institutions, and during her years in office she took a vengeful delight in shaking them up and putting them down. In public, at least, she always made an exception for the monarchy, of which she spoke with scrupulous respect. But some of her followers (like Norman Tebbit) showed no such restraint. And the new-style, right-wing Tory press which came to prominence during her premiership was even less deferential.

To the extent that there has been a collapse of deference in this country during recent years, it is the Tory governments themselves that have been primarily to blame. But there is a second irony. For it is not just that Conservative ministers are themselves most responsible for the state of affairs which they now so regret. It is also that the Tory party itself, as another of the nation's historic institutions, has been undermined by the very forces of destabilisation that it was so happy to see let loose elsewhere. And it is not John Major's leadership, but this destructive Thatcherite legacy, which explains why the Conservatives are in the mess they are in today.

Appropriately enough, the collapse of deference seems to have gone further in the Tory party than anywhere else in the country. When Mr Portillo complains about 'the disintegration of respect', and when Mr Hurd fears that the questioners and the critics have become too strident, they need look no further than their own back benches for corroboration. In the aftermath of Thatcher, it is Conservative MPs who have perfected the new concept of the actively disobedient political party. The days when loyalty was the Tories' 'secret weapon' have long gone. MPs no longer do (or think) what they are told. As an ex-minister recently remarked, 'The old levers don't work any more.'

No wonder the right-wing press is baying for Major's blood, and that so many backbenchers are so discontented. The Prime Minister is the focus of these disgruntled feelings, but not the cause. The enduring legacy of Thatcherism is that it elevated institutional resentment into a political programme and an acceptable state of mind. What was not foreseen in the heyday of her handbag was that the Conservative Party would itself become the victim – indeed, the prisoner – of this corrosive ideology. Does anyone seriously suppose that, if Michael Heseltine or Kenneth Clarke or Michael Portillo took over, order would be restored in the ranks, and deference return?

From this perspective, it is clear that Mr Major is no more to blame for the Tory party's present disarray than he is for its continuing unpopularity. In the present climate of panic and anxiety, it is understandable that some Conservative backbenchers feel that a change of leader would result in a change of fortunes. After all it is much easier for a party to sack its skipper than to rethink its policies or to restore some semblance of corporate purpose or to rediscover a sense of collective responsibility. But there is little evidence that such a solution would work. If the ship is heading inexorably for the rocks, then changing the captain is not going to avert disaster.

So Mr Major's luck should continue to hold: this does not mean that he will win the next general election (although there remains an outside chance that he might), but it does mean that he will probably still be there, leading his troops into battle. Whatever the limitations of our unwritten constitution, Britain is still a democracy of sorts. Which means that party leaders are chosen by MPs, and that British governments are elected by voters. It is an understatement to observe that this is not a perfect system, and that it often produces the wrong results. But it is still better than leaving the choice of prime minister to Paul Johnson or Lord Rees-Mogg.

It is rumoured that, among former prime ministers, John Major's favourite is Stanley Baldwin. Unlike Major, Baldwin went to Harrow and Trinity College, Cambridge. Although the son of a Midlands industrialist, he was far from being non-U. But he was endlessly patronised by cleverer politicians (Lord Birkenhead called him 'the dud', and Winston Churchill was no more complimentary), and newspaper proprietors like Lords Beaverbrook and Rothermere went after him with relish. Yet Baldwin survived, not least because the press lords were much more disliked than he was, and he left 10 Downing Street at a time of his own choosing. John Major may himself yet do the same.

The removal of the Prime Minister would not solve the Conservative Party's problem, because he is not the Conservative Party's problem. The Conservative Party's real difficulty is the Conservative Party itself. In recent years it has simply ceased to function, or to have any sense of itself, as a great or serious institution of state. Pandora's box has been opened, and as the winds blow unchecked from the left and the right, it is not at all clear who can put the lid back on, or when. The party is now a deregulated free market of independent and often undisciplined individuals. It is neither an edifying spectacle nor an effective vehicle of government.

The trouble with Thatcherism was that it weakened faith in the established institutions of this country but was utterly devoid of any creative vision as to what should be put in their place. It claimed to be arresting the nation's century-long decline, but achieved no such thing. In the process of accomplishing these non-triumphs, it also wilfully set out to destroy many admirable British virtues, including tolerance, decency, fair-mindedness and public-spiritedness. It may yet destroy the Tory party itself. It would be poetic justice if it did. But if this does happen, John Major will not himself be to blame, whatever the press may say. He is a very lucky man.

16 April 1994

DIARY

Robert Harris

Modern life holds few greater pleasures than flying first class at some-body else's expense. Personally, if I had to pay for the privilege myself, I wouldn't enjoy it. I'd spend the entire flight thinking how much more wisely I could be spending the money. But if somebody else is paying – in my case, the occasional foreign publisher – flying abruptly ceases to be a chore and becomes a luxury. My heart was therefore touched last week when I heard the story of Albert Goldman, the American biographer of Elvis Presley and John Lennon notorious for dwelling on the more sordid aspects of his subjects' lives. It seems that at the end of last month Mr Goldman agreed to fly from Miami to London to give an interview to *The Late Show*, but only on condi-tion his seat was first class. Imagine his distress on arriving at the check-in desk and discovering his reservation was only for club class. Mr Goldman promptly threw a tantrum of epic proportions – so epic the BBC had to be telephoned and his seat upgraded. Alas, the author's victory was short-lived. Possibly as a result of his exertions at the ticket desk, Mr Goldman suffered a heart-attack and died mid-flight.

This cautionary tale was fresh in my mind last Thursday night when I emerged from BBC Television Centre having just appeared on Mr Goldman's least favourite programme – *The Late Show*. It was half-past midnight. A car had been promised to take me home. But instead of the usual Ford Sierra, there waiting was a black cab, its driver under orders to take me 'as directed' and charge the fare to the BBC's account. 'Where to?' asked the cabbie. 'You're not going to believe this,' I said. 'Hungerford.' Seldom in my life have I seen such an expression of awe and gratitude on a human face. It turned out to be a surprisingly comfortable ride up the M4, most of which I passed in a kind of trance, my eyes riveted on the meter. At 1.30 a.m. we stopped to refuel just off Junction 13. By that stage there was £104 on the clock and the driver was in a state of ecstasy. 'This is the best job I've had in nine years of cabbing,' he murmured. 'This is like winning the pools. I'll always watch the BBC from now on.' When we arrived home – at a cost of £123 – he insisted on opening the door and escort-ing me into the house. 'Mr Robert Harris,' he said, looking lovingly at the docket, 'I shall never, never forget your name.'

I am writing a novel – or trying to write a novel – set in Britain and Germany during the second world war. Occasionally I feel rather guilty about this: shouldn't I be tackling something of more contemporary relevance? But then I look at the newspapers and it seems to me that the war is not diminishing in importance but growing. Whoever would have guessed that nearly 50 years after his death England wouldn't dare play football against Germany on Adolf Hitler's birthday? The tenacity of the man's grip on our imaginations is astonishing. The same is true of Winston Churchill, judging by the reaction to Andrew Roberts's article about his alleged racism. At first I was tempted to agree with Lord Deedes, who wrote a reply in Saturday's *Daily Telegraph* arguing that Churchill's views had to be set in the context of his time. But Lord Deedes's assertion that some of Churchill's 'more outspoken sayings' were mere jests, uttered 'with a twinkle in the eye', made me think again. I defy anyone, in any age, to joke about blacks dying in their thousands of measles, or being scalped in South Africa, and do it 'with a twinkle'. I can't think of any of Churchill's major contemporaries who would have been capable of such callous remarks. Halifax? Chamberlain? Baldwin? I doubt it. Equally bizarre is Lord Deedes's argument that Churchill couldn't have been a racist because he admired the Jews. One could more easily argue that Churchill's particular veneration of Jewish people ('the most remarkable race which has ever appeared in the world') was simply another facet of his racism. Still, the fact that this debate is taking place at all is a tribute to Churchill's enduring capacity to fascinate. I can't imagine there'll be much interest in the views of any of our current rulers half a century hence – a comforting thought to those of us writing novels set in 1943.

On Saturday I received an unexpected letter from a Church of England priest with whom I was at Cambridge nearly 20 years ago: 'I note from last week's *Spectator* that, like most of my agnostic contemporaries, you live in an old parsonage. I just want you to know that when Britain becomes "Great" again, the plot to serve a writ of praemunire against Dr Carey is successful, and Neil Hamilton MP is Prime Minister, we will claim all our rightful property back. *Dominus Tecum.*' It's true that I'm an agnostic. But this splendid clergyman – not so much High Church as stratospheric – is one of the few who might yet persuade me to see the error of my ways. A few years ago, at the wedding of a mutual friend, I watched him tiptoe up behind a young Tory parliamentary candidate who was droning on about something, and slowly tip a glass of beer over his head. 'Why did you do that?' spluttered the sodden guest. 'Because,' replied his newly ordained assailant, 'you're so fucking boring.'

16 April 1994

BOOKS

MORE CHIPS OFF THE OLD BLOCK

Alan Clark

CHURCHILL
by Clive Ponting
Sinclair-Stevenson

These days 'chip' means very-high-speed-integrated-circuit. But it can also *(arch.)* signify what a certain type of academic carries on his shoulder. David Cannadine comes to mind. And so, after boring my way through this latest 900-page biography of Churchill, does Clive Ponting.

Come to think of it, wasn't he something to do with the *Belgrano* at one point? Like Mrs Thingummy, the 'Cirencester housewife', never heard of again. All of them (except the crew of *Conqueror)* wankers.

So there is something strangely unsatisfactory about this book. Perhaps it is because, while the author may be an academic, he is not a scholar. The style is that of a reasonably competent *Grauniad* feature-writer, complete with time-honoured lapses – *squardon, feleing,* and adjectival adverbs. Favourite word, 'virtually'.

Sweeping assertions abound – many of them quite significant in terms of Historic Revisionism – but with very little corroborative support. The footnotes are sparse, perfunctory and, for the lay reader, almost unverifiable. There is all the difference between being 'provocative' like, say, A. J. P. Taylor, where it is stimulating because founded on real historic perception, and just being WRONG.

Ponting: 'Before the war the Admiralty had insisted on giving priority to battleships rather than the less glamorous convoy escorts.' Fact: No 'battleships' were laid down after the signing of the Washington

Treaty in 1922. The three King George V class were incomplete even at the outbreak of war. But in that period seven aircraft-carriers, 51 cruisers and 133 destroyers were added to the fleet.

Ponting is ludicrously Francophile. He peddles the Vichy line that Britain, and particularly Churchill, let them down in 1940. But his figures for French casualties during that very short period – 370,000 dead and wounded – are as slipshod as his scrutiny (if any) of the Naval Estimates.

All this is a pity, because scattered about the book there is enough to hold the attention of all that wide body who are still hungry for 'insights' on Churchill. Interesting and entirely believable is the account of how much order/counter order/disorder there was in several days of indecision over how many RAF squadrons should be 'thrown into' the Battle of France. Churchill made a lot of bad strategic decisions but at least (runs the folklore) he got this one, the most critical of them all, right. But in fact the Cabinet had on three occasions to restrain him from making an 'emotional' (in more than one sense, one suspects) commitment that would have irreparably crippled Fighter Command.

Ponting dodges the big issue. Or perhaps it is simply that his Correctness obliges him to regard the survival of our 'Island Race' (ugh) as being less important than the theoretical welfare of coloured immigrants and the congenitally disabled. (He sneers at Churchill's use of the word wherever it occurs, and the class-war mask slips disconcertingly often: '. . . one of his [Churchill's] millionaire friends who had been close to Oswald Mosley '.)

November 1940 Ponting rightly identifies as the one moment in the war when we had a breathing space before – just before – we were irretrievably bust. But the logical conclusion – that this was the time when, unlike the Cabinet panic in May of that year, we could have got excellent peace terms – goes virtually (sic) unexplored. Paradoxically, it was the sickness and death of Neville Chamberlain that finished us. Until his operation Chamberlain blocked Churchill's efforts to move Halifax from the Foreign Office (from where he could have conducted, even initiated, the negotiations). But after Chamberlain's death Churchill assumed, against a background of considerable party unease, the leadership and lost no time in packing his principal rival off to Washington. Thereafter we were committed on a long and bloody trek towards a desert of bankruptcy and disillusion. This huge, geostrategic miscalculation is barely addressed. Nor is the secondary question of how Churchill managed to make so many errors of command and deployment when *virtually* throughout the war he was reading the enemy cards by means of the Ultra decrypts.

The bibliography cited is impressive. But as far as his understanding of the Tory party goes, Ponting might just as well have asked for a reading list from Camden Borough library:

> Churchill [was cautious about] the Draconian powers given to the Minister of Works in case they were used against the interests of property-owners.

This kind of right-on shorthand is pamphleteering. A serious historian would have adverted to the very difficult balancing act which Churchill, Liberal opportunist and turncoat, deeply distrusted by most Conservative MPs, had to maintain. And the huge difficulties in toppling a sitting Premier (and the lessons therefrom, which should be of some comfort to John Major) are referred to, bereft of any feel for the workings of the Tory Party.

The two authors of whom I am reminded by Clive Ponting are Margaret Thatcher and David Irving. Like them he has written a work of 900 pages. Like *The Downing Street Years* there are nuggets of information to be found, plus a lot of pre-warmed material for the scissors and a shallow PhD paper.

And like Irving's biography, underrated (as well as, in this country, effectively suppressed by the book trade), it is far too informed by racial prejudice. Ponting is obsessed by black people, and loses no opportunity to 'disclose' how Churchill disliked them, even trying to refuse entry to black US infantry convoyed to Britain in 1942. 'Next time tell him to bring his banjo along' was Churchill's advice to some dignitary who complained that a black aide was turned away at the door of his club. Irving in the same way is obsessed by the Jews, and frequently seeks to demonstrate how they made Churchill their puppet. There may well be something in both of these assertions. But they cannot be more than ancillary to the main conundrum. Who was Churchill? An impetuous romantic who blundered about bumping into things, or a patient visionary surveying events from a deep historic perspective? A big selfish baby who stamped his foot and blubbed if he couldn't get his way, or an inspired patriot and saviour of his people?

Dr Charmley and, in the more specialised field of military operations, Mr Richard Lamb have already done much to clear the air. But for a full and balanced assessment of this great genius we must await the pen of one who has actually himself dabbled in the black arts.

Churchill: A Study in Failure remains the best of all the biographies. I for one am impatient for that sequel which only Sir Robert Rhodes James can provide.

23 April 1994

BOOKS

A GREAT ENGLISHMAN

John Osborne

JOHN BETJEMAN: LETTERS, VOLUME 1, 1926–1951
edited by Candida Lycett Green
Methuen

I say! What a fulsome letter . . . Gosh! I did enjoy myself . . . My God it's exciting, ain't it duckie!

And so it is. Into the black well of last week, the stone rolled back, light appeared and this gorgeous book thumped me into remembrance of the possibility of redemption from sloth and despair, a bolting revelation which has left me blinking and dazed with delight.

I know next to nothing of the technical problems of such things, but it seems to me that Candida Lycett Green has achieved a miraculous service of homage to her father's head-down genius in her editing and annotation of his letters from 1926 to 1951. All is lean, clear and informative. When she told an enquiring, dusty don what she had undertaken, he replied, 'Mmm... That should take you 15 years or conceivably 20.' Blessedly, she blew hot against this academic frost and took Michael Holroyd's gentle counsel: 'You just have to love your subject, that's all.' To have had to wait for the appearance of such a heavenly comet, as precious and exhilarating as the explosion of Boswell's *Life of Johnson*, would have been a cruel deprivation and a graveside blow struck to the very heart of J. B.'s own glorifying immediacy.

What an almighty and uncloying marveller he was. Unforced gales of grateful laughter sweep up line after line of these incontinently exuberant pages, exploding in postscripts, inspired, ridiculous nicknames, dark, mischievous fantasies and the joyous doodledums of

happy and affectionate sketches. To Lionel Perry: 'My Dear Old Lil . . .
You filthy old thing with your round head like an 18th-century gate-
post.' To Nancy Mitford: 'Your handwriting is like that of a maid . . . I
have had to call up what the telephone operator calls Sloone sex-four-
seven-sex'. Or, of his wife, Penelope, in 1950:

> I am getting on very nicely with Propellor who has gone in for a new hair-
> style called, I believe, 'windswept'. She had it done in Wantage where
> 'Marguerite' the perm specialist is an RC. The brain and face beneath the
> hairstyle are happily the same.

He breathed in the island ozone of his own curiosity, fantasy and
invention and it exploded into the air above his friends, like Spring
squalls at the end of Southend Pier. He had the supreme clown's gift of
holy self-deflation. He signs himself off:

> Tonkety, tonk old boy . . . Your's in Calvin's name . . . Ever your adoring
> fag . . . From that poverty-stricken old rip, J. B.

It is hard to think of anyone whose company incites the word 'merri-
ment' itself, who could pipe, dance and lead his correspondents from
devout solemnity to girly-giggling irreverence back to the awesome
delights of molecular divinity to be found even in a brand of smokers'
matches – England's Glory. J. B. writes to a public school prefect:

> I like England's Glory for the jokes, yes. Wasn't it frightful when they
> gave up the jokes and had reviews of the Cabot Tower, Brakes Statue etc!?
> I wrote and complained. They said it was only an experiment and now
> I'm glad they've gone back to the jokes again.

Without drawing breath, he informs this young stranger:

> I think I am Catholic in a low way. Red velvet and a couple of candles for
> illumination. Prayer book version of the Mass. In fact Georgian 'High'
> Church. Erequent mass, celebrated in a long surplice and black scarf at a
> red velvet covered communion table. Clear glass. Box pews. There was
> once a man at St Mary-le-Bow who thought like that.

Reading or, rather, clinging to these pages like a whirling carousel
horse, the image of that elegant rotundity of mind, body and spirit
braces, astonishes and infuriates the blood in a month when the dismal
Dr Carey attempted to betray the nation's history and common intel-

ligence with his Slough-like slouching towards incantations of his imagined 'ordinary little country'. What an Archbishop would have been John Betjeman, with his English gift of turning the inconsequent into circumstance and the ordinary into the divine. Oh, contemptible Carey, how I wish J. B. Cantuar were here to mock you gently for the cuntuar: he would have had a few larks with Carey, hairy, Mary, dairy, fairy. Only he could do it, entertainer that he was, in boater or panama, natty vaudevillian of the heart's true ease. Why a 'minor poet'? Another fiction, like 'flawed masterpiece', the babble of eunuchs who have no idea of the cost and usage of a storm-room of energy. In his case, it was prodigious.

How could anyone possibly accept the fairground roundabout spectacle of his lurching folly and hate-clutching curiosity as anything but a superb and mocking pantomime? This was a sportive, dolphin god-on-earth, sonically beamed into sight and sound beyond the range of most mortal apprehension. His instinct for parody was unerring, the invitation for ridicule masterly. The selective aloofness of Archibald, his bear, was tuned as finely as everything else in that dolphin wavelength. In 1940, he wrote of him: 'Archie is very well, and pro-Hitler, I am sorry to say. It is the Nuremberg manufacture that must have done it.'

Mrs Lycett Green plaindeals:

> I want to show the world how great he was how he was, unlike most of us, interested in things other than himself; how he laughed an inordinate amount and when he put his head back and shook with laughter, you couldn't help laughing too.

He was also a great Englishman. I keep thinking of this common grocer-divine, Carey, when reminded of the 29-year-old J. B.'s list of interests: ecclesiastical architecture, three-decker pulpits, Irish peers, Irish architecture and pre-Celtic twilight Irish poetry (or 'Oirish', as he would have it, signing himself Sean O'Betjeman), Salkeld's Catalogue, branch railways, suburbs, provincial towns, steam trains. His dislikes, sniffed out and exposed by that rooting terrier passion, included aeroplanes, main roads, insurance companies, 'development', local councils, and materialism, dialectical or otherwise. His hopes were for 'a Triumph of Christianity and a town plan for England'. It is an agenda that makes one think of Sir Christopher Wren, discouraging calls while designing St Paul's.

But, I say! This book is full of surprises. To me, at least. J. B. and Penelope Chetwode were married, unknown to the bride's disapproving parents, at Edmonton Registry Office. They then spent a few days at the Green Man pub in Braxted, Essex. 'Oooh, I did enjoy Essex,' said the bride. Then off she went to Berlin. J. B. wrote: 'Oi am thinkin of you at the moment quiverin loike a jelly on the English Channel. Oi do hope you won't be orribly sick.' Upset and insecure, he bought a farmhouse and employed a pretty girl with dark brown hair, one Molly Higgins. He confessed to his bride in Germany. 'I did not realise until I got yours this mornin that you were actually in love with Molly H.', she replied. By the time P. B. returned for Christmas 1933, the affair had faded and, adds J. B.'s enchanted daughter, 'my mother was very much in command'.

In 1929, J. B. wrote:

> I have got to go out with a lot of jolly girls now – oh God I wish I were dead . . . As usual, I am on the rocks . . . I wallow in the pleasures of Melancholy . . . I have been at the door of death . . . I have discovered a rather beautiful girl here and my sex becomes rampant. I think I must be a bit better.

Miraculously, he never really changed. I hope to learn from this book for years to come and not simply mourn my own misspending and that imposed upon me by those who have empowered themselves over my life.

In the meantime, would Mr Patten distribute this monumental history of the ineffably unordinary to every sullen, ignorant teacher in the land and force them to read it aloud above the ethnic clamour and drown the general grudge?

My hat! What a fulsome review. Gosh! I did enjoy myself: My God it's exciting, ain't it, duckie?

23 April 1994

BOOKS

MR POOTER BUYS A COMPUTER

Julie Burchill

HUNTING PEOPLE: THIRTY YEARS OF INTERVIEWS
WITH THE FAMOUS
by Hunter Davies
Mainstream

In every hack, a heartache, a hero we can never hope to measure up to, but who comes sometimes and sneers over our shoulder when the midnight oil is all but consumed, 'Are you *sure*? You *really* want to use "smorgasbord" again? Well, go on ... but people are *laughing* at you, you know.' The hero of the hack is not as benign or free with blessings as the hero of a novel is; he's a hardhat, heavy on the kibosh. But we like him that way; he makes us better.

But looking on the right side, a lot of us also have an anti-hero; a hack we know that we will never, never in a million years, or its equivalent intake of alcohol, be as bad as. We cannot look at this mark without our jaws dropping in sheer molten awe and our celestial semaphore appealing: 'Oh God, don't make me like that – please! Make me a stringer from Strathclyde, if you must! But please, please, don't make me like that!' My stop-sign, my scarecrow, is Hunter Davies.

He is 58. He has written more than 30 books. This one, subtitled *Thirty Years of Interviews with the Famous*, takes its pieces from the *Sunday Times*, *Mail on Sunday*, *Observer* and *Independent*. Which really does make you think, has talent got anything to do at all with Making It in newspapers? I'm a success; Hunter Davies is a success. I don't want to come over as the little boy swinging on the lamp-post and giggling at the Emperor, but what does this make me?

One can only hope – and actually believe, on the evidence supplied here – that journalistic standards have changed quite dramatically for the better over the last 30 years. Surely no one would trust a young Hunter Davies with a major interview these days? Someone – probably me – once said that the key to understanding Jeffrey Archer's prose was simply to accept that English must be his second language; it would appear to be Hunter Davies's fourth. The quite singular gracelessness of his writing can be sampled in a few sentences from the introduction (which reads much more like an extremely painful induction):

> Over these last thirty years I have had the possibility, pleasure, nay privilege, of interviewing many of the household names of the day. They were often interesting and important enough to be still remembered today, from Noël Coward to Salman Rushdie. Or later events have retained our interest in them, such as Christy Brown.

Not since last year's wonderful Giles Gordon autobiography has the ghostly hand of the Grossmiths so hovered over a book; Mr Pooter buys a computer.

His unintentional humour knows no limits. In the course of the introduction, he actually asks two of our greatest interviewing journalists – Zoe Heller and Lynn Barber – what makes them so good. But when they reply that it is a tape recorder, endless transcribing and at least a week's worth of work on each piece, he makes his excuses and leaves: 'I was surprised, in talking to the women interviewers, how long they take to write their pieces.' Try it! is the only possible reaction. But dismissing the hard graft of Heller and Barber, Hunter lets us in on his tricks of the trade: 'I'm a notebook man myself. Always have been.' Tell me more. 'Little red notebooks, the soft sort which fit flat into the pocket.' And what, O Great One, do you fill them with? 'A few shorthand abbreviations, of my own devising, but mainly it's a mad scribble.' Phew!

Davies divides these pieces by decades. The Sixties section is probably the funniest, a helter-skelter of non-specific fame; because the interviews are chronological, U. Thant sits sandwiched between Paul McCartney and Bill Naughton. Mr Thant, you'll be amazed to hear, was 'not a great one for casual chat', and appeared to be unsportingly preoccupied by the American war in Vietnam. Still, as Davies writes robustly of the UN, 'As long as there's confidence in U. Thant, people will meet there.' Vera Lynn couldn't have put it better.

I do feel a certain louche loathing for the likes of Keith Waterhouse, endlessly fidgeting with words as though they were doilies set out to protect a prized table from stains, but his fogeyism is positively energising when one reads Hunter on Nancy Mitford: 'She doesn't do nothing. She just moons around.' Innocent little full stops seem like furniture he cannot help but blunder into: 'Not stupid,' he says of one subject. 'Hard not to get good stuff out of,' he says of another. This is a fine style for, say, sending telegrams; as writing proper, it just won't do.

Judge for yourself: on Noël Coward – 'You couldn't be snide about him, could you? He's a living legend.' On Yoko Ono, promoting her tragic film *Bottoms* – 'You might think it's ridiculous, but at least the people making it are convinced intellectually about what they're doing.' Or how about 'Is Marshall McLuhan a genius? In North America many people think he is.'

Just think, Hunter Davies *sat down and read these stinkers*! What were the pieces he rejected like, you can't help but wonder. He uses the word 'potty' a lot; a sure sign of a resigned wretch who knows he will never make words sing. And he uses the abbreviation 'etc'. 'Etcetera, etcetera, etcetera' is just about acceptable from the King of Siam; it is not acceptable in grown-up journalism. Occasionally, humanity cannot help but shine through; on a minor note there is the ever-adorable Paul McCartney admitting that, yes, he did question the wisdom of putting his wife in his band: 'I did once say in a row that I could have had Billy Preston on keyboards. It just came out. I said I was sorry about an hour later.' (Also, amusingly, we experience Linda cooking the family a huge egg-and-bacon breakfast as late as 1976: 'We don't get cholesterol!')

Then there is Christy Brown. Spotting a newspaper picture of Davies's wife, Margaret Forster, and taking a shine to her, he becomes a pen-pal. Eventually they meet, and Brown is left alone with Davies for a while. What did he think of her husband? Miss Forster asks him. 'Naïve,' says Brown. *I'll* say; if you are as bad a writer as Hunter Davies is, is it really smart to include the brilliance of a man who has to type his words with the toe of one foot?

Hunter Davies has the moustache of a Seventies San Fran homosexual, and the sad eyes of a man who hangs around iceskating rinks staring mournfully at the little girls. Because he is neither, he accentuates his ordinary-bloke persona to an excruciating extreme, and tries to turn everyone else, from James Baldwin to J. R. R. Tolkien, into an ordinary bloke too. Salman Rushdie becomes 'a bearded speccy bloke' wearing 'a boring anorak'. But if these people are as relentlessly ordinary as Davies seeks to make them, why on earth would we want to read about them? Surely not for the sheer pleasure of the prose?

23 April 1994

THE LOWEST COMMON DENOMINATOR

Andrew Gimson

If St George had slain the dragon sooner, would the maiden ever have been in such peril? It is not my wish, least of all in an issue of this magazine which appears upon his day, to criticise the saint. But if he was anything like the people, the English, who long afterwards adopted him as their patron, he will have been quite amazingly slow to detect, let alone respond, to danger.

One almost feels sorry for the dragon. From childhood onwards, it behaved in a thoroughly antisocial way, but George was always kind to it. The weapons and suit of armour in the hall of George's house seemed purely decorative. The dragon grew larger and larger, and began to commit quite serious offences, but George refused to give it a custodial sentence. At most, he chided the beast.

And then the dragon went too far, and George killed it. By that stage, the whole thing was touch and go: the dragon had become so strong, it might have killed George. But the knight, by good fortune or divine providence, vanquished the dragon and established himself as the very type of chivalry.

There you have our national myth in all its glory and ignominy. The English (not the Scots, Welsh or Irish) are a nation of procrastinators. We proclaim our love of compromise and know backwards all the wise arguments in favour of settling disputes by mutual concession. But love of compromise is very often our excuse for appeasement and defeatism.

We have grown so addicted to compromise that we seem, at times, to be blind to any other truth. The satirical item known as 'Thought for the Day' on Radio 4's *Today* programme illustrates this condition. The producer of the feature seems to have only one thought, which is that no listener must be upset. Contributors from an amazing range of traditions are therefore asked to deliver, day by day, the following compromise formula: we ought to be nicer to each other. The satire, such as it is, arises from the fact that the programme is supposed to be about religion. Christianity, Judaism, Islam, Hinduism and psychoanalysis are all reduced to a single matey platitude. One learns without surprise, but with a certain feeling of discouragement, that the head of religious affairs at the BBC, Ernest Rea, is particularly proud of the programme.

When compromise, which can be such a noble thing, descends to such mindless banality, several evils flow. One is boredom. Another is ignorance. We can no longer learn much, or impart much, when our main motive is to say what we think other people want to hear.

The Archbishop of Canterbury cannot be accused of that fault, unless, that is, he has some very odd ideas about what we want to hear. As I write, it occurs to me that perhaps he does have some very odd ideas about what we want to hear. Consider his recent throw-away remark: 'We're a pretty ordinary little nation and yet we don't realise it.'

This happens to be the opposite of the truth, which is that we're an extraordinary nation and don't realise it. The Archbishop would surely agree that each individual is extraordinary, if only one has eyes to see. The same is true of nations. There is no such thing as an ordinary nation.

But to compromise junkies the idea that we're 'a pretty ordinary little nation' comes as welcome news; for the more ordinary we are, the less hope we have of standing up for ourselves, so the more reasonable it is to compromise. There is, incidentally, no doubt that the Archbishop had the question of whether we could stand up for ourselves in mind. The poor man had observed in his previous phrase that 'we have lost nearly all our navy and air force and so on'.

To leaders who have lost their nerve, the revelation of weakness comes as a blessed relief. It gives them an excuse for not trying to make a fight of things. During the several years I attended editorial conferences at the *Independent*, one of my colleagues inveighed on an almost daily basis against 'losing-side psychology'. The phrase was horrible, but the phenomenon could be found in almost every area of British life.

When the Duke of Wellington was asked what the test of a great general was, he replied that it was to know when to retreat, and to dare to do it. That is very likely true of great generals, who would not, by definition, be defeatists. It has not (with some salient exceptions) been true of the British ruling class in this century, which has generally had the utmost difficulty knowing when not to retreat, let alone daring (not) to do it.

Our present Prime Minister is too good an example of this to be ignored. John Major was elected party leader because Conservative MPs considered him the best compromise. He is an almost flawless specimen of our national predilection for the lowest common denominator. Untainted by privileged background, university education, oratorical brilliance or other unfair advantages, he sets great store by feeling 'at ease with oneself' and has a genius for bringing any meeting he chairs to a compromise. One of his strengths in that respect is an apparent absence of any deeply held views of his own. He can without difficulty shift his position to wherever he feels the centre of gravity lies.

On becoming Prime Minister, he was encouraged, for form's sake, to develop one or two ideas of his own, and hit on the concept of class-lessness. His choice is instructive, for here is another valuable source of comfort for leaders who have lost their nerve. By indicating that they are themselves of no higher rank than those they lead, classlessness helps them to imply, however unwittingly, that no greater courage can be expected of them. This is the opposite of the traditional under-standing of leadership, exemplified by the second lieutenant who (however incompetent he may actually be) is expected, on occasion, to take greater risks than his men. At Westminster, an ordinary man leads a nation certified as ordinary by his spiritual equivalent.

A parody of compromise has ensued. Mr Major is trying to bring peace to Northern Ireland by reaching agreement with a gang of terror-ists who have come quite close to assassinating him. He is trying to bring peace to the Conservative Party by agreeing with both sides about Europe. It is not, I hope, necessary to share my views about either Ulster or Brussels (Unionist and anti-Union respectively) to agree that in neither case has the pursuit of the lowest common denominator proved a satisfactory policy. In neither case does a lowest common denominator exist.

'But what is the alternative?' the political class cries, and thereby betrays its gutlessness. Much the greatest difficulty of pursuing differ-ent policies in Northern Ireland and Europe would be making the deci-sion to do so. We could act differently, if the political will existed.

Weak men bent on compromise are inclined to develop a bogus doc-trine of necessity, according to which the only practical policy is the one into which they have allowed themselves to be pushed. They use this doctrine partly to hide their cowardice from themselves, partly to hide it from other people. Liberal commentators endeavouring to pose as men of the world are particularly liable to fall for this pseudo-prag-matism. A British minister who has let himself be compromised into telling lies to the House of Commons about negotiations with terror-ists can rely on the full support of the liberal press. Truth becomes one of the first casualties of compromise.

It might be thought from all this that I am pessimistic about Britain's future, especially as I have just moved to Berlin, but nothing could be further from the truth. There has never been a time when the British political class did not show grievous failings of one kind or another.

Twenty years ago, when I started reading the *Times*, it was full of magisterial articles by William Rees-Mogg and Peter Jay which demonstrated that the end of the world, or at least the British part of it, would take place next Tuesday afternoon at the latest. On Wednesday they would duly print our obituary, without realising we had somehow managed to survive another night.

One reason why they were wrong was that they were right. Relations with the trade unions were so disastrous in the Seventies that during the Eighties a serious, frequently wrong-headed but at least not defeatist attempt was made to put things right. It is a pity things were allowed to get so bad, and one should not forget the pain and loss caused to many people, but if things had never grown so bad we would never have summoned the determination to mend them.

Water must, metaphorically speaking, be pouring in through the roof before the British Government will even consider making repairs. Otherwise we bumble along, doing not very well. Our railways have been a compromise for many decades, denied commercial freedom but not run with the ruthless dirigisme of France. Now they are being subjected to a compromised privatisation. As for the link between the Channel tunnel and London, one loses count of the number of compromises it has been through before work even begins.

London itself is a monument to architectural compromise. We don't have a dramatic number of skyscrapers, like New York, or virtually none, like Paris, but a scattering of mediocre blocks. At Victoria Station there are three escalators to the Victoria Line, because we could not quite bring ourselves, in the early Sixties, to build the necessary four. The hopelessly crowded M25, a lane short of its original, uncompromising design, is another testament to the short-sightedness of the halfway house.

The Sizewell B nuclear power station rises above the Suffolk coast. One gets a good view of it from the Harwich to Hamburg ferry. It is the latest in a long line of British nuclear compromises. A strong case could be made for building none of these pressurised water reactors, or else for building an economic number, but not, as we did, to pitch our nuclear industry awkwardly between the bespoke and the mass produced.

Some compromises are so clearly disastrous that we have at least reached the stage of wondering (though not yet very productively) what we should do about them. The welfare state, a grand collective compromise with our consciences, falls into this category. It gives millions of unemployed people enough money to reduce their incentive to seek work, but not enough for a satisfactory standard of living. There's a fine

'I think we've got a leadership problem'

compromise for you, one which discontents those who give and those who receive.

Crime is worse than it has been in living memory. I recently asked some middle-aged Jamaican immigrants why they thought it had got so bad. They said that when they were growing up in Jamaica they were given a traditional English education. If they did something wrong at school, they were beaten, and when they got home they were beaten again by their fathers for getting into trouble at school. But now, if their own sons get into trouble at school, no serious punishment is meted out, and when fathers try to discipline sons, the sons report them to the police or the social services. Young black men run riot because middle-class English liberals, than whom no class is more addicted to compromise, have destroyed the means by which their schools and families once kept them in order.

Young white men run riot for the same reason, and millions of old people live in fear of going outside. On housing estates on the edges of our large cities, gangs of children as young as ten or twelve run wild at three in the morning. Not that decadence is the preserve of any one class. When one looks at the Duchess of York and her friends, one can only say, with Matthew Arnold, 'What a set!'

So it would be easy enough to argue that there has been a general and disastrous collapse of authority, honesty, standards of behaviour etc. in Britain. But the argument would be overstated, and a symptom of the very defeatism I have tried to attack. The test of our society is not whether it makes mistakes, but whether it has the strength to learn from them.

The slowness with which our ruling class learns anything is frustrating. It has donned protective camouflage – men like John Major and

George Carey – for want of anything better to do. It would rather buy off any threat and avoid any difficult decision. It felicitates itself (with justice) on averting revolution, but left to its own devices it would quite soon compromise itself into extinction.

It will not be left to its own devices. Events will not leave it alone (which is why Harold Macmillan feared them). And in the end the English people will not leave it alone. We are quite ridiculously slow to become excited. Nobody can tell when the scorn we feel for our government will turn to uncontrollable anger. The cause will probably be something much less worthwhile than a maiden chained to a rock. And only then we shall find whether we have left it too late to slay the dragons at home or abroad with whom we tried . . . hard to compromise.

23 April 1994

A SHAMEFUL AND INSECURE EXISTENCE

James Buchan

My theme is the unhappiness of Englishwomen, a grim and bizarre feature of our society. Driven out to work in the paid economy either to feed themselves or to attract respect, they must also manage their households, this time unpaid. They differ from their sisters in the old Soviet Union only in their degree of misfortune and their access to contraception.

I first wrote on this subject in an article called 'The Redundant Male', which appeared in *The Spectator* of 25 July 1992 and was subsequently reprinted in the *Daily Mail*. The article was magisterially denounced by the editors of *Cosmopolitan*, and every month or so I still get calls from television production companies who hope and believe I am a misogynist. 'You see, James, we've got this new studio discussion programme, very gritty and upfront, we're calling it *Scratch Your Eyes Out!* and we thought maybe you could come on and say what you said in the *Daily Mail*, about how women have got to get back to the kitchen and give men back their jobs. Of course I haven't read it myself'. I generally reply that absolutely the last place you want an Englishwoman is in the kitchen, and they say, 'What?'

I am not often asked out to dinner, but when I am I go. I arrive with my wife at half-past eight, always the first, and while the others straggle in there is conversation in a sitting-room: upstairs in North London, street level everywhere else. Sometimes a fire is burning. A dim champagne is served, sometimes by a temporary servant. At half-past nine we sit down. The food looks all right, but has been prepared without care or affection. The wine, well, of the wine least said soonest mended. I have already talked to the ladies on each side of me, in the room with the fire, and bumped up against the limits not of their intelligence, but of the cultivated parts of it: beyond is desert and misery. Pieces of a life story spill down on to the rocket salad: an education in the distant past, even a project for the future (a shop, a book), but for a future that is also now past. I carefully avoid the word 'work', but, in truth, every subject is trip-wired with embarrassment: children, school, houses, ideas, money, cookery. Across the table, the ladies' husbands talk rudely to each other, for women bore them; and, I confess, sometimes I get so sad I excuse myself, and I go into the kitchen and ask for an ashtray and sit on the kitchen table and smoke.

These women are miserable because they do not work. Nobody told them, when they were young, that they would be expected to work for money to enjoy any standing in society; and that looking after a house, a husband, children and all wasn't occupation enough for one life. They sense only dimly, because they find it hard to think in economic categories, that the tidal draw of English society is pulling them into work, that the country needs them in peacetime as badly as it once needed their mothers in war; and that's why housework has been mechanised and the fridge is stocked with M & S recipe dishes and the birth-rate is so low.

What they sense sharply, and painfully, is that their life's work has been wasted: what's the use in defending a place in society for their family when society itself has disintegrated? Anyway their husbands, who are supposed to know about money, borrowed three times their salaries at a real rate of interest, or started underwriting at Lloyd's in 1988 – everybody was doing it. So these women are, as well as everything else, stony broke. They are bad cooks and housekeepers. They envy their mothers but also women who work.

But working women are also unhappy. For nobody told them that the world of paid work would be so unforgiving; that men are such bastards; and that in their professions – perhaps the law or journalism – there would be no time out for them to have children and get them started, just six or seven years, and then return to the battle. Everything they do they do by halves: half to job, half to children; or rather less than half because in moving from one sphere to another they use up time and their vitality. They see, very clearly, that the counterpart of their paid labour is male idleness. In the working class, it is male unemployment. Among professionals, it is male laziness. For the men of the house enjoy not just the financial fruit of their wives' paid labour but also a few extra hours a week doing nothing; they do not, except in the most trivial or symbolic way, help bring up their children and anyway aren't to be trusted. Indeed, they will not even fix the shed door, for under their breath they say, 'You tore up the old marriage contract, my sugar, fix the damn thing yourself'. So these women work all day, at home and in an office, and it's better than not working and anyway they are also in debt; but I doubt if, as in previous generations, they'll outlive their husbands. They are bad cooks and housekeepers. They envy their mothers and also women who don't work.

In an article that appeared in the *Times* last week, Mary Ann Sieghart complained of the misery of being a working mother; and what was striking about the article was not so much its intelligence but, from an individual so gifted, its despair. She pleaded, rather half-heartedly, for the problem to be socialised – surely a lost cause in a country so reluctant to pay taxes as ours – and then, rather guiltily, for male consideration.

But the English gentleman culture is, we are told, dead and anyway thoroughly worthless; and the *Times* of Mr Murdoch seems a quixotic address from which to launch its restoration. I imagine the gentlemen of the *Times*, skimming through Ms Sieghart's plea, will shout, 'If you can't take the heat, get out of the kitchen!' and then, seeing that they had made a joke, 'Arf-arf!'

This is a bad situation, but I don't think it will last. I know that it is an axiom in this country and the United States that only women may justly pronounce on the condition of women; but if that were sense, we'd have to forgo Shakespeare's heroines and Daisy Miller; and anyway you can't speak of women in society without also speaking of men. (Fortunately, I have picked up some intellectual fag-ends from my wife; and since she disapproves of *The Spectator* and of articles such as this one, and won't read it, I am on wholly safe ground.) Also, the clamour of messianic feminism has stilled to a murmur of conformism and censoriousness, and many women I speak to recognise their condition has not improved in the past 25 years but got worse. A flag of truce was raised in, of all places, the *Independent*, and by Camille Paglia, of all people. In an interview with that newspaper in March, she said that the penis had some role to play in relations between men and women. Now this truth has been known to all men and all women for all time, except one, and has now struck that last as a blinding epiphany. Behold, this thing we made, we call it a wheel, it goes round and round, we invented it, all by ourselves! What do you mean, here's one you made earlier?

Many women appear to believe they have a right to equal representation in the paid economy, as if this had some Jeffersonian authority, even though there is no such amendment to the American constitution and none is likely in our lifetime. In reality, there is no authority whatever for any model division of labour between the sexes (except maybe in Scripture, but very few people in this country read Scripture, and none in bourgeois London). There is only custom and the economic forces that continuously pound society and throw up its manners and habits like outcrops made by geological action. The eruption of women into the paid economy, so that they now, if we include part-time workers, out-number men, has less to do with a feminine notion of liberty than with the grinding requirement of a mature economy to find the cheapest sources of labour and brainpower.

Nowadays, only the very richest societies can afford not to put women to paid work: the chief example in our times is Saudi Arabia. Outside the Wahhabi kingdom there is a compulsory aspect to women working which is, as always, better grasped by the working class than by its betters; though many middle-class men, scrambling to afford ponies and public schools – badges of class membership which came effortlessly to their parents – are getting the message that they need a wife with earning power.

The economic forces I mentioned, those old economic forces, are destroying the male occupational clubs; and since they have reached down to the troglodyte fastnesses of Lloyd's of London and the British officer corps, we can be sure that they are pretty powerful. The true nightmare facing Englishwomen is not, as the lady columnists tell us, that they will be excluded from the economy when they want to have babies, but that women will end up doing all the work, paid and unpaid; and men will watch television or do dope, as in Harlem, or sing, as in Sumatra.

This probably won't come to pass, for this reason. Provided women don't overprice their labour and ability by demanding six years' paid maternity leave and crèches at every corporation they will eventually be scattered as widely over the heights of the professional economy as they are in, for example, book publishing; and, by their numbers and power will oblige men to be more considerate of birth and babies and to fix that damn door.

But the task of men and women in their maturity is not the

accumulation of exclusive goods or the search for some chimerical emancipation. It is the production and upbringing of children. Children are best brought up as they are conceived, in an intensive engagement of both parents; and one that lasts, unlike the moment of conception, a period of perhaps half a dozen years. Children brought up by strangers or by one parent may flourish, but are less likely to. In all questions of the domestic and national economy, the good of the child stands supreme; and must be the criterion in all judgments of law in such matters as divorce, fostering, single parenthood and so on.

This is self-evident, because small children, unlike their parents, cannot help themselves. And it is not a mere grind: for this attention, I believe and hope, will rain cascades of benefits on parents and children right through to old age and death. For a man or woman voluntarily to forgo these benefits, merely to climb the greasy pole at Cherne & Byrne of Leadenhall Street or grub a shameful and insecure existence on the *Daily Error*, seems to me daft, or whatever comes after daft.

What does the child need from its parents? Security, obviously, and in a society that includes economic security; and love, because only a child that has been loved can love, and love is the gateway to contentment in the world. How love and economic security are delivered doesn't really matter, only that they are delivered.

Once this truth is understood, or rather recollected (since everybody has learned it), the problem vanishes. The married woman who farms out her children will be as much reviled as the married man who returns one evening, after 30 years in the City, to find his wife in weeds and his children flown.

23 April 1994

CITY AND SUBURBAN

AN ELEGANT HOLE IN THE GROUND IN EC3 – THROW YOUR MONEY IN HERE

Christopher Fildes

I have a new and improved plan for Lloyd's of London. It fits in with my proposal to dismantle Lloyd's impractical head office, and re-erect it at Sydenham, on the site of the Crystal Palace. When it has gone, it will leave a large hole in the ground, conveniently located in the City. On the edge of this hole I shall put up a notice, which will say: THROW YOUR MONEY IN HERE. Below this, in smaller but still legible lettering, I shall add: AT YOUR OWN UNLIMITED RISK. It will go with a roar. People will come up from their country estates and take taxis from Paddington to Lime Street, EC3, with boxes full of money. Throwing it in will carry a marked social cachet. It will help the toilers at the bottom of the hole to pay for their expensive suits, and keep them in smoked salmon sandwiches. I shall recycle some of the money, which can be used to pay for school fees or holidays in the West Indies. These will serve as sprats to catch mackerel. The great thing is to keep the money pouring in. This is technically known, I believe, as a Ponzi scheme, and can be made to work with pigs and even with British Government stock. Something of the kind seems to have worked very well, on the site of the hole, for a long time. Of course the time will come, as it has, when the second line of my notice turns out to mean what it says. Then there will be grief and umbrage and litigation. I shall excavate another hole, conveniently located near the Inns of Court. Beside it I shall put up another notice, which will say: NOW THROW YOUR MONEY IN HERE.

Lawsuits at Lloyd's

This is the popular idea of the moment. Already a dentist has successfully sued his Lloyd's agent for exposing him to unwanted risks. This week 3,062 members of Lloyd's have opened their case against the Gooda Walker agency and against 71 different agents who put them on to its ill-fated syndicates. Some agents and agencies are more worth suing than others. (Gooda Walker has been in liquidation for some time.) If they lose in the courts, they must be expected to fall back on their own insurance. Some will be better insured than others. Much of this insurance has been placed at Lloyd's. With its reinsurers outside the market, the buck may at last stop. By that time my new hole will be filling up nicely. All that the members can hope from it is to win damages from Lloyd's professionals who let them down. No court – not even an American court – has yet found that the members of Lloyd's are not liable for their commitments. They went into the insurance business on their own account and without limit. For many of them, it has proved disastrous. Disasters, though, are what insurance is about.

All Betsy's fault

Thirty years ago Hurricane Betsy blew in from the Gulf of Mexico and left tankers stacked one on top of another like cars on a scrapheap. Asked to comment, Sir Paul Chambers, chairman of Royal Insurance, said simply: 'If there weren't any hurricanes there wouldn't be any insurance companies.' Betsy plunged Lloyd's into three years of losses. Its response was to replenish its capital by letting in foreigners, for heaven's sake, and even women. This, Adam Raphael thinks, is where it all went wrong. In his new book *Ultimate Risk* (Bantam Press), he argues that Lloyd's mistake was to dilute its membership – 6,000 when Betsy struck, 32,000 at its peak six years ago. Too many of the new members ought never to have run the risks of the insurance business, and when the next round of disasters struck, at the end of the 1980s, they were broken reeds. The big insurance companies were hard hit, too. Their mortgage business alone, in one year, cost them £2 billion in losses. (Lloyd's stayed out of that one.) The difference was that they had the capital and the reserves. Few members of Lloyd's had spent the 25 years since Betsy squirrelling up reserves to meet the next set of mega-bills. Their cheques had dribbled away into school fees and holidays. Indeed, for most of those years, they could not have saved much from income taxed at a top rate of 98 per cent. Instead they enjoyed the unique tax advantages of Lloyd's. When Nigel Lawson as Chancellor set the top rate at 40 per cent, their chairman, Murray Lawrence, told them that they might have joined a tax haven but were now in an insurance market. They should have taken warning. Some of them were unlucky, some were greedy, some were gulled. Some are ruined. None of them had to join Lloyd's. They had plenty of sound homes for their savings and plenty of scope for investment and enterprise. They would have found it difficult to lose more than the sum of their investment. Lloyd's was a way to do that, which was one reason why their cheques kept on coming so effortlessly. They had total liability combined with minimal control. One way and another, some people who run risks like that are going to lose their boots. When some of them do, it may set off domestic tragedies, or serve as a convenient excuse for faltering prep schools or disheartened Conservative associations, but it is not the end of the world or the country or the City, or even of Lloyd's. It is, though, a deeply unsatisfactory way to run an insurance market.

Quaint old British custom

Lloyd's always argued (and wrote into its own Act of Parliament) that the unlimited commitment of its members was one of its strengths. I have long thought it a weakness and a delusion – one of those quaint old British customs so widely envied that nobody copies it. When that commitment must be called, Lloyd's is not going to pay its mega-bills out of a quick sale of Old Rectories and Old Masters. That lesson is now being learned the hard way. Lloyd's needs a capital base appropriate to the risks it runs, and if the risks are innovative and specialised, all the more reason for the capital to be orthodox and solid. The policy-holders pay their premiums because they know that disasters can happen. When they do, insurers like the Royal and the members of Lloyd's lose a great deal of money. That is not a scandal. If the policy-holders did not get their money, that would be a scandal. At Lloyd's, that has not come into question – but its business needs a better foundation than an elegant hole in the ground.

30 April 1994

FOOD

IMPERATIVE COOKING: THE MORAL OF THE BARBECUE

Digby Anderson

By the time you've found out, it's too late: 'Glad you could come. No, no, don't come in, let's go round to the garden, it's so glorious we decided to have a barbecue.'

It's tempting to rehearse the legion of unpleasant thoughts that rush to the brain once one realises that indeed retreat is impossible. There are the things people put on barbecues: bits of plastic chicken or fillets of farmed salmon that couldn't stand a clove of garlic and some olive oil in a frying pan, let alone charcoal; kebabs deliberately assembled to combine four ingredients which require four different times of cooking, so you wind up with raw pork, squashy tomato which falls off, onion burnt at the edge and uncooked near the skewer, all in sequence, with three slices of perfectly cooked aubergine liberally sprinkled with scorched rosemary.

There's the barbecue itself. At one primitive extreme this may be a few lumps of charcoal ignited by firelighters which leave everything reeking and tasting of paraffin, at the other a huge gleaming monster on wheels and with shelves and wood panels. Barbecues, like lawn-mowers, seem to get bigger and less like their originals each year – if you, like me, find it difficult to tell the difference between the two, the lawn-mowers are green. There are now barbecues which do not even smell or taste of wood or charcoal: why not give up and go back to the cooker indoors? Barbecues are also like overhead projectors: they never work first time. And the more each proud owner tells you this one is different, the less it is. Then, by their method of operation or their size, barbecues are designed to ensure that no food is ready when you want it, so chaps wander off, then it's suddenly ready and no one can be found, or they're all tight and past eating.

The thoughts quickly clear as you find your hostess has not finished the awful news: 'And Peter's taken charge – you know how he loves his barbecues.' And there Peter is, a man never seen in the kitchen for 365 days a year, proudly standing by his new monster. He has a butcher's apron on, and a pair of gloves with 'Barbecue Gloves' written on them (lest he forget what he is up to). He is staring at a rack of implements – various fish-slices, tweezers, forks, knives and grips, deciding which instrument he needs. Peter knows nothing about cooking.

The combination of him and the barbecue means the food will be doubly dreadful.

But the point is why? Why do non-cooking men seize on barbecuing? To be factual, it is not quite the only thing they do. Men who never cook, and literally don't know a duck's arse from its elbow, still proudly like to seize a bone-handled, blunt carving knife and fork and carve at the dinner table. If the bird is, as usual, plastic, they might as well just flick it with a towel; it will meekly fall into pieces. If not, they wind up hacking away where no joint has ever been and complaining, 'It's a little on the tough side, dear.' If someone has been daft enough to give them one of those new electric hedge-trimmer carvers, it simply makes matters worse: every time the teeth hit a bone, the duck shoots round

in a circle, showering juices and potatoes – with which someone has sabotaged its every side – on to the table-cloth that was brought back from Tenerife.

The only other occasion when such men 'cook' is when they adopt a dish as their own: 'George loves his curries, he's got a whole set of books on them and a special place to himself for his ingredients in the larder. I don't know whether he loves cooking them or eating them more.'

It's easy to see what is wrong with Peter and George. They are happy to leave their wives to do what those wives call the chores of daily humdrum cooking, but when any opportunity turns up to show off and play with fire and sword or the exotic secrets of the East, they want to be centre stage. They love their bit of cooking but won't do regular hard cooking work.

Their wives are the opposite. They do the regular work but treat it as a chore. Today's working woman – and not a working woman does not highly value cooking on a daily basis – is resentful of the demands it involves and has herself turned it into a chore. Cooking needs to be both highly valued and worked at. It is difficult to know which produces the worse food, Peter's rare and incompetent spectaculars or Mrs Peter's daily chore cooking. All one can say is that she does harm more often.

7 May 1994

BERNARD, HAND BACK THE MONEY

Jeffrey Bernard

One morning last week, I woke up and it was ominously dark. I hadn't woken too early, it was just a storm coming in from the west. I spent some time reading *How We Die* by the bedside light to review for the *Telegraph*. And so I was feeling a little gloomy by the time the district nurse, a flash of lightning and the first roll of thunder arrived. The district nurse, Trudy, was her usual cheerful self – she comes every day to dress my so-called good leg – and although it looks fairly hideous to me she keeps saying it is getting better. Of course, in the back of my mind I fear that Mr Cobb will get his hands, saw and scalpel on it one of these days. The thunder rolled on and I began to feel as though I was playing a minor role in a Wagner epic.

Just as Trudy finished with my foot there was a knock on the door and a collector from the Inland Revenue presented himself and asked me for £9,660 there and then. Lightning flashed appropriately at this crazy demand and I have earned no money to speak of since Peter O'Toole stopped playing me for the last time. Although a court judgment has been made already against me and the date for an appeal has gone by some time ago, the collector was nice enough to say that he would try and arrange for me to make an appeal rather late in the day. He spent quite a bit of time sitting at my table writing God knows what, and finally Trudy left without taking my foot with her.

As soon as she had gone, the phone rang and it was an agent from London Management answering a complaint I had made about not getting any money from the Dublin production of *Jeffrey Bernard Is Unwell*. I remember the opening well although I wasn't there because it was on 8th February, the day I had my right leg off. Anyway, I said it had been a long time in coming, the money I mean, and she said, there isn't any coming. It seems that the Irishman who leased the play from Michael Redington who first put it on at the Apollo had gone broke, maybe bankrupt, and more or less done a bunk. The tax collector went on with his writing and the thunder, now in the east, continued to rumble. Then the agent told me the surname of the Irishman who had absconded with the loot. It is Bernard. That came as no surprise, in fact it seemed quite appropriate and I would guess that, at this minute, that particular Mr Bernard is propping up a Dublin bar and laughing about having got away with not paying Keith Waterhouse and myself.

All the time this dreadful morning was unfolding, I had that book, *How We Die* at the back of my mind. By the time I got to the end of it, I found myself not giving a damn how I am going to die as long as it is without pain. At tea time my daughter telephoned. Then her mother telephoned from Spain, pleasantly enough as it happened, but it still felt like a Wagnerian day. It was all so absurd that I fell asleep laughing.

I was quite interested that the Inland Revenue collector told me that he got a fair amount of verbal abuse in the course of his duties but I was surprised to hear that he should have been hit a couple of times. What on earth for? You might as well hit the milkman on Saturday mornings when he gives you the week's bill. This could be another one of those days. The F.state Office has just telephoned to tell me that it will cost me £80 to have my entryphone mended. I can't imagine what visitors I'm missing at the moment but they should pay for it themselves with the disability allowance. Creeping bureaucracy is not only killing the National Health Service but also making the Westminster Council behave like lunatics. All I hope for now is that the Inland Revenue collectors should behave like a lot of lemmings.

14 May 1994

DOCTORS, PATIENTS AND OTHER NUISANCES

Theodore Dalrymple

Five years ago there were three offices for nurse administrators in one of the hospitals in which I work. Now there are 26, filling two corridors. When you enter one of these offices unannounced, you sense the same blind alarm as when you lift the bark from a damp rotting log and the woodlice and other small creatures scurry for humid cover. I do not think it an exaggeration to say that guilt and bad faith are written on the faces of the inhabitants of these offices: the guilt and bad faith of people who draw a salary to perform a task, which is unnecessary and quite possibly harmful, but who must nevertheless pay their mortgage like the rest of us.

Another of the hospitals in which I work has recently increased the staff of its finance department from three to twenty-one (without counting their secretaries). Moreover, one of the original three members of staff has been made redundant and given a generous golden handshake. In the National Health Service, even reducing expenditure is a very expensive business.

Now there may be some among you who see the influx of financial controllers, financial accountants, finance managers, management accountants, management accountants' assistants, exchequer services managers and cost accountants into our hospital (to name but a few) as a sign that at last the Health Service is taking financial matters seriously, and also that its profligacy is being curbed; that at last some sense of the importance of what things cost is being instilled into those who work in the service. When demand so far outstrips supply, after all, financial discipline is of the essence.

This view was expressed to me by a chief executive at the head-quarters of a nearby health authority (not my own), who told me that we all had to live henceforth in 'the real world'. But I wasn't interested so much in what he had to say as in the building in which he said it. It was large, on three floors; and it was as protected from the malign influence of the outside world as a bathyscape from the pressure of the ocean. One entered through a kind of airlock arrangement, visitors communicating with the doorkeeper by means of microphones and loudspeakers. All the windows were triple-glazed to keep out the noise of the real world, and were sealed so that they could not under any circumstances be opened; the temperature was eternally controlled to within a degree or two and the ventilation was by means of a faintly humming draught, expelled through aluminium grilles in the polystyrene ceilings. There were fire doors every ten feet in the corridors, suggesting either a surfeit of potential arsonists or an excess of timidity among bureaucrats. The atmosphere was monastic, calm and otherworldly; but, instead of illuminated manuscripts, the bureaucrats were producing pie and flow diagrams, and tables of such vital statistics as the proportion of women in the district between the ages of 16 and 35 with intrauterine devices, or of men over the age of 75 who required Zimmer frames, analysed by electoral ward.

What these bureaucrats of the health authority could not explain to me was how their financial interests could be reconciled with those of my own hospital. I have a patient with a frequently recurring illness who is usually treated in my ward: a service for which, under the new arrangements, the health authority has to pay. Therefore the more frequently the patient is admitted, and the more intensively he is treated, the better for my hospital but the worse for the health authority, which frantically tries to deflect this patient to an inferior facility on grounds of cost. So much energy now goes into shifting the cost of treatment from one part of the health service to another, with no thought of reducing the cost to the service as a whole, and certainly none with regard to the convenience of the patient.

Information, we are told, is the key to efficiency. Maybe so, though I suspect that, in the absence of intuitive perspective, information is but a higher form of ignorance. To know what proportion of hospital porters have shoulder-length hair or tattoos on their necks, for example, is not to improve the survival rate in the coronary care unit, though it is undoubtedly information of a kind. But to help us gather allegedly 'relevant' information, we now have in one of the hospitals in which I work no fewer than nine medical audit facilitators, two audit supervisors and one director of medical audit. Their salaries and other costs must be at least £500,000 per annum. One cannot help but wonder what audit facilitators did before they were employed as such. Or is there now a four-year university course leading to a B.Med.Aud.Fac. degree?

According to one government publication, medical audit is 'the systematic, critical analysis of the quality of medical care, including the procedures used for diagnosis and treatment, the use of resources, and the resulting outcome and quality of life for the patient'. Participation in medical audit is now an obligation placed on hospital doctors by the Government. According to my contract, for example, fully one-tenth of my time must be taken up with evaluating what I do in the other nine-tenths of my time.

There is no doubt that medical audit can be useful, especially when answering highly specific questions, such as whether it is necessary or not to do routine chest X-rays on young people before operations. But the vaguer and more general the questions asked, the less certain the answers, and the more room for bureaucratic overemployment.

Some problems do not require audit facilitators for their elucidation, but are a matter of constant, everyday experience. In my department, for example, it often takes four weeks to get a letter typed to general practitioners about our patients. This is because we have too few secretaries. Moreover, the computers in our department were bought not by the hospital, which claimed, at the very time it was recruiting audit facilitators and handing out management contracts for hundreds of thousands, that it had no funds to do so, but by a public-spirited physician. If he had not bought them, we should have been able to send no letters at all, ever.

Whether one should spend the hospital's limited money on audit facilitators or on word processors and medical secretaries is, of course, a question for medical audit. Thus the need for medical audit is logically prior to any other activity whatsoever. But who audits the auditors? No one: audit is now a matter of blind faith, against which the urgings of common sense are quite useless.

In practice, I have not found the audit facilitators to be of immense use. This is not entirely their own fault. About three months ago, I asked one of them to provide me with the number of patients from one of my clinics who had failed to attend for their appointments. A simple matter, said the facilitator enthusiastically. Two weeks later, she returned to me, slightly downcast, to tell me that the figures were not available because in the meantime all the hospital computers – £900,000 worth – had been stolen, actually for the third time, and this time the loss was uninsurable. Unfortunately, the back-up disks had disappeared along with the hardware, but she had every hope of recovering the information from elsewhere. Three months later, I still don't know how many patients failed to attend for their appointments, and in reality I don't much care. I had only asked because I had to ask something.

But the facilitators, informationless, are still employed: our hospital thus suffers from a variant of the London Transport syndrome, in which automatic ticket machines are installed but ticket inspectors and collectors are retained.

A colleague of mine runs four outpatient clinics a week, which he administers himself with the aid solely of a diary and one nurse. He thus sees vast numbers of patients weekly. The hospital administration is unaware as yet of any of this *clinical activity*, as they would no doubt call it. But when they do get to hear of it, they will demand, in the name of efficiency, that it be organised through the normal channels, which are so bureaucratic that the *clinical activity* will have to be reduced by three quarters, and the numbers of staff to do it tripled. My colleague will find his time filled up with such essential procedures as putting requests for appointments in writing to outpatient clerks who will then write – or fail to write – to the patient. This procedure alone takes – when it works – more than two weeks. Thus my colleague can either provide the administration with the information about his work which it requires, or he can see many patients – but not both. There are no prizes for guessing which option the administration will choose.

The Health Service is presently suffering from a form of medical Leninism. The assumption is that if decisions have to be made about the allocation of resources (and apparently they do, since demand out-strips supply), they are best made explicitly and 'rationally'. This, of course, is precisely what the Marxists thought about the economy as a whole, with what results we now appreciate. The Health Service is probably bigger and more complex than the entire Russian economy was in 1917, yet health economists and others assume that it can be organised on a wholly rational basis, its output for use rather than for profit – or, indeed, public benefit as defined by doctors.

Increasingly, the Health Service resembles the Soviet Union. The managers are apparatchiks (down to their bad suits), and will arrogate more and more privileges to themselves. It is not in the least surpris-ing that the bill for Health Service company cars has risen so dramat-ically of late. Furthermore, it is not implausible to see information-gathering as an excuse for the development of a Health Service NKVD: again, it hardly surprises me that a hospital consultant recently had his telephone tapped by a hospital manager. This is the wave of the future.

The public-spiritedness which undoubtedly existed in hospitals will soon be destroyed utterly, just as public-spiritedness was destroyed in Russia. In my experience, most doctors and nurses do far more throughout their careers than they are paid to do; but their attitude will change if they are asked to account for and justify every task they perform.

Of course, the Government will claim by way of refutation that it has introduced the rigours of the market-place to the Health Service. This is a straightforward lie. The customer in the new Health Service is not the patient, but a bureaucracy allegedly acting on behalf of the patient. I mean no personal disrespect to professional bureaucrats, but it is simply not in their nature to act in the interest of others. Doctors and nurses often do so act (though not always), because they have direct contact with people, and natural human sympathy prevails.

What the Government has done is not so much to introduce market relations, with all their efficiency, as to introduce a system in which two monstrous and uncontrolled bureaucracies speak to each other, with all the incompetence and rigidity which bureaucracies usually bring in their wake. The goal of the present Health Service is not to serve the patients, but to eliminate them altogether as an unnecessary complication in the running of hospitals. Indeed, hospitals themselves are increasingly superfluous to the need for offices.

We are often told of the alleged need for professional management. In all the myriad circulars I receive – several pounds avoirdupois every week – the word *professional* is invariably used as a term of approbation. But nothing could be further removed from the truth than the need for professional management. On the contrary, what is needed is amateur management – by which I do not mean, of course, that it should be *amateurish*. No: I mean the running of public institutions such as hospitals should, as far as possible, be deputed to retired colonels and commodores, bank managers and accountants, businessmen and surgeons, who, for a very small emolument, would be prepared and indeed delighted to devote themselves to the public good.

Such people would have no careers to make, and no ambitions requiring the employment of scores of underlings; they would have no vested interest in mistaking activity for work, they would not imagine that the production of circulars, with flow diagrams running from *users' and carers' needs* to *resource implications, service agreements, client information systems* and *aligned operational co-ordination* (an actual example taken at random), was in itself productive of anything except profound irritation in the recipient; and they would have a great fund of experience of running important undertakings, private and public.

Moreover, a return to management by amateurs would do much to restore public spirit and civic pride, which vast public expenditures and the absurd attempt to put everything on a supposedly rational basis have done so much to destroy. It is characteristic of our age that in the name of reason we have created absurdity.

21 May 1994

CENTRE POINT

PERHAPS I SHOULD JOIN THE MOONEYS ON THE FIELD OF CLOTH OF DENIM

Simon Jenkins

Bel Mooney – Mrs Jonathan Dimbleby – jets down from Granadaland to fast for Mother Earth. Women in designer jeans drape over JCBs. Travellers weave daisy-chains and hold pagan weddings. Bob Dylan and Joni Mitchell rise with the smoke from the yurt camp. Rednecks shout,

'Get an effing job!' The Swainswick bypass is the D-Day festival of the Sixties generation. Ms Mooney is their laptop Vera Lynn, warbling each day in the *Mail*, the *Times* and the *Guardian*.

Nimby direct action lends itself to satire. Here are the beautiful Dimblebys ensconced in their home from home. They have found a lovely valley near lovely Bath, where the locals are no less lovely and 'do for you' in Somerset accents. The faxes, modems and portables all work. Every field has a crop circle. And, joy of joys, the M4's fashionable exit 17 is just over the hill. 'We're really amazingly close to London.' It was for havens such as this that England was made.

But somebody else wants their own highway to Heaven and it passes slap through Ms Mooney's nirvana. Where she communes with Jane Austen, sips cider with Rosie and romances with the shades of ancient Britain, she now confronts £75 million of earth-moving equipment. Essex man could be forgiven a smile. The Dimblebys did not fast for four days when the M4 smashed through Osterley. They did not summon Fleet Street when it raped the water meadows of Windsor, careered through the Berkshire Downs and gouged the White Horse Hills, on its royal route to their Cotswold doorstep.

Now the transport department is no longer a boon and a blessing to them. It has grown horns. Innocent III has summoned a crusade. The cross of St George is raised over the feature pages of the land. No self-denial, no humiliation, no publicity is too much. 'A fever set my adrenalin going,' reported Bel from the field of cloth of denim. As the digger approached, 'I removed my pretty straw hat and lay down too.' Cue the fashion pages, the starvation experts, the aerobic advice on how to be dragged through the mud. (Lie parallel to a ley line.)

So far, so much fun. But what is it that makes reasonable people – for such is Ms Mooney – take leave of her respect for democracy, break the law and encourage her daughter to do the same? Would I, or you? I sense that until somebody has driven a motorway through our back garden we had better not answer. I would go berserk if government action threatened my child or my health. I might take the same view of my garden. When the local council refused me a side-wall alteration, but approved a restaurant with late-night music directly opposite, I certainly pondered a contract killing. (Camden Council wisely denied me details of the relevant committee.)

Roads are no less sensitive. Many years ago, the then Greater London Council decided to push something called the West Cross Route behind my house. I was incredulous, as if numb with bereavement. I joined some campaign and eventually the road was abandoned. The poor citizens of North Kensington were less lucky. At the same time the transport ministry wanted an elevated motorway linking Marylebone to Shepherd's Bush. This fitted no plan, being inside the GLC's ringway. It was simply some official's extravagant idea. 'Yes Minister' later claimed the road was for officials to get to Oxford dinners more quickly. That road was indeed built, largely because the houses destroyed were poor and cheap to demolish. It is called Westway.

Such sagas destroy any faith I might have in British road planning. It is a crudely authoritarian corner of public administration. The Swainswick road is not a bypass. It is part of a trunk road being driven by stealth across the landscape, proceeding as the Victorian railways did by local skirmishes and skulduggery. Every now and then a hapless minister is pushed forward to 'deny any plans' for a trunk route. These are mere words. There is no 'plan' for the Trans-Europe Route Network from East Anglia to Wales. It is merely being threaded across middle England, to the rage of such grandees as Lord Bullock, Sir Evelyn de Rothschild and the planning lawyer Sir Frank Layfield. Its younger sister, the Southampton-to-Bristol link, has fallen foul of the Dimbleby clan. There is a mighty battle ahead.

I have a little sympathy for officials in Whitehall's roads directorate. They are not their own masters. At least the railways had to say where they were going. The trunk roads are not revealed for fear of prejudicing some local inquiry or other. The resulting secrecy makes arms-for-Iraq look like a paragon of open government. Road planning is reduced to a series of crude deals, the planners trapped between the Treasury and the construction lobby. Road inquiries are designed to enrich planning lawyers. They never advise against a road or ask strategic questions. As for senior officials, they know their jobs depend on keeping in with the Treasury. Ministers come and go and are of no account.

Nothing can cut this Gordian knot. Most traffic jams can be relieved by junction widening or by mini-flyovers, such as the efficient and economical one at Chiswick's Hogarth roundabout. These structures are hated by the roads lobby as cheap. It prefers huge, land-hungry interchanges. Yet this same lobby cannot be mobilised for tunnels, such as might long ago have relieved the pressure on Bath. So transport officials ask the Treasury for the cheapest project that satisfies the roads lobby, gets permission and then goes on a war footing to defend it at inquiry. At the 1990 Bath inquiry, the department dared not admit its Southampton-Bristol highway. Instead it pretended it was building a £75 million bypass for the village of Batheaston, a bypass worthy of an egomaniacal African dictator.

Ever since Chesterton's rolling English drunkard finished work, our roads have been a disgrace. The absence of tolls means that ministers and officials feel no obligation to the convenience of drivers, for instance by doing nocturnal maintenance. Roads are built that are expensive in land but cheap in landscaping. Services are standardised, sparse and ugly. Information is non-existent. Only recently did Whitehall even think of apologising for delays.

Dump one of these roads in my back yard and I sense that I would do a Mooney. Those who sneer should visit the last road that the hippies and harpies tried to stop, the M3 through Twyford Down above Winchester. This great chalk gash above the Itchen Valley is an outrage. The M3 should have been in a tunnel and in any other European country it would have been. Roads there must be. But let them be fair in their planning and discreet in their execution. As long as Whitehall is staffed by secretive philistines, I am for direct action. The English landscape is the sum of a million back yards. Thank God for their defenders.

21 May 1994

THE FRENCH SOLUTION TO THE LOO PROBLEM

Miles Kington

To celebrate the opening of the Channel Tunnel, the Foreign Office is publishing a glossy brochure full of articles commemorating the links between France and England, cultural, commercial and historical. I was asked to contribute a piece to it, a lighthearted article on the cultural differences between us. I did contribute such a piece, but it was never used; I was given to understand that the Foreign Office did not approve of its sentiments. This is the article; if any reader can spot the offensive material, please let me know, as I can't.

I have once, and once only, given an after-dinner speech to a gathering of Frenchmen. It was a very valuable learning experience. The most important thing I learned was that I would never again agree to give an after-dinner speech to a gathering of Frenchmen.

The event took place last year, at Claridge's hotel in London. Some of the directors and executives of Gaz de France, the state-owned gas company, were coming over to London for a big meeting and dinner, and they wanted someone to give a light-hearted after-dinner speech on some of the cultural differences between France and England. They asked me. The money was generous. I said I would. A few days before the dinner, the organiser rang to inform me that not all the directors and executives of Gaz de France spoke English, so could I do my speech in French?

The money seemed a little less generous suddenly, but I felt I could manage it. I rewrote the speech in French. The day came. I went to Claridge's. I sat between two very senior Gaz de France executives. I tried to make small talk with them. How is your small talk about gas? About French gas especially? Mine neither. But I did my best. I spoke to the man on my left, in French, just in case.

'*Alors, comment ça va avec le gaz en France?*'

He shrugged. Evidently not all was going well with gas in France.

'*On a des problèmes,* ' he admitted.

What problems? I wanted to know.

'*Pour commencer, il n'y a pas de gaz en France.*'

No gas in France. I hadn't thought of that. Apparently they have to buy it all from abroad. It cast a cloud over the evening as far as I was concerned. He seemed quite cheerful. Finally it came to my turn to speak and I did my 20 minutes, and it didn't go too badly. Then the (English) chairman rose and said, '*Et maintenant M. Kington veut accepter des questions en français.*'

This was a lie. I had no wish to accept any questions in whatever language. But I was trapped. The first few were not too bad but then came this one – in French, remember.

'Mr Kington has made the good point in his address that the British have always had a reputation of being more pragmatic and practical, while the French have a reputation for being more intellectual and theoretical. I get the impression that in recent years this has started to change, and the two nations are exchanging characteristics with each other, with the French becoming more pragmatic and the British more theoretical, etc., or at least more ideological. Does Mr Kington agree with this and, if so, how does he think that it will affect business in the 1990s?'

My mouth opened and closed as various possible answers flashed through my mind. (*'Je m'en fous'* was first. 'Look, mate, I'm a humorist not an economic guru' was the second.) I can't remember now what I did say, if anything, but what struck me was the intense revelation that I had just witnessed a prime example of the cultural differences

'Ms Wilson's a temp, she's only with us for today'

between the French and the English. It was unthinkable that any Englishman I know could have asked that question seriously – it showed an interest in theoretical analysis that is absolutely foreign to us. And if by some terrible miracle an Englishman had wanted to ask that question, he would never have directed it at an after-dinner speaker. Only a Frenchman would imagine that an after-dinner speaker is there to provide information and enlightenment. An Englishman knows that his purpose is sheer amusement. To the Frenchman, sheer amusement can never be a worthy purpose.

If you dispute this, I call one Frenchman as a witness. Some years ago, the famous French scriptwriter Jean-Claude Carrière edited a book called *Humour 1900*, an anthology of turn-of-the-century French humour, and in his introduction he said that humour hardly existed in France because its purpose was solely to amuse, and the French mistrusted anything with no useful purpose. The period of the 1890s was one of the few eras in French history when humour had flourished in France, as I came to learn when I did my first book, which was a translation of humorous pieces written by Alphonse Allais. Allais wrote solely to amuse. He was very funny. He might have been English. I find it inexplicable that he was not English.

But then Allais found the English inexplicable. He relates how one day he visited London and discovered to his horror that he couldn't find a public lavatory in Leicester Square.

'You would think,' he says, 'that the English with their love of *le confort* would have public conveniences all over the place. Not a bit of it. And there was I, with eighteen pints of best porter sloshing around inside of me, desperate . . . '

Allais' solution, by the way, was brilliant. He spots a chemist's shop in Tottenham Court Road, goes in and says to the man 'I fear I may have diabetes.'

'It shouldn't be hard to find out,' says the pharmacist. 'But I'm afraid I shall need a sample of your water.'

'No problem,' says Allais, and is ushered into the back room and to intense relief.

This illustrates another great difference between us and the French: the different ways in which we go about problem-solving, whether the problem is finding a lavatory or building a high-speed rail link to the Tunnel. Whereas the English bumble along, patching up as they go and refusing ever to have an overall strategy, the French believe in the big plan. It was because the French had a big plan, and carried it out, that they now have a booming nuclear energy programme, and we don't. It was because the French conceived their big high-speed plan that they have a TGV network, and we haven't even started to build our fast rail-link to the Tunnel. (And has anyone noticed that the French call it the Eurotunnel and we persist in seeing it as the Channel Tunnel?)

At the highest level this manifests itself in the way the French have a constitution, and we don't. The French constitution is the biggest plan they have. Of course, this also explains why they have revolutions and we don't – the revolution is caused by the break-down of the big plan, and the tremors involved in replacing it. And it is at this point that my mind goes back to a meeting I had two or three years back with a man who ran a horse farm in Provence, somewhere near Carpentras, a farm which was about to be cut in two by the projected TGV line from Paris to Marseilles.

'There is nothing I can do to stop it,' he told me. 'We do not have the planning inquiries that you have, none of the democratic checks. They issue the plan, and bang! They build through my place. But I too have a plan. I am writing to Colonel Gaddafi. I am asking his advice on how to make bombs. I am asking him how to make a bomb big enough to blow up a main French railway line. I am very serious about this.'

It was his plan against the government plan. I wish I knew if he ever carried it out. It's not the sort of thing I would ever have done. But, then, I would never have thought of feigning diabetes in a chemist's, and, if I had thought of it, I would never have done it. But, then, I am not French. It will take more than a tunnel to erase differences like this.

28 May 1994